Fintech, Small Business & The American Dream

Karen G. Mills

Fintech, Small Business & The American Dream

How Technology Is Transforming Lending and Shaping a New Era of Small Business Opportunity

Second Edition

Karen G. Mills
Harvard Business School
Harvard University
Boston, MA, USA

ISBN 978-3-031-55611-1   ISBN 978-3-031-55612-8   (eBook)
https://doi.org/10.1007/978-3-031-55612-8

Cover illustration: Oksana Chaban/iStock/Getty Images Plus

This Palgrave Macmillan imprint is published by the registered company Springer Nature Switzerland AG
The registered company address is: Gewerbestrasse 11, 6330 Cham, Switzerland

Paper in this product is recyclable.

To Will, who was brave and wise

Preface

It was a cold day in Arkadelphia in the spring of 2010, and we were shivering out in the muddy grounds of the sawmill. As part of my new role in Washington, I had gotten up at 4 AM, taken two planes to land in Little Rock, then driven two hours south to visit Richie and his wife Angela at their business, Shields Wood Products. I was not in a good mood. Then Angela, who was also the business's bookkeeper, turned to me and said the words that changed my whole perspective on the day and probably led to the writing of this book. "You know," she said, "you saved our business."

I heard these words dozens of times over the next year as we worked to get capital flowing to small businesses that were suffering because credit markets had frozen during the 2008–2009 recession. Banks that had become overextended stopped lending, making loans guaranteed by the U.S. Small Business Administration (SBA) a lifeline for many. As the head of the SBA, I was the member of President Obama's Cabinet who was responsible for all of America's entrepreneurs and small business owners. It was a terrific job. But it sometimes required pounding the table to ensure the voice of small business did not get lost under the mass of other priorities.

I thought at the time we were facing the greatest small business crisis of my lifetime. I was wrong. In March 2020, the Covid-19 pandemic shut down the U.S. economy in a matter of weeks. Lockdowns for public health and safety forced small businesses to close their doors, and with an average of only 27 days of cash on hand, many faced the possibility that they would soon be permanently out of business. Fortunately, the U.S. government acted quickly, authorizing over $1.2 trillion in aid. Though far from perfect, the response kept millions of small businesses alive and protected our economy from a dark outcome.

I have always known how important small business was to the economy. My Grandpa Jack had come to America from Russia at the turn of the last century with nothing. Starting with two machines in the back of a shoe shop in Boston, he built a textile business that not only provided for his family and extended family but also grew to employ hundreds of people. When I worked for him in the mill during my college years, he would tell me not to go to work for a big company. "Our family," he would say, "doesn't work for other businesses. We build our own."

Grandpa Jack's story was the story of the American Dream. Our country is one of the few places in the world where it is possible to lift oneself and one's family to a new set of opportunities and a new life by starting and growing a small business. This path to opportunity, however, is not evenly distributed and is becoming more and more threatened. Access to capital for small businesses has been under pressure, not only during the recent crises, but also for decades, due to consolidations in community banks and the difficulty banks have in making profits with small loans, particularly those given to the smallest businesses.

Beginning around 2010, however, fintech entrepreneurs came on the scene. Using data and technology, they brought a new experience to small business borrowers, massively improving a process that had essentially not changed since the time when Grandpa Jack sought a loan. Though it has proven more complicated than originally anticipated, these innovators are transforming the small business lending market. Large global banks and small community banks have woken up to the fact that small businesses are looking for a more responsive, more innovative set of products and services focused on their unique needs. Platforms as varied as Square, Stripe, and Shopify have demonstrated the power of data to overcome the information opacity that has long made small businesses difficult to understand.

This book explores the current and future states of small business lending. It asks, "What do small businesses want? Who will be the winners and losers? And how should regulators respond?" It seeks to define a new state—Small Business Utopia—a world of innovative solutions that will help small businesses get the capital and financial insights they need to grow and succeed. But mainly this is a book about the role of small business, its importance to the economy, and the prospects that technology brings to overcome some of the fundamental barriers to a better small business lending market.

At the center of this book is a basic premise that small businesses matter. They matter for economic growth, they are fundamental to our communities, and they are critical to the future of the American Dream. This has been my experience as a venture capitalist and a small business owner, and during my time in government. And it is confirmed by the stories of Richie and Angela, Grandpa Jack, and the owners and employees of so many of America's 33 million small businesses.

*   *   *

In October 2009, I was standing with President Obama in a warehouse in Landover, Maryland, filled with small business owners. The President finished his speech, looked into the faces of these entrepreneurs who were suffering in the aftermath of the 2008–2009 financial crisis, and said:

> I know that times are tough, and I can only imagine what many of you are going through, in terms of keeping things going in the midst of a very tough economic climate. But I guarantee you this: This administration is going to stand behind small businesses. You are our highest priority because we are confident that when you are succeeding, America succeeds.[1]

Small businesses are better off today than they were in the midst of recent crises, but obstacles remain. The rise of technology will help small businesses overcome these challenges, forging transformative new products and services and a renewed pathway to the American Dream. In this period of change, we must ensure that innovations flourish in ways that enhance the prospects and prosperity of small businesses. Because when small businesses succeed, America succeeds.

Boston, MA, USA   Karen G. Mills

---

[1] President Barack Obama, "Remarks at Metropolitan Archives, LLC" (speech, Landover, Maryland, October 21, 2009), Government Publishing Office, https://www.govinfo.gov/content/pkg/PPP-2009-book2/pdf/PPP-2009-book2-doc-pg1555.pdf.

Acknowledgments

When my terrific publisher Tula Weis called with the idea of writing a second edition, I was reluctant. A book is a long effort, and I had written one that reflected my knowledge and experience regarding the possibilities for technology and small business lending. Yet, when I sat down that weekend and reread the book from cover to cover, I changed my mind.

Published in 2019, the first edition had come out before the extraordinary challenge of the Covid-19 pandemic and associated lockdowns that, while necessary for public health and safety, imperiled the small business community. In those difficult months, I had engaged in the government response from afar, pushing hard for modifications that ensured federal programs reached the smallest and most vulnerable businesses. Eventually, several rounds later, with the help of many fintechs, money reached about 13 million of America's small businesses and likely saved the nation from shuttered storefronts on Main Streets for years to come. That story, with all the proper facts, needed to be told.

The landscape of small business lending had also evolved. Platforms like Stripe and Shopify had grown, and financial products began to be embedded in the stream of a small business owner's daily activity. I had traveled around the world asking audiences who would be the winners and losers in small business lending. There were many opinions. Thus, we embarked on the second edition, which takes the core analysis of U.S. banks and small business lending markets and reexamines each aspect of how technology will change the game. This book includes two new chapters which assess the pandemic response, including issues of fraud, and chapters on competitors (old and new) in the marketplace, including a new playbook for banks.

The journey required more than a year and benefited from the input of many wise and generous colleagues. I thank Sophia Alj, Dane Atkinson, Jo Ann Barefoot, Ismael Belkhayat, Sean Carmody, Gilles Chelma, Charlotte Crosswell, Mercedes Delgado, Robert Fairlie, Isabel Casillas Guzman, Sabrina Howell, Pete Lord, Gabby MacSweeney, Chip Mahan, Ramana Nanda, Hicham Oudghiri, Jim Poterba and the NBER community, Peter Renton, Jackie Reses, Liz Reynolds, CeCe Rouse, David Snitkof, and Gina Taylor for their wise and helpful comments and ideas. I thank Morgane Herculano who traveled with me to London, Morocco, and Washington interviewing fintechs, bankers, and regulators and updated every graph and every page of the manuscript.

Brayden McCarthy had the original idea to write about the gap in small business lending, after working at the SBA and in the White House and was my coauthor on two Harvard Business School white papers that form the basis for Part I of the book. I thank Annie Dang and Aaron Mukerjee for their work on the first book. I am especially grateful to Annie for reading and editing every chapter of this second edition.

This book had its origins in the time I spent in Washington running the SBA during the 2008–2009 financial crisis. I want to thank the team at the SBA for their inspiration and dedication, particularly those in the field offices who spend every day getting capital into the hands of small business owners. The impact we made would never have been possible without the vision and hard work of the SBA leadership team, especially Jonathan Swain, Chief of Staff, who continues to work with me on these issues. Those that have worked in Washington know that nothing gets done without support from the White House and Congress. To this day, I am grateful to President Barack Obama and to Larry Summers, Gene Sperling, Valerie Jarrett, and Pete Rouse for their commitment to small businesses and to me. Senators Mary Landrieu and Olympia Snowe set an example of bipartisan leadership by working together to pass critical legislation that is still helping small business owners.

Harvard Business School has been my intellectual home for almost 10 years and created the opportunity for this journey. I thank Srikant Datar, Nitin Nohria, Jan Rivkin, and my colleagues in the Entrepreneurial Management Unit for their ideas and encouragement. The Division of Research and Faculty Development provided significant and much appreciated support. I am grateful to Tula Weis and the team at Palgrave Macmillan for the opportunity and for all their help. Glenn Kaplan and Rebecca Uberti provided design and wise counsel on the book cover.

The inspiration for this work on small businesses comes from watching my family, particularly my parents Ellen and Melvin Gordon, and my grandparents, go to work each day in offices just off the factory floor and build businesses. I am grateful to them, and to those who work in those businesses for all they do.

I am especially thankful for Barry and for our family. To Henry, Annie, Molly, George, and Grace, each of you is strong and wise, and in your work and how you live, you make the world a better place. I am grateful for your support and encouragement in this book and in all endeavors. To Will, who was brave and wise, we will miss you forever.

Contents

1

The Story of Small Business Lending

Almost half of the people who work in America own or work for a small business. These 33 million small businesses underpin not only our economy, but the fabric of our society.[1] Small businesses are everywhere. They operate across all the states and exist in every industry, from retail to oil and gas exploration. The small business owner might be the community-minded citizen who supports the local Little League or the immigrant entrepreneur who builds a life of opportunity. Each one has a story.

Every small business is different, but they face a common challenge: it is often difficult to get access to the capital they need to operate and succeed. Until recently, lending to small businesses hadn't changed much for over a century. A small business owner would compile a stack of paperwork, go to their local banker, and often wait weeks for a response. If the answer was "no," they would go down the street to the next bank and try again.

While this might sound like a frustrating process, there are many who say that there is no serious problem. They argue that many of the small businesses that have trouble accessing capital should not actually get it because they are not creditworthy, and that most small businesses don't want to grow, so have no need for external financing. They also argue that banks are fully meeting the needs of creditworthy borrowers in the marketplace. These statements have some truth to them. Not every business who wants a loan should get one, and many businesses don't want to grow. However, these views are blind to the significant market failures in small business lending, which have only worsened over recent decades. The problems are the most intense for the smallest businesses, particularly those that are minority and women owned.[2]

K. G. Mills, *Fintech, Small Business & The American Dream*, https://doi.org/10.1007/978-3-031-55612-8_1

Small business lending is hard. In this book, we will meet small business owners—from Miami to Manhattan to Maine—who are struggling to get the right loan in the right amount at the right cost. We will meet lenders— from New England to North Carolina to Silicon Valley—who are trying to figure out which small businesses are creditworthy and how to lend to them profitably. These are not just isolated anecdotes, but rather, they represent the experiences of small business borrowers and lenders in a market filled with frictions. According to the International Finance Corporation (IFC), small businesses globally face over $5 trillion in unmet credit needs.[3] Using the best available research and data, we will identify the gaps in access to capital for creditworthy small businesses in the United States, and the barriers that have made many traditional lenders less willing or able to meet their needs. And we will describe how innovations in financial technology are creating new solutions that address these problems.

Transforming Small Business Lending

Many industries, from music to telecommunications, have been transformed by technology, but small business banking has been slow to evolve. That is changing. Financial technology, or "fintech," has become a common term, but it represents a very broad category that includes innovation across banking, insurance, and financial services, as well as activities like crypto-currency. This book uses a narrow fintech lens: we focus just on the way technology will affect small business lending.

Lending does not happen in isolation. Other fintech products, particularly those in payments, will have a related impact as they evolve. But, for the purposes of this narrative, the innovations in lending, and in data and intelligence related to lending, provide a rich environment for exploring the ways in which technology will bring transformational change to the world of small businesses.

The cycle of fintech innovation in small business lending is not yet complete, but we can already see its promise. As technology opened the doors to vast troves of data, opportunities emerged to create new insights on a small businesses health and prospects. These inputs have the potential to resolve two defining issues that have faced lenders and borrowers in the sector: heterogeneity—the fact that all small businesses are different, making it difficult to extrapolate from one example to the next—and information opacity, the fact that it is hard to know what is really going on inside a small business.[4]

From a lender's point of view, the smaller the business, the more difficult it is to know if the business is actually profitable and what its prospects might be. Many small business owners do not have a great sense of their cash flow, the sales they might make, when customers will pay, or what cash needs they could have based on the season or a new contract. Small businesses have low cash buffers, and a miscalculation, late payment, or even fast growth could cause a life-threatening cash crunch.

But what if technology had the power to make a small business owner significantly wiser about their cash flow, and a lender wiser as well? What if new loan products and services made it easier to create what one investor calls a "truth file"—a set of information that could quickly and accurately predict the creditworthiness of a small business, much like a consumer's personal credit score helps banks predict creditworthiness for personal loans, credit cards, and mortgages?[5] What if a small business owner had a dashboard of their business activities, including cash projections and insights on sales and cost trends that helped them weave an end-to-end picture of their business's financial health?

This future is appealing because it responds to the fundamental need of small business owners to be able to see and more clearly interpret the information that already exists, helping them navigate the uncertain world of their businesses on their own terms and plan accordingly. And it provides an opportunity for lenders to better understand the creditworthiness of their potential customers and provide lower lending costs as a result. But what if there was more?

What if this dashboard was part of a portal from which the business owner could operate all their financial activities? What if this intelligent platform knew when the business might need credit and could offer relevant options which were prequalified? And better yet, what if the platform came with a digital small business assistant who knew all about the business, including the goals and preferences of the owner. What if this bot could respond to requests in plain English to perform daily tasks and improve sales and marketing. Marshaling the predictive power of artificial intelligence and machine learning amassed from data on thousands of business owners in similar industries, what if this bot could help a business owner head off perilous trends and chart a plan for success?

We call this future state "Small Business Utopia."

It may be that this name overpromises the outcome. Small businesses are perhaps too varied to be predictable, and entrepreneurs run their businesses with so much ingenuity and peculiarity that their insights cannot be replaced or augmented by artificial intelligence. It could be that small business owners are too set in their ways and will resist the new technology driven solutions. Yet, evidence suggests the opposite.

If new intelligence is developed that will help them succeed, small businesses will find a way to adopt it. Small businesses are hungry for new solutions. They responded so positively to the early fintechs' quick turnaround times on loans and the ease of online applications that they spurred traditional lenders to action. The next set of advances are proving to be even more accessible. Platforms are built in the cloud and come ready to help a business owner do everything from paying their bills to building their website. AI-powered intelligence can engage in a comfortable format and quickly provide valuable assistance. And credit options are being embedded in the workflow of their existing systems and are tailored to the needs of the business.

Many of these advances are not fully available, but the path to their arrival has been set. In this book, we trace the progress of the fintech innovation cycle and explore what will be next and who will provide it. We build these predictions for the future on a fundamental foundation of elements we can see today: the needs of small businesses as they access the capital they require, the challenges traditional lending has faced in meeting these needs, and the opportunities that technology is providing for new solutions.

Three Myths of Small Business Lending

In the course of this journey, this book takes on three commonly held misconceptions about small businesses and small business lending. There are often good reasons why countervailing narratives exist. Sometimes, they are partly true. Often, there is not enough data to know definitively what the actual situation is or to prove causality. This is often an issue with small business, as data sources are scarce. Fortunately, in the last several years, more research and analysis has been conducted on the importance of small business to the economy, the role of access to capital for small businesses, and the gaps that exist in the market. We take advantage of this new research as we explore three myths of small business lending.

The first myth is the view that small businesses aren't that important to the economy, and that most small businesses fail and probably shouldn't be financed. This narrative argues that the small businesses that succeed largely don't need external financing, and those that should get financing are already well served by the market. In contrast to this narrative, the early chapters of this book pull together evidence of the barriers which are preventing small businesses from getting the financing they need and describe the underlying market gaps in small business lending.

The second myth is that traditional lenders were "dinosaurs" that fintech start-ups would soon replace. Subsequent events have shown that this initial expectation about fintech disruption was too simplistic. Technology is revolutionizing small business lending, but the landscape of players and solutions is much more complex than we originally anticipated. The contribution of this book is to pull apart where disruption will occur and where it will have the most impact, both on the health and well-being of small businesses and their finances, and on small business lenders. Based on an understanding of the kinds of products that will best serve small businesses and their needs, we predict what will determine the winners in the future small business lending environment.

The third myth is that regulation is the enemy of small business lending, and that the Dodd-Frank reforms had a particularly negative effect.[6] Some have argued that if these regulations were reduced or eliminated, community banks would return to their former role as the critical providers of small business loans, particularly through relationship lending. There is truth to the claim that small banks suffered disproportionately from the burdens of regulations post the 2008–9 financial crisis and that changes that were subsequently made did ease the regulatory burdens on small banks. However, these reductions in bank oversight also contributed to more recent crises such as the failure of Silicon Valley Bank in 2023.

The future we have imagined for small business lending will never be achieved without a stable foundation of rules and safeguards. The new world involves large flows of highly sensitive data traveling continuously between third parties and financial institutions, which must be kept secure. At the same time, lending will be highly automated through algorithms that will need to be monitored for bias and transparency. The arguments for more versus less regulation must be replaced by striving for "smarter" regulation—regulation that promotes the safety and security of customers and the underlying banking system, while still encouraging innovations that fill market gaps.

Taking on these three arguments is an ambitious journey because it requires delving into the data and evidence in three distinct areas of economic work. First is the macroeconomic and microeconomic debate over the importance and role of small business and the gaps in small business lending. Second is the innovation literature, which helps explain how cycles of innovation work and what outcomes we can predict for the fintech revolution. Third is the policy and regulatory arena, which requires an understanding of both the current state of financial regulation and the debates over the future of regulation as it relates to data and artificial intelligence. The constant thread in this journey is the narrow lens of small businesses and their need for capital.

Small businesses are the key actors in our narrative, but not all small businesses are the same. This heterogeneity is the source of much of the complexity in small business lending, and in future solutions. In this book, we introduce a new categorization of the country's 33 million small businesses. We define four distinct segments: sole proprietors with no employees, Main Street businesses, suppliers, and high-growth start-ups. This book focuses on bank-dependent small businesses that fall mostly into the first three groups. We do not cover the capital needs of the relatively small number of high-growth firms that are backed by venture capital. They are vitally important, as they are the firms that could grow to be the next Google or Amazon, but they largely operate in a different market for equity capital.

There are a few other areas that are not covered. *Fintech, Small Business, & the American Dream* is the story of U.S. small businesses and their available capital markets. The United Kingdom and China play a small role as examples of countries with different regulatory approaches, but the promising developments in global fintech, particularly in developing nations, is largely left for future exploration. Additionally, this book is about innovation activity in the lending markets and how technology might help these markets operate more efficiently. Government policy is covered in reference to the response to the 2008–2009 recession as well as the Covid-19 Pandemic, and recommendations regarding the regulatory environment receive substantial attention. However, this effort does not suggest specific government interventions to further close market gaps or fully explore how technology might optimize government efforts to improve lending options to underserved segments, an area with much potential.

Book Overview

This book is organized into five parts. Part I begins with the problem: small businesses are important to the economy and access to capital is important to small businesses, but banks, which have been the traditional lenders to small businesses, face both cyclical and structural pressures. The result is a gap in access to credit, particularly for the smallest businesses, who seek the smallest loans. Part II describes the rise of fintech innovations and the new and old players who have stepped up to fill this gap. Although the fintech innovation cycle has moved in fits and starts, it is now accelerating and shows the potential to be truly transformative, for both small businesses and their lenders. The section ends with a review of the Covid-19 Pandemic government programs designed to help small businesses through this extraordinary crisis, and the important role fintechs played in those interventions.

Part III envisions the future of small business lending, the environment we call "Small Business Utopia" where new data and artificial intelligence create transformational products and services. We explore which actors have the potential to be the winners in the new small business lending landscape, and what a successful playbook for banks might look like. Part IV takes on regulation, discussing issues with the current state of regulatory oversight, and the principles on which a better, more efficient regulatory scheme can be built. The book concludes with a look at eternal truths about small business lending and predictions for the future.

Part I—The Problem

Small businesses are the backbone of the U.S. economy. While most politicians and the public say they agree with this statement, small businesses are excluded from many economists' models and exert little influence in Washington policymaking circles. Yet small businesses contribute disproportionately to job creation and innovation. Moreover, the ability to start and own a small enterprise embodies the American Dream. Small businesses support a vibrant middle class, strong communities and provide a pathway for social mobility. However, small business policy is difficult because not all small businesses are the same. This section describes four distinct small business segments, each of which has different needs, particularly with regard to access to capital.

Capital is the lifeblood of small businesses that depend on credit to start, operate, and grow. Historically, small businesses relied on banks to access capital. But during the 2008–2009 financial crisis, credit markets froze, and banks temporarily stopped lending even to businesses with good credit. This crisis hit small businesses hard and credit conditions were extremely slow to recover. The economic downturn significantly devalued collateral—especially home equity—that small business owners use to secure credit. Lenders and business owners became risk averse due to lost sales and the trauma from the crisis. Short-term cyclical factors made securing credit particularly hard for small businesses during the recovery, opening the door for the entry of new technologies and lenders.

After the recovery, there was still a gap in access to capital for small businesses. It is tempting to blame this on regulation or other cyclical issues, but longer-term structural factors had been putting pressure on banks for decades. Community banks, which traditionally devoted a disproportionate amount of their capital to small business lending, had been declining since the 1980s. The concentration of assets in large banks reduced the focus on small businesses. Larger banks tend to prioritize consumer banking, mortgages, and investments, often viewing small business loans as less appealing. Indeed, small business loans are riskier, have transaction costs that do not scale, and are difficult to securitize. These structural factors have reduced small business access to capital over several decades and do not seem likely to disappear.

Against this background, we ask several crucial questions: What do small businesses want? Why do small businesses seek capital, what kind of capital do they need, and where are the market gaps? The majority of small businesses are looking for small-dollar loans, but the lending market is plagued with frictions that make it difficult for banks to deliver small loans efficiently and profitably. The gaps in the bank-focused small business lending ecosystem and the nature of the capital challenges small businesses face set the scene for the transformative role of fintech.

Part II—The New World of Fintech Innovation

In Part II, we explore how technology is changing the game in small business lending. Joseph Schumpeter, an influential twentieth-century economist, posited that innovation was the fuel that energized the economy through a process of "creative destruction." In his theory, new inventions would be applied in economically useful ways that disrupted traditional industries. Later scholars built the theory of the innovation S-curve, where new innovations live for some time in a stage of ferment, as markets become accustomed to new products and services, followed by a period of acceleration and market adoption. Fintech entrepreneurs, when first entering the market, appeared to have an opportunity to dramatically change the landscape of small business lending at the expense of banks. The process, however, proved to be more complicated.

The second phase of the innovation cycle, takeoff, did not occur as expected. The initial excitement around the entry of hundreds of new fintechs produced rapid growth and a loosely regulated environment that allowed for high prices and hidden fees, which caught some small business borrowers unawares. While the first fintech wave laid the foundation for greater changes, it soon became clear that the innovations brought by the new entrants were largely linear improvements focused on customer experience and could be replicated by traditional lenders more easily than initially anticipated. Banks and other existing lenders also had significant advantages over the newcomers, particularly in the form of large customer bases and low-cost pools of capital from deposits.

The aborted takeoff phase led to a second rich period of market development. Newly available data streams created game-changing insights and reduced some of the frictions that have made small business lending so difficult. With these new tools, it became easier to see inside a small business and predict its future cash flows and ability to repay a loan. And with data on thousands of companies in each sector, it was easier to create a model that determined whether the coffee shop in question was a high, or not so high, performer. The new age of small business lending began to take shape. Then in March 2020, the unthinkable happened.

Part II concludes with a detailed look at the government aid programs for small businesses impacted by the Covid-19 Pandemic and the related lockdowns. Over $1.2 trillion was distributed in a series of massive small business relief efforts, through government agencies and financial institutions. Fintechs played a critical role in increasing access to these programs, particularly for smaller businesses and those underserved by traditional banks. Many have criticized these programs for being costly and vulnerable to fraud. However, a review of the available economic research reveals that these programs were highly effective in meeting their stated objectives.

Part III—Technology Changes the Game

In Part III, we explore the future world of small business lending and the products and services that comprise "Small Business Utopia." These offerings are truly transformational thanks to the application of advanced data analytics and artificial intelligence. The solutions in small business lending involve advances in three distinct areas: the creation of (1) streams of standardized, relevant data available securely through Application Programing Interfaces (APIs), (2) new underwriting models that are highly predictive across different small business segments, and (3) customer interfaces that are easy to use, individualized and available in a platform that is already part of the business owner's routine.

Within the context of this changing technology environment, we review the evolving landscape of small business lending and assess who might be the winners and losers. We identify four key categories: Traditional Banks and other financial institutions such as credit card providers; Big Tech; Challenger Banks; and Infrastructure Players. Each one has a robust story of competitive advantages and challenges. We chart the rise of new platform players like Shopify and Stripe and show how embedded financial offers and the evolution of "Banking as a Service" will change the competitive landscape.

We then return our attention to the traditional banks and develop a playbook for existing lenders to innovate in the new ecosystem. Using Massachusetts-based Eastern Bank as an example, we address the key question: How should banks and traditional lenders evolve their small business lending products and services? This section also discusses the difficulties of bringing disruptive ideas into a traditional institution and proposes structures through which to overcome these obstacles.

Part IV—The Role of Regulation

In Part IV, we ask how the regulators should respond to these changes. The fragmented "spaghetti soup" of the current U.S. regulatory system is ill equipped to support the future of small business banking. While these problems have long existed, the emergence of fintech has made solving them more urgent. Drawing on lessons from the United Kingdom and China, we propose a set of principles for oversight of the future of small business lending, particularly in the era of big data and artificial intelligence. A new regulatory framework should both protect small businesses and encourage innovation while recognizing that many of the new players will look different from traditional lenders. Regulators must also confront thorny questions such as data security and algorithmic bias raised by the use of new technology in lending products and services. Collecting timely data on the small business loan market is a lynchpin of any new system, allowing regulators to identify market gaps and "bad actors."

Part V—Conclusion

This book is the story of the transformation taking place in small business lending, and the impact these changes will have on the financial sector and the small business economy. The new technology is more powerful than we ever imagined, but the problem is more complex. There is great variation in the kinds of small businesses, the loans they need and the objectives of lenders. It will take longer to see the full picture, but we predict that there will be more than one winning strategy. A wide variety of products and lending solutions will be successful, each filling different parts of the current market gaps.

In the optimum market, there will be more lenders and more lending options each serving different small business needs. But across the entire landscape, improved data and intelligence will allow lenders to identify and serve more creditworthy borrowers, and small businesses will gain key insights to manage their cash and operate their companies. The right regulation will enhance borrower protections for small businesses and create a more transparent environment. An ideal future does not mean that all small businesses will get loans. Instead, the ultimate goal is a better small business lending market with fewer stresses, frictions, and gaps. As this small business lending transformation occurs, the prospects will improve for more small business owners to succeed and achieve the American Dream.

Part I

The Problem

2

Small Businesses Are Important to the Economy

In 2017, late night star John Oliver began a segment by noting something interesting about politicians and small business. First, he showed former Democratic presidential candidate Hillary Clinton saying, "Small business is the backbone of the American economy." Cut to former Republican vice-presidential candidate Sarah Palin making almost the same statement. Then a split screen of former presidents Barack Obama and George W. Bush intoning the same small business mantra in tandem. More screen mitosis followed until, in total, 34 politicians from across the political spectrum appeared, each touting the importance of small business in almost exactly the same words (Figure 2.1). In an increasingly partisan political arena, support for small business is a rare point of bipartisan agreement.

It's not just politicians who express support for small business—it's also the public. According to a Gallup survey, 65% of Americans have a "great deal" or "quite a lot" of confidence in small business—twice the average rate for all major institutions surveyed. Only 7% said they had "very little" confidence. Small business has consistently ranked first in public trust, ahead of the military, media, government, religious and criminal justice institutions, and large businesses.[1]

Americans have great affection for small businesses and believe in their importance. But what exactly does it mean to say that "small business is the backbone of the American economy?" Are we referring to the importance of innovators and entrepreneurs who develop new ideas and start companies that grow rapidly to become the next tech giant? Or are we describing the Main Street shops and other small businesses that make up the fabric of our communities? How do we measure the impact of small businesses on

© The Author(s), under exclusive license to Springer Nature
Switzerland AG 2024
K. G. Mills, *Fintech, Small Business & The American Dream*,
https://doi.org/10.1007/978-3-031-55612-8_2

Figure 2.1   "Small Business is the Backbone of the Economy" from John Oliver's Last Week Tonight
Source: "Corporate Consolidation: Last Week Tonight with John Oliver (HBO)," September 24, 2017.[2]

economic growth and on the quality and quantity of employment? Since half of U.S. employment is in small businesses, we know they are important, but exactly how relevant are they, and why?

To understand how small businesses fit into both the economic growth and employment picture, we must focus on an issue that often leads to confusion among policymakers: not all small businesses are the same. High-growth tech businesses play a different role in the economy than the dry cleaner or restaurant on Main Street, yet each has an important place in helping America prosper. Supporting each type requires a different policy perspective, as each one has different needs, including for capital.

In this chapter, we draw up a new way to categorize small businesses and quantify the different types of firms that make up the small business sector. This construction helps us better understand the significance and role of America's small businesses and sets the stage for exploring the markets where they access capital and evaluating how technology is changing those markets.

Is Small Business Important to the American Economy?

Surprisingly, economists have no analytical framework to understand the contribution of small businesses to the economy. Macroeconomists tend to focus on broad indicators, such as GDP, average wages, and the unemployment rate. In Keynesian models, consumption, investment, and government spending drive the economy. Since so much spending power lies with consumers, and larger businesses drive most of the investment, small businesses receive little attention from these economists. In fact, the contributions of small businesses are largely absent from most macroeconomic models.

Monetary economists pay attention to inflation and what the Federal Reserve (Fed) does. In their assessments, small businesses are not relevant, as small business policy does not drive monetary flows or outcomes. That is the province of global markets, where small companies seldom participate.

When macroeconomists think about the contribution of entrepreneurs, it is often through the lens of innovation or productivity. As one economist observed, "No amount of savings and investment, no policy of macroeconomic fine-tuning, no set of tax and spending incentives can generate sustained economic growth unless it is accompanied by the countless large and small discoveries that are required to create more value from a fixed set of natural resources."[3] In this framing, the contribution of entrepreneurs who invest in and market new products and services should be captured as inputs to innovation and reflected as improvements to productivity.[4] But this contribution is difficult to measure. For example, it is hard to know how the advances that allow us to Google information instead of reading a newspaper—or order on Amazon instead of shopping at a brick-and-mortar store—translate into productivity measures. Arguably, posting on social media and binging shows on streaming services have reduced productivity for many of us. Nonetheless, we know that entrepreneurs and the innovations they produce are important because they contribute to the "creative destruction" of the status quo that economist Joseph Schumpeter once argued was the price for a nation to keep or attain leadership in the global economy.[5]

Even with accurate productivity measures, this analysis of small businesses' contribution to the economy would be incomplete. There are only a relatively small number of high-growth small businesses, the ones we often think of as the influential innovators in the U.S. economy. Some economists have argued that these are the only ones that truly matter and should therefore constitute the majority, or even be the sole focus, of government policy. For example, Pugsley and Hurst write that policies that encourage risk-taking and support access to capital for all small businesses might be better aimed at a smaller set of businesses that expect to grow and innovate.[6] Others go one step further, arguing that "the focus of entrepreneurship policy should be squarely on spurring more technology-based start-ups."[7]

It is true that these high-growth innovative businesses contribute much to the economy. But try this thought experiment: imagine a world in which we fully subscribed to the belief that the other kinds of small businesses didn't matter much. If policymakers could identify the high-growth firms early on, they might reasonably decide not to waste time providing licenses to any other small businesses or support their efforts to start and grow. The economic argument would be that small businesses like the shops on Main Street were not worth government or market attention, as they fail at a high rate, are replaced by other businesses, and don't appear to add much to the economy. In this imaginary world, small businesses and the loans and other services that support them would not exist. Without a small business lending market, there would be no private financing for small businesses, other than a few venture capital firms focused on innovative, high-tech industries. The economy would be driven by large businesses. Every Main Street shop would be a chain restaurant or store. Except for a few high-growth entrepreneurs, sole proprietorships would not exist. The Uber driver would be an employee of Uber and the small-town lawyer would be an employee of a large law firm. The path of starting your own business and building generational wealth would be replaced by an entry-level job at a large company. A world without small businesses would dramatically alter the fabric of our communities. It would certainly change the way we lived and worked and would affect the image and culture of America—and the American Dream.

When faced with the prospect of even an imaginary world without small businesses, the average American becomes upset. People inherently know the value of small business. A national survey found that 94% of consumers said that doing business with small businesses in their communities is important.[8] And despite the fact that many consumers shop at Starbucks and Walmart, another survey found that over 70% of respondents expressed a willingness to go out of their way, and perhaps even pay more, to support their local small businesses.[9]

When politicians say that "small businesses are the backbone of the economy," or when former NBA superstar Shaquille O'Neal stars in an ad for Small Business Saturday, they aren't focused on the high-growth firms.[10] They are talking about the corner grocery store or the mom-and-pop coffee shop. But, given the lack of importance of small businesses in macroeconomic models, is their economic value just a myth?

Contributions of Small Business to the Economy

A deeper look shows us that the sentiment many attach to small businesses is reflected in economic reality. Small businesses do, in fact, matter to the economy. In contrast to macroeconomists, microeconomists see many ways that small businesses contribute to the larger economic picture. Their reasons fall into three major arguments: small businesses provide jobs, drive innovation, and act as a path to achieving the American Dream.

Small Business and Job Creation

The most basic argument has to do with the size of the sector and how critical it is to employment and job creation. As Nobel Prize winning economist Robert Solow points out, jobs are the main way our economy has chosen to distribute wealth and other benefits.[11] Small businesses employ about half of all working Americans. As of 2023, over 61 million jobs were accounted for people who worked for themselves or for a company with fewer than 500 people.[12] In addition, small businesses created 63% of net new jobs from 1995 through 2021.[13]

The sheer number of employees in the small business sector warrants close attention from a U.S. policy perspective. If small businesses are under pressure and begin to cut jobs, the impact on national employment and well-being can be significant. This was the case during the 2008–2009 recession. From the first quarter of 2008 through the fourth quarter of 2009, small businesses shed 5.7 million jobs, 60% of the jobs lost during that period.[14] This sent leaders in Washington scrambling to figure out how to stem the damage. In the United Kingdom, the financial crisis elevated small business policy, particularly with respect to access to capital, to a central place in the government's agenda—an action that continues to have a positive impact on the UK's small business and fintech economies.

In the Covid-19 Pandemic, small businesses suffered disproportionately from the mandatory business closures required for public health and safety. Governments around the world recognized the importance of the small business sector and implemented emergency programs. None were larger than the $1.2 trillion in small business pandemic aid distributed in the United States. (The impact and efficacy of these programs will be assessed in some detail in Chapters 8 and 9.)

Some economists and political theorists argue that small businesses are important because they provide stability to the economy. This theory has traction in other nations that build their small and medium enterprise (SME) policies around promoting a robust small business segment that can grow and support a thriving and stable middle class.[15,16] Saudi Arabia, for example, began an SME fund in 2017 with the objective of stabilizing its economy and providing jobs to its growing middle class in the face of falling oil prices.[17]

Small Business and Innovation

Even among skeptics, there is widespread agreement that some small businesses play an important role in innovation. A subset of high-growth small businesses are led by innovative entrepreneurs who create competition for established firms and markets by developing new ideas that keep the economy from becoming stagnant.[18,19] In fact, small businesses with five to nine employees received over 50% more patents per employee than any category of large businesses.[20] In a review of related economic literature, Mirjam Van Praag and Peter Versloot concluded that entrepreneurs account for significant "employment creation, productivity growth and produce and commercialize high-quality innovations."[21] Entrepreneurship and the experimentation it engenders are important underpinnings of economic growth and success.[22]

Small Business and the American Dream

Small businesses and entrepreneurship also provide a path for upward mobility. Research suggests that self-employment increases intergenerational mobility.[23] In addition, studies found a positive link between small business lending through the U.S. Small Business Administration (SBA) and future per capita income growth in a local economy.[24]

Small business has long been a critical part of the American Dream for new Americans, who often start businesses soon after they arrive. Immigrants inject a greater share of economic dynamism than their numbers would suggest. According to recent research, immigrants make up just 17% of the U.S. college-educated workforce, but constitute around a quarter of its entrepreneurs, and account for a similar share of inventions.[25] A Kauffman Foundation index shows that, going back to 1996, immigrants have consistently punched above their weight when it comes to entrepreneurship.[26] From 1995 to 2005, immigrants founded a staggering 52% of new companies in Silicon Valley.[27]

Yet, despite these attempts to quantify the impact of small businesses in the local and national economies, there is no clear framework that captures the contribution of all small businesses. This can lead to economic policy largely focused on taxes, research and development, and trade promotion, and geared primarily toward larger companies, leaving small businesses with the policy crumbs. Creating smart and powerful policy geared toward small businesses is a worthy objective, as it can have a positive impact on a large segment of our economy.

What Is a Small Business?

One key to economic insights when thinking about small businesses is to eliminate the confusion about the kind of small business being discussed. When we do, it becomes clear that each type of small business has a role, and each needs to be considered separately in terms of product needs and policy approaches. In response, we have segmented small businesses into four categories, quantifying the size and activity of each group. As the old saying goes, "What gets measured, gets done." But a corollary ought to be, "What gets categorized, gets measured accurately." The following categorization can help us measure, create policy, and assess the capital markets for the different types of America's small businesses.

The Four Types of Small Business

There is no generally agreed upon way of defining a small business. Most of us have a rough notion of what a small business looks like based on our own experiences. Economists, governments, bankers, and others each categorize small businesses by different measures: their number of employees, their annual revenues, or even the size of their loans. "What are you calling small?" is a frequent question.

Throughout this book, unless otherwise noted, we will rely on the definition of small business used by the SBA, the U.S. Census Bureau, the U.S. Bureau of Labor Statistics, and the Federal Reserve, which all classify a small business as one with fewer than 500 employees. By that definition, there are 33 million small businesses in the United States, constituting more than 99% of all American companies.[28]

To illustrate the different types of small businesses, let's take a walk through a typical American town—Brunswick, Maine. Located near the coast, Brunswick's primary employers are the shipbuilder Bath Iron Works (owned by General Dynamics) and Bowdoin College. New businesses have been opening in the industrial park, located at the former Brunswick Naval Air Station. One manufactures composite aircraft parts and another makes healthcare equipment. These businesses supply goods and services to larger customers. Their employees are happy to get their lunch from the Big Top Deli, where Tony makes the best sandwiches at his shop on Maine Street (spelled with an "e" in Brunswick). Tony had the chance to open another shop nearby but decided against expanding. Next door, however, the entrepreneurial owners of Gelato Fiasco had bigger plans. With growth capital from investors and a local bank, they opened a wholesale plant and began selling Italian ice cream as far away as San Diego.

The aircraft parts supplier, Big Top Deli, and Gelato Fiasco are all small businesses, as are the fast-growing tech start-ups moving in down the coast in Portland. Although they are all small, they are different in many ways including the ways they require and access capital. Some need money to invest in equipment and buildings. Others like Tony are content with where they are but may need a credit line to smooth out operating expenses. Each is an important component of the U.S. economy, but none alone paints the full picture of the small business ecosystem in America.

The 33 million U.S. small businesses fall into four main categories: non-employer sole proprietorships, Main Street firms, suppliers that primarily serve other businesses and organizations, and high-growth companies (Figure 2.2).

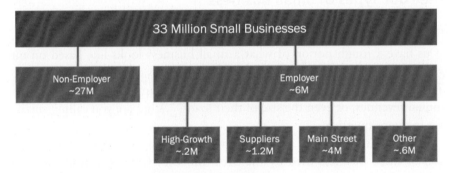

Figure 2.2   The Four Types of Small Businesses
Small businesses by number of firms in the United States (Millions)
Source: Author's calculations of 2017 Economic Census data. This analysis is based on the work of Mercedes Delgado and Karen G. Mills, "The Supply Chain Economy: A New Industry Categorization for Understanding Innovation in Services," Research Policy, Volume 49, Issue 8, October 2020.

Non-Employer Firms

Most small businesses, around 27 million of the 33 million, are sole proprietorships without paid employees. These "non-employer" businesses include consultants and a range of independent contractors and freelancers, from ride-share drivers and painters to real estate agents and hair stylists. Around half of these businesses are full-time jobs for their owners, while others are side businesses.[29] Some people start such firms intending to eventually hire employees and expand, but many start them to accomplish other goals, such as having more flexibility over the hours they work. For many Americans looking to supplement their incomes, these businesses provide an attractive opportunity in addition to their traditional work.

Non-employer firms make up a growing share of U.S. businesses. Between 2007 and 2019, the number of non-employer businesses increased by more than 24% (Figure 2.3). Faster and more ubiquitous broadband and post-Covid-19 remote work trends have made it easier for people to work from home or the local coffee shop. Innovation has also promoted growth in the "gig economy," where people increasingly use online platforms to find independent contractor work as drivers at Uber or Lyft, as freelancers at Upwork or Fiverr, or even as social media influencers on TikTok.[30]

The growth in non-employer businesses has been driven in large part by people working full-time jobs with a part-time business on the side.[31] Whether this development is positive or negative is debatable. On the one hand, individuals now have more opportunities to earn money, and the hours of these part-time businesses tend to be more flexible. However, this may also indicate a structural issue in our economy, in that many people feel the need to take on an additional part-time business because their full-time employment does not pay enough. It could also be that many of these individuals would like to make their side business full-time, but do not have the resources, such as the capital or the skills, to grow the business.

Main Street Firms

The second largest category of small businesses is what we call Main Street firms. These are the local restaurants, gift shops, car repair operations, and other storefronts that come to mind when we imagine a small business. Most of these Main Street businesses, like florists and cafés, do not dramatically increase their employment from one year to the next, but together, these firms provide jobs and benefits for tens of millions of people.

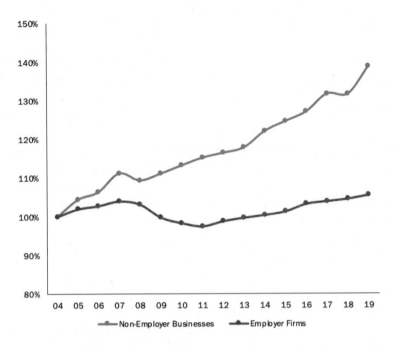

Figure 2.3   Non-Employer Businesses Have Grown Compared to Employer Firms
Growth rates from 2004 to 2020, indexed to 2004
Source: Author's calculations based on U.S. Census Bureau Business Dynamics Statistics and Non-Employer Statistics data.

Although e-commerce is allowing some small firms to ship their goods across the country and around the world, Main Street businesses generally produce goods for local consumption. This contrasts with firms that engage in what we call the "traded" economy, in which businesses sell goods or services outside of their regions. However, the local and traded economies are linked through a "multiplier" effect. For every new traded job, two or more local jobs are created due to the demand of the employees at the traded firm to go out to dinner and use other local services.

Supply Chain Firms

A third category of small business is important but often overlooked: small firms that supply large firms and government clients. There are about one million of these supplier firms, which are often focused on growth and managed with greater sophistication than Main Street firms. An example is Transportation and Logistical Services (TLS) in Hoover, Alabama, just

	Supply Chain Traded	Supply Chain Traded Manufacturing	Supply Chain Traded Services
Small Firms (#)	1,190,385	150,604	1,039,781
Small Firm Employment (M)	12.7	3.5	9.3
Small Firm Wages	$68,728	$51,577	$75,187

Figure 2.4   Supply Chain Employment and Wages (2019)
Source: Author's calculations of 2017 Economic Census data. This analysis is based on the work of Mercedes Delgado and Karen G. Mills, "The Supply Chain Economy: A New Industry Categorization for Understanding Innovation in Services," Research Policy, Volume 49, Issue 8, October 2020.

outside of Birmingham. Started in 2003, TLS employs about 30 people and provides trucking and logistical services to companies as large as Coca-Cola.

New research allows us to identify and separate supply chain industries from business-to-consumer ones for the first time. This work has shown how important small suppliers, which account for almost 13 million jobs, are to the U.S. economy. Although most people just view suppliers as manufacturers of parts, the number of suppliers of traded services is growing rapidly and delivering innovation and high wages[32] (Figure 2.4).

Supplier firms play an important role in local economic growth and development. Cluster theory suggests that strong suppliers impact the ability of both large companies and start-ups to succeed and co-location of companies and their suppliers leads to more economic growth and innovation.[33,34] Support for these small suppliers needs to be an important policy element of the efforts to rebuild U.S. supply chains for critical components such as chips.

High-Growth Firms

The smallest category of the four kinds of small businesses, at least numerically, is high-growth firms. There are about 200,000 of these companies in the United States, but they contribute a disproportionate share of job creation. An MIT study showed that 5% of firms registered in Massachusetts delivered more than three-quarters of growth outcomes and had specific qualities that were evident even as early as the time of their original business registration.[35]

Most of the jobs at these high-growth small businesses are traded jobs, meaning where these firms are incubated or decide to locate greatly impacts the local economy. Cities have long recognized this and have provided incentives to attract these high-growth firms. As one economist argues, "Because a few, typically young firms grow rapidly and account for much of job creation, finding an effective way to support their growth is important."[36]

*   *   *

Each of these four kinds of small businesses plays a different role in our economy, and each has its own needs. A mom-and-pop Main Street shop has different financing needs than a tech start-up. The former might be best served by a bank loan, while the latter might need a patient angel or venture capital equity investor. A sole proprietor such as an Uber driver might need a loan to buy a car, while a supplier might need a short-term advance to hold them over until they are paid by the companies to which they are selling. It is not "one size fits all." The key to robust capital markets for small business and to effective government policy is to understand what it takes to meet the needs of each type of small business.

Economic Dynamism

Economic research has shown that new and young firms are important drivers of job creation in the United States.[37,38] But before 2020, the rate of small business creation had been declining for several decades. Researchers who identified this trend raised the concern that less firm creation would result in reduced economic "dynamism"—the fuel that keeps the American innovation engine pumping.[39] Economic dynamism means new ideas replacing old ideas, and new and energetic companies replacing incumbents. Surprisingly in June 2020, in the midst of the Covid-19 Pandemic, the negative trend reversed and small business applications skyrocketed to unprecedented levels.

The Decline

Between 1977 and 2020, the share of new firms in the U.S. economy declined by almost half (Figure 2.5). The long-term decline in new firm creation was accelerated by a sharp drop during the 2008–2009 recession from which there was never a full recovery.

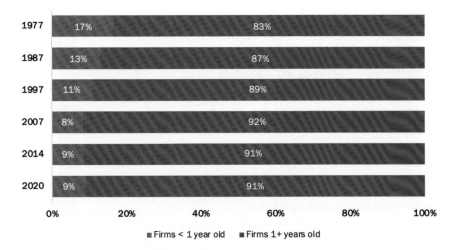

Figure 2.5 New Firms as a Share of Total Firms Declining Since 1977
Employer firms: Firms <1 and Firms 1+ Years Old
Source: Author's calculations based on U.S. Census Bureau, Business Dynamics Statistics, Firm Characteristics Data Tables—Firm Age.

Between 1994 and 2020, the average number of new firms created annually decreased from a peak of more than 550,000 to about 450,000 and the number of jobs created by new firms declined as well (Figure 2.6).

There is no single explanation for these declining trends of small business formations in the United States.[40] Several economists believe the declines were a result of the simple math of having a smaller labor force.[41] As baby boomers retired, there were fewer working-age people, meaning there were fewer candidates to start small businesses. Another explanation may have been the proliferation of "big box" stores in areas like grocery, hardware, and pharmacies. These chains could undercut pricing and offer a wider selection of products, making it harder to start small businesses in these sectors. The high cost of health care and increasing levels of student debt are also often cited as barriers to entrepreneurship.[42,43] In addition to these issues, the market frictions dampening the ability of small businesses to access capital are much more pronounced for younger firms. Whatever the explanation, the trend was worrisome.

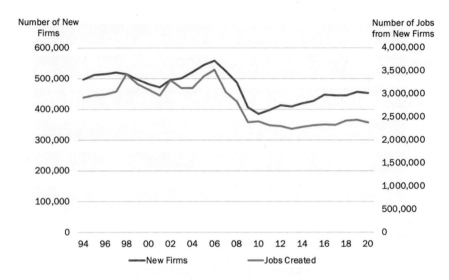

Figure 2.6   Decline in New Firms and New Firm Employment
Annual number of new firms and jobs created by new firms <1 Year Old (1994–2015)
Source: Author's calculations based on U.S. Census Bureau, Business Dynamics Statistics, Firm Characteristics Tables—Firm Age.

A New Spike in Business Applications

While the economy as a whole was slowing down due to the pandemic, an unexpected thing happened: applications to start a new business spiked. Nationally, business applications went from about 300,000 per month to over 500,000 in June 2020 and remained at these high levels throughout the following years (Figure 2.7). This phenomenon happened in all regions of the country and included business from every sector with an emphasis on Retail Trade which comprised over one-third of the applications in 2020.[44]

Economists have been unable to find a concrete explanation as to why new business applications suddenly soared and then stayed at such high levels. However, some interesting hypotheses have been put forth: first, is the theory that there was a restructuring of the economy due to changes in consumer behavior. The pandemic accelerated shifts toward more e-commerce, delivery services, and remote work, building on pre-pandemic trends. This created opportunities for new businesses catering to these changes, as reflected in the large jump in new applications for nonstore retail, professional services, and food delivery.

Research also showed that applications for likely non-employer businesses surged, reflecting a countercyclical increase in self-employment during downturns as unemployed workers start their own businesses.[45] For workers who

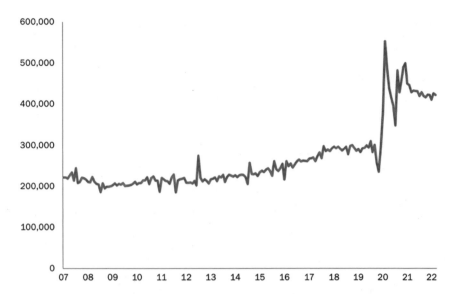

Figure 2.7 Monthly Business Applications, Seasonally Adjusted
Source: Author's calculations based on U.S. Census Bureau, Business Dynamics Statistics, monthly business applications 2004–2022.

lost their jobs in the pandemic, and were already at home, why not turn a longtime side hustle or personal passion into a real business. The surge was larger than in past recessions, reflecting an existing rise in the gig economy.[46]

Finally, in contrast to the 2008–2009 recession, financial markets and access to capital remained strong during the pandemic. This liquidity was augmented by small business government stimulus programs, which helped many businesses pivot to new business models and increased unemployment insurance which may have funded some of the new start-ups.

Although the full data does not yet exist to see if these applications turn into a sustained level of higher business starts, the trends are promising. Research by John Haltiwanger indicated that, based on historical patterns, the 20 percent increase in total applications from 2019 to 2020 "should result in a surge of new employer and nonemployer businesses."[47] Other economists have found that this growth was more significant in regions with a "higher proportion of Black residents," particularly those where median incomes were high.[48] The overall trend in increased applications continued through 2023, indicating that the change in attitudes toward entrepreneurship that began during the pandemic had been sustained and could have had a long and important impact on new business formation trends.

* * *

The health of the U.S. economy depends on the small businesses that create the majority of net new jobs, drive innovation, and secure economic mobility for millions of Americans. This makes it critically important to identify and address frictions that impact small firms. In the next chapter, we explore one area where such frictions plague the ability of entrepreneurs to start and grow a small business in America today: the ability to access capital.

3

Small Businesses and Their Banks: The Impact of the 2008–2009 Recession

In 2015, Pilar Guzman Zavala was down to her last chance to seize the opportunity she and her husband had worked years to achieve.[1] She had to convince Jorge Rossell, the Chairman of TotalBank in Miami, to give her and her husband Juan a loan to open a new restaurant at Miami International Airport.

As she drove into the parking lot of the bank, she ran through her story one more time. Pilar would explain how she and Juan had rescued their business, Half Moon Empanadas, from the brink of failure during the 2008–2009 recession. She would show Rossell how they were now consistently exceeding sales targets, and how they had won the competitive bid to open a new location at Miami International Airport. The new location would be a godsend and was a perfect place for selling their delicious empanadas. Yet, despite their recent success at other locations and even with the airport contract in hand, they had been declined for loans everywhere they went, including at Total-Bank. She hoped against all hope that this personal appeal to Rossell might make the difference. As she walked through the doors and up to the C-suite, she took a deep breath, reminding herself that no matter the outcome of this meeting, she and her family, and their business, were far better off than they had been just a few years ago.

The Zavalas were both immigrants to the United States—Pilar from Mexico and Juan from Argentina. Hoping to achieve the American Dream, they opened Half Moon Empanadas in a fashionable dining room in South Beach. The couple also had plans for a delivery business and ultimately wanted to create "a new category of food."[2] Pilar and Juan poured their savings into the idea and borrowed additional money through a bank loan

K. G. Mills, *Fintech, Small Business & The American Dream*, https://doi.org/10.1007/978-3-031-55612-8_3

to start the business. But soon after opening in South Beach, the Zavalas realized that they had misjudged the market for delivery, and they failed to hit their expected sales. They also had the bad luck of opening their restaurant just before the financial crisis cratered the Florida real estate market. As they struggled to find a workable sales model and weather the recession, they missed payments on a $350,000 bank line of credit. Attempting to make it good and gain financial flexibility, they used an injection of money from their family to make a $125,000 payment. Instead of stabilizing their financing, the bank responded to their show of good faith by cutting off the Zavalas' line of credit.

A few years later, having put $1 million into the business, including all their savings plus bank loans, they could no longer afford to pay rent. They were evicted twice from their business location and then, unthinkably, from their own home. Devastated, the Zavalas questioned whether they should continue with the business. They believed their concept could still work, because although the full-service restaurant had failed, when they took their empanadas to open-air markets and festivals, they could barely keep up with the demand.

Pilar and Juan didn't take a paycheck for nearly four years and avoided the temptation to declare bankruptcy. They adjusted their business plan, got out of their restaurant lease, and took over a food cart at the University of Miami. The previous occupants of the cart had struggled to make $100 per day, but the Zavalas averaged $1,500. Through trial and a fair amount of error, they found the kinds of locations where they could succeed. As Pilar said, "We dusted ourselves off, we tightened our belts, and we survived, never abandoning our bigger dream."

By 2015, when Pilar walked into Rossell's office to request an expansion loan, the Zavalas were operating three storefronts at the University of Miami and had the winning Miami airport bid in hand. Given their credit history since 2008, it was understandable that banks were hesitant to lend to them. In fact, they had only gotten the meeting with Rossell due to a timely introduction from Pilar's mentor. Fortunately for the Zavalas, Rossell looked past the numbers and saw that they really had turned things around. He decided to provide them with the financing for the new location. That bet paid off, with Half Moon increasing its revenues from $500,000 in 2014 to $3 million in 2017. By 2023 the company had 22 stores, 15 in Miami and 7 others in airports across the country.

* * *

Many small business owners across the United States could tell similar stories to that of Pilar and Juan. Getting a small business loan is tough enough on a good day, but during and after the 2008–2009 recession, it became nearly impossible for many businesses to access the financing they needed. Even armed with a good idea, hard work, and a willingness to go to great lengths to fund their business, many small business owners were not as fortunate as the Zavalas. With bank credit frozen, small businesses lacking the additional cash to weather the storm were forced to close their doors. Those that stayed open often found themselves in the same position as Pilar and Juan—with rebounding sales, but an inability to access additional financing because the crisis damaged their credit and because of the long and uneven recovery of bank lending to small businesses.

The Impact of the 2008–2009 Recession

The 2008–2009 financial crisis was a wakeup call for Washington and governments around the world, as policymakers saw the effects of a lack of access to capital for small businesses. Although it was generally understood that access to capital was important to the small business economy, the United States had not seen such a shutdown in the bank credit markets since the Great Depression. In fact, from 2006 to 2007, credit markets for small business loans were so robust that the White House wondered if the government's role in guaranteeing small business loans was still necessary. The impact of the credit crisis on small businesses was unforeseen and devastating. In the first three months of 2009, the economy lost 1.8 million small business jobs, and more than 200,000 small businesses closed between 2008 and 2010.[3]

In Chapter 2, we saw that small business is important to the U.S. economy. But how important is access to capital to small businesses, and what happens when that access goes away? In this chapter, we will explore why the 2008–2009 financial crisis was particularly devastating to small businesses to better understand the importance of a highly functioning small business lending market. The lesson of this recession is one we know from the work of economists: firms that depend more on credit suffer more from a financial crisis.[4] Small businesses depend largely on banks for their credit needs. When banks froze their lending, small businesses had nowhere to turn. Without the liquidity they required, many had to shut down their operations, adding to unemployment and deepening the crisis.

While the financial decline in 2008 was sudden, the recovery in small business credit was slow and bumpy. Banks had sustained severe damage to their balance sheets from overinvesting in bad mortgages, and they were reluctant and often unable to take on risk. At the same time, the deep recession that followed the crisis dealt heavy blows to many small businesses' sales and profits. As a result, small business capital was extremely hard to obtain for a very long time.

The difficulties in the recovery of small business credit were also an indication of a deeper problem. As we will discuss in Chapter 4, structural forces over previous decades had created permanent changes to the traditional bank landscape, resulting in even more difficulties for those trying to access small business loans.

Why Focus on Access to Capital for Small Businesses?

Running a small business requires strong products or services, skilled workers, access to the right markets and customers, a trusted brand, and more. But underlying everything a business does is access to the cash necessary to operate and grow. The liquidity needs can range from working capital to run daily operations to capital to fund investments. While many owners of new businesses finance themselves or rely on friends and family to help, a significant number do not have those options or choose not to use them. In those cases, getting access to capital another way, most often through a bank loan, can be the difference between starting the business right away, putting it off, or not starting it at all.

Even once they begin operations, small firms tend to have more volatile sales and profits than larger businesses, as well as thinner margins for error. According to a study by the JPMorgan Chase Institute—which tracked daily cash flows for more than 600,000 businesses—the typical small company only holds enough cash in reserve to last 27 days.[5] The median cash buffer varies substantially across industries. For instance, the restaurant industry in which the Zavalas operate holds only a 16-day buffer period. This means that a poor month of sales or an unexpected expense can put a small business in a cash squeeze. Securing a line of credit for operational funding can smooth out volatility and provide a source of liquidity when cash is needed.

Access to capital is also important for expansion. When a sole proprietor decides to add their first employee, they might incur incorporation fees, have to purchase a payroll system, or need new office space. When a restaurant owner identifies a market opportunity and expands from one location to two, they will likely need new equipment, furnishings, and a point of sale system. According to the 2022 Federal Reserve Small Business Credit Survey, 53% of firms that sought financing in 2022 said they did so to expand or pursue a new opportunity.[6] These firms required a one-time investment that would often exceed what their businesses could generate internally, or what their owners' personal resources could handle. In these cases, they had to turn to outside sources of financing.

The 2008–2009 Financial Crisis

For many years, little national attention was paid to the issue of small business access to capital. The U.S. economy, including small businesses, seemed to be doing well in the mid-2000s. Economic growth had been consistent, if not spectacular, for several years. Few financial policy experts, much less small business owners, understood the risk building up in the financial system due to soaring home prices, exotic financial products, and highly leveraged investment banks. They certainly did not foresee that in 2008 it would all come crashing down, sparking the most severe economic downturn since the Great Depression. The ensuing recession harmed the economy broadly, but small businesses were hit harder than most sectors. In 2008, small businesses employed 50% of the private sector workforce, but accounted for over 60% of the net job losses as the economy dipped (Figure 3.1).

Many of us thought at the time that we were facing the greatest small business crisis of our lifetime. Yet, in 2020 the Covid-19 pandemic and the

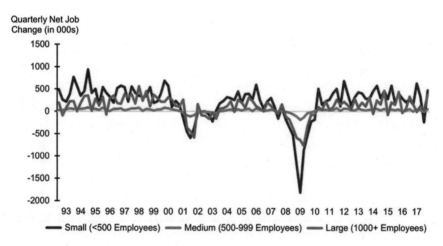

Figure 3.1   Small Firms Were Hit Harder in Crisis, Representing Over 60% of Job Losses
Net job gains or job losses by firm size ('000s of Jobs)
Source: Bureau of Labor Statistics, Business Employment Dynamics, Table E—Quarterly net change by firm size class, seasonally adjusted.

subsequent public health crisis and shutdown of the economy created a challenge that made the job losses from the 2008 financial crisis appear like a small blip (Figure 3.2). Clearly, the Covid-19 pandemic was a different situation. It was not a credit crisis, and the small business impact was collateral damage from necessary actions to ensure public safety. The massive and rapid government response in small business aid recognized the need to keep small businesses liquid and bridge them to a post-pandemic environment and resulted in a more rapid recovery of small business jobs post-Covid-19, than we saw in the aftermath of the financial crisis. (The impact of the pandemic on small business and the efficacy of the response will be covered in some detail in Chapters 8 and 9.)

In 2009, the epicenter of the crisis was the banks. Small businesses depend on banks, and when banks are in trouble, as many were during the 2008–2009 recession, they tap (or slam) the brakes on lending. In the first quarter of 2009, small businesses lost 1.8 million jobs, more than twice the job losses of larger business. Small businesses were hurt more, in part, because they had fewer financing options than larger firms. Large companies can raise money by issuing and selling debt to investors in capital markets (and in this recession, they could take on this debt at historically low interest rates). Larger firms have these options because they usually have longer, more established track records, less volatile income and profitability, and are considered less risky to lend to than smaller firms. In addition, they borrow in the larger amounts that debt markets have traditionally required.

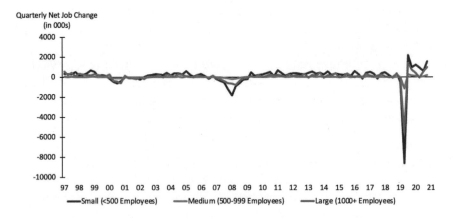

Figure 3.2 Small Firms Were Hit Harder in Crisis—Covid-19 Era
Net job gains or job losses by firm size ('000s of Jobs)
Source: Bureau of Labor Statistics, Business Employment Dynamics, Table E—Quarterly net change by firm size class, seasonally adjusted.

During the 2008–2009 financial crisis, banks and their regulators realized that the huge numbers of mortgages and financial products based on mortgages on their books were much riskier than they had previously thought. As the value of these assets dropped, banks didn't have the capital and reserves they thought they had. To get back into regulatory compliance, some banks ended up allocating less money to small business lending. In particular, the four largest banks—Bank of America, Citigroup, JPMorgan Chase, and Wells Fargo—dramatically reduced lending to small businesses. Loan originations for these top four banks fell to just 50% of pre-crisis levels and remained there through 2014.[7]

In addition, many community banks failed during the crisis. From 2007 through 2013, the number of U.S. banks declined by 800, including a 41% drop in the number of the smallest banks (those with less than $50 million in assets).[8] Since community banks are disproportionately large lenders to small businesses, this was an additional disruptive force preventing small businesses from accessing capital during the recession.[9]

Economic research demonstrates that credit markets act as "financial accelerators" that amplify both periods of growth and downturns for small businesses that rely on bank financing. One influential 1994 study showed that small firms contract significantly more than large firms when credit conditions are tight.[10] More recent research found that firms that are more dependent on banks for their financing suffer more during banking crises.[11] The 2008–2009 fit the pattern of previous financial crises in which the risk of unemployment was higher for people working in a sector that was more dependent on external financing. In effect, firms that couldn't secure enough capital from banks to fund their operations had to downsize.[12] Another analysis of the crisis found that, among all firms dependent on bank financing, small and medium-sized firms experienced the greatest drops in employment, partly due to the costs of switching lenders when their original lender ran into trouble.[13] The research consensus is clear: in a credit crisis, it is credit-dependent entities like small businesses that suffer the most.

Government's Response to the 2008–2009 Recession

By January 2009, it was clear that there was a crisis in small business lending. Lehman Brothers had failed, and banks were suddenly facing uncertain futures. Some of the most important U.S. banks were calculating their balance sheets every few hours to see if they were bankrupt or could continue operating. Small business credit markets were frozen. New lending came to a standstill, and, even worse, many small businesses received a surprise phone call from their banker: their lines of credit had suddenly been cancelled—often not due to anything those businesses had done wrong. Without access to liquidity from their credit lines, small business owners were forced to cut back on spending. This meant anything from delaying an expansion to missing a rent payment to laying off employees.

In the United States, the federal government knew that small businesses were in trouble, but the full extent of the problem was hard to quantify. In the West Wing of the White House, we on the economic team gathered in the early days of 2009 to discuss what should be done. The debate was fierce: should banks be forced to lend to small businesses? Should the government step in and lend directly? Were small businesses still creditworthy? What level of defaults should the government be willing to risk? The discussion was difficult because the exact data needed to define the state of the crisis did not exist. Despite bank regulation and quarterly call reports, there was no real-time collection of small business loan originations.[14] Anecdotes, however, were pouring into the White House and into congressional offices from small businesses like the Zavalas' who were caught in a credit squeeze and had nowhere to turn.

As the head of the U.S. Small Business Administration, my job was to understand and communicate the impact the banking crisis was having on small businesses and ensure the response was a top priority across the administration. Because of the lack of data and the fact that many economists don't see the importance of small businesses (in part because they don't show up in the macroeconomic models), this took some effort.

In the United Kingdom where bank concentration was very high, George Osborne, the Chancellor of the Exchequer, noted that during the crisis, there was not a day that went by when he did not hear from small business constituencies about the depth of their plight.[15] As a result, the U.K. government made small business lending a priority, coming to the aid of their four major banks that together made up over 80% of small business lending. For the United States, the situation was more complicated, in part because of a more dispersed banking system.

In late 2008, the U.S. government implemented the Troubled Asset Relief Program (TARP), a bold plan to provide capital to banks and prevent their collapse. However, TARP legislation did not require that a certain amount of the capital infusion be used to lend to small businesses and keep their credit lines active. This turned out to be a mistake. Although some banks used the capital for small business lending, most had what they viewed as more pressing needs. Between 2008 and the first quarter of 2012, outstanding small business loans (defined as the stock of commercial and industrial (C&I) loans under $1 million) dropped by 17%.[16]

In the face of the devastation, the United States had at least one often overlooked asset: a widespread loan guarantee network through the Small Business Administration (SBA). The SBA had relationships with 5,000 banks throughout the country and the ability to guarantee loans—a powerful tool that did not exist in the United Kingdom or many other countries. However, as the financial crisis peaked, even SBA-guaranteed lending had ground to a near halt, as banks pulled back and SBA securitization markets froze. In response, starting in early 2009, we at the SBA took aggressive steps to boost credit availability for small businesses.[17]

Before 2009, the SBA generally guaranteed 75% of the value of a loan. In early 2009, Congress passed the American Recovery and Reinvestment Act—popularly known as the stimulus bill—which temporarily raised the guarantee to 90% of the loan value, making these loans less risky for lenders to offer.[18] In addition, the bill eliminated almost all SBA fees. The combination worked. Using the new guarantees, more than 1,000 banks that had not made an SBA loan since 2007 made at least one during the next six months. The turnaround helped many businesses survive and contributed to three record years of SBA-backed lending from 2011 to 2013.[19]

More legislation followed. The Small Business Jobs Act of 2010 contained additional lending and tax support for small businesses. One program, the Small Business Lending Fund (SBLF), provided capital to community banks, with the stipulation that they increase small business lending. According to the U.S. Department of the Treasury (Treasury), the SBLF invested $4 billion in 281 community banks and 51 community development loan funds. Small business lending increased by almost $19 billion at those institutions from the time the program began.[20,21]

Another important program came directly from the voice of a small business owner. In August 2011, President Obama and I sat down with small businesses at Northeast Iowa Community College in Peosta, Iowa. One owner was visibly unhappy. His business had a government contract but had not been paid for nearly a year, and he was running out of money. From that meeting, the QuickPay program was born. The thesis was that late payment was exacerbating already tight cashflows among small business contractors. On September 14, the White House directed all government agencies to speed up federal payments to small business contractors from 30 to 15 days.[22]

This acceleration of payment was designed to increase the cash liquidity of federal small business suppliers and offset their need to seek credit in the still tight post-crisis markets. The program worked. Payment times were cut in half, significantly reducing the cash required for working capital for the affected small businesses (see box). Years later Harvard Business School researchers studied the program data and found that it had had a positive impact on recovery. Firms that received the quicker payments showed higher growth in employment, although the impact was less pronounced in tight labor markets.[23]

> **Impact of QuickPay**
>
> Necole Parker is the Founder and CEO of The ELOCEN Group LLC, a construction and renovation project management firm located in Washington, employing 47 people. The company works with a number of federal agencies, including the Food and Drug Administration, the Bureau of Land Management, and the General Services Administration. Before QuickPay, Necole was constantly in touch with her contracting officers to make sure she got her invoices paid within 30 days. In addition, she had to frequently check to make sure she had enough in the bank to meet payroll. QuickPay's reduction of the payment cycle from net 30 to net 15 days allowed The ELOCEN Group to have a significant buffer of cash in the bank on a more regular basis. Necole reported that as a result of QuickPay and better cash balances, she was able to convince her bank to increase her line of credit from $250,000 to $1 million. In her words, QuickPay "had an incredible impact, [allowing] us to … provide a better service not only to our clients, but to our subcontractors who help us with our capacity."[24]

The Slow Post-Recession Recovery for Small Business

Government action helped spur small business lending, but the recovery still took time.[25] Employment growth returned in 2010, but it took until mid-2014 for jobs to reach pre-crisis levels[26] (Figure 3.3). Similarly, lending was slow to come back, as compared to past recessions (Figure 3.4). The levels of total loans in the economy, even eight years after the crisis, were below the recovery levels of any of the previous seven recessions.

The story of post-crisis bank lending was different for small and large businesses. The volume of C&I loans under $1 million dropped substantially during the 2008–2009 recession, and only reached its pre-crisis level in 2016. Larger loans, usually made to larger businesses, also dropped during the recession, but recovered more quickly and continue to grow at a rapid rate (Figure 3.5).

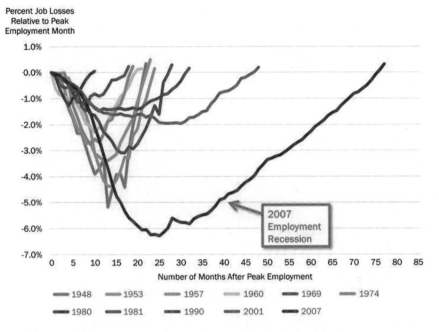

Figure 3.3   Change in Unemployment for Post-World War II Recessions
Source: "Current Employment Statistics," "Bureau of Labor Statistics; US Business Cycle Expansions and Contractions," National Bureau of Economic Research; Adapted from Bill McBride, "Update: 'Scariest jobs chart ever,'" Calculated Risk Blog, February 2, 2018.

Why was the recovery so slow for small business lending? One reason is that the financial crisis caused cyclical damage to both small businesses and small business lenders, which was deep and lasted well beyond the official end of the crisis. As a result of this trauma, small businesses became less creditworthy and banks became more risk averse, in ways that took years to reverse.

Cyclical Damage to Small Business Lending

One version of the narrative in the period after the financial crisis was that the market was functioning as it should: banks were not providing loans to small businesses because they weren't creditworthy. In the post-recession period, bankers believed that they were making loans to all viable small business owners.[27] At the same time, small business owners were telling stories of

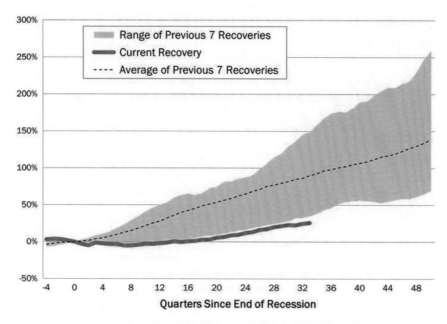

Figure 3.4   Growth in Bank Lending Since the End of the Recession
Source: "Financial Accounts of the United States," Federal Reserve; Adapted from Steven T. Mnuchin and Craig S. Phillips, "A Financial System That Creates Economic Opportunities: Banks and Credit Unions," U.S. Department of the Treasury, June 2017

going from bank to bank and being rejected. The reality was likely a combination of a decrease in demand by recession-damaged small businesses and a slow recovery of supply by the banks.

Lending has always been simple at its core: banks make loans when they are reasonably confident they will be repaid. Banks ask themselves many questions when deciding whether to lend to a small business: does the firm have a good chance of sustained profitability? Is it managed well? Can it put up collateral to reduce the risk of making the loan? Can it find the workers it needs to start or expand? Do the owners have a track record of success and paying their debts on time? Is the economic outlook positive? During the 2008–2009 recession, it became harder for banks to get to "yes" on these questions. The prime culprits were cyclical issues: declining revenues, damaged collateral for potential borrowers, and more risk-averse lenders facing new regulatory pressures.

Dec 2008 = 100

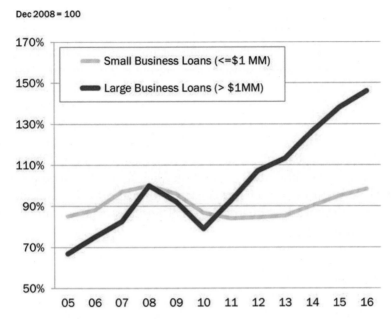

Figure 3.5 Comparison of Change in Small vs. Large Business Loans
Source: FDIC Quarterly Banking Profile Time Series Data; Adapted from Steven T. Mnuchin and Craig S. Phillips, "A Financial System That Creates Economic Opportunities: Banks and Credit Unions," U.S. Department of the Treasury, June 2017.

Declining Revenues

During a recession, revenues can decline even for otherwise healthy companies. For about four years after August 2008, small businesses reported disappointing sales as their biggest problem.[28] The Wells Fargo/Gallup Small Business Index shows that, from 2004 to early 2008, 40–50% of small businesses reported increased revenue in the previous year. That metric plummeted to 21% following the crisis and did not return to above 40% until the second half of 2014.[29] These revenue issues had lasting effects. Even when revenues improved during the recovery, the tough times that many small businesses went through in the recession made potential borrowers, like the Zavalas, look less attractive to banks.

Collateral Damage

If a bank can take possession of collateral assets when the borrower defaults on a loan, the loan is less risky to make. Home equity has traditionally played an important role in financing small businesses.[30] Unfortunately, the financial crisis wreaked havoc on this collateral, in large part because the crisis was built on an unsustainable bubble in the value of home prices. Once the bubble burst, home values dropped substantially, erasing trillions in asset value.

We do not know for sure how many small businesses finance themselves using their homes as collateral for a loan or a home equity line of credit (HELOC). In 2007, at the peak of U.S. home prices, the estimate was as high as 56%.[31] However, in 2011, after the collapse, a survey by the National Federation of Independent Business (NFIB) found that only 22% of small business employers either took equity from their homes and used it for their businesses or used their homes as collateral to finance their businesses. The collapse also left nearly a quarter of small business owners underwater on their home mortgages.[32]

Risk Aversion

In late 2007, with their balance sheets reeling and the devastating effects of risky loans like subprime mortgages fresh in their minds, banks began to tighten their credit standards. At the peak of the crisis in 2009, over 70% of senior loan officers surveyed by the Federal Reserve said that they were tightening their credit standards, including higher collateral requirements, calling in loans ahead of maturity, increasing the amount of equity businesses needed for new loans, and increasing personal credit thresholds. Credit standards remained tight until 2010 and only loosened slowly in the following years (Figure 3.6).

Regulatory Overhang

An increased regulatory burden was partly to blame for the slow post-crisis recovery in small business lending. The Dodd-Frank Act required hundreds of new rules and regulations to be written, and U.S. regulatory agencies opted to develop others. One study found that regulation after the recession reduced the incentives for all banks to make very small loans, and also reduced the viability of banks with assets of less than $300 million. After Dodd-Frank, the small loan share at larger banks fell by nine percentage points, while the magnitude of the decline was twice as great at small banks.[33]

A 2016 Bipartisan Policy Center paper found that while post-crisis reforms had generally made the financial system and consumers safer, they also created unintended consequences. Some regulations were unnecessarily duplicative,

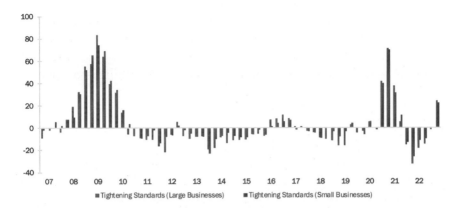

Figure 3.6 Tightening Credit Standards for Small Businesses
Quarterly percentage of bankers reporting net tightening or loosening of loan conditions
Source: "Senior Loan Officer Opinion Survey on Bank Lending Practices", The Federal Reserve, accessed June 2023.

or even in conflict with each other, causing firms to stop offering certain services.[34] Attempts have been made to quantify the costs of compliance to banks.[35] Rice University's Baker Institute estimated that the Dodd-Frank Act had imposed costs to be $50 billion and the American Action Forum estimated in 2016 over $36 billion in final rule costs and 73 million hours of paperwork. Estimates published in the Federal Register pegged the cost much lower, at $10.4 billion. Other estimates of the total compliance cost to the industry vary widely.[36,37]

What is clear is that increased regulation raised costs for banks, which made it costlier to lend and likely caused some financial firms to reduce or eliminate their lending to small firms. The regulatory burden seems to have fallen on smaller banks the hardest. In a 2013 paper, the Federal Reserve Bank of Minneapolis found that the smallest banks, those with assets of less than $50 million, suffered the greatest hit to their profitability from having to hire compliance staff.[38] This makes intuitive sense because the smallest banks have the fewest employees, so having to hire one more person for compliance costs relatively more than it does for a large bank that already has a robust compliance department. A 2016 paper from the Federal Reserve Bank of St. Louis presented evidence confirming that "compliance costs at banks with assets of less than $100 million represented more than 8% of noninterest expense, while the same costs at banks with assets of between $1 and $10 billion represented less than 3% of noninterest expense."[39]

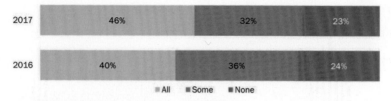

Figure 3.7 Small Business Funding has Improved
Amount of financing approved (percentage of applicants)
Source: "2017 Small Business Credit Survey: Report on Employer Firms," Federal Reserve Banks, May 2018.
Note: Values may not total 100% due to rounding. Data from the 2014 and 2015 surveys is not included due to differences in sampling.

An Improved Funding Environment

Despite these issues, credit markets eventually improved. The 2017 Federal Reserve Small Business Credit Survey showed that over 46% of respondents said they had received all of the funding they applied for, up from 40% of respondents in the previous year[40] (Figure 3.7).

It is important to note that this number should not be close to 100%. Some small businesses are not creditworthy enough to qualify for the full amount they request, and lending to them would likely result in poor outcomes for both the lender and the small business owner. However, we also do not want a market gap in which many creditworthy small business borrowers are being turned away.

Unfortunately, there is evidence that, despite the improved environment, a credit gap did continue. Even as late as 2017, small business loan assets held at U.S. banks had not reached pre-recession levels. In fact, by 2017, the share of small business loans as a percentage of all business loans at banks had dropped to about 20%, down from over 30% before the crisis (Figure 3.8).

* * *

If the cyclical pressures had receded, then why was bank lending to small business still so low? Small business lending was also affected by structural changes, which had begun before the 2008–2009 recession, were exacerbated by the crisis, and continued in its aftermath. In Chapter 4, we will explore changes in the structure of the banking industry beginning with the decline over the last 40 years of community banks in the U.S., on which small businesses have historically relied for their capital needs. Then in the following chapters, we will see how these changes opened the door to fintech

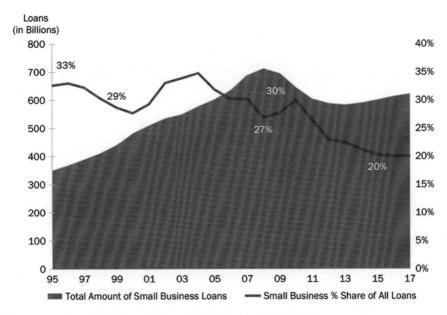

Figure 3.8   Small Business Loans at U.S. Banks, 1995–2017
Source: Author's analysis of FDIC Quarterly Banking Profile Time Series Data.
Note: Small business loans are defined as those under $1 million.

entrepreneurs who responded by using technology to serve the unmet needs of small business owners seeking capital.

4

Structural Obstacles Slow Business Lending

In 2016, Rich Square, North Carolina—population a bit south of 1,000—found itself without a bank branch for the first time in more than 100 years.[1] Nearby Roxobel had lost its only branch in 2014, forcing small business owner Tommy Davis to drive 25 minutes each way to make deposits at his bank. Davis was not the only time-strapped small business owner facing this issue. Local banks are the lifeblood of many communities—rural and urban—and their small business ecosystems.

The 2008–2009 financial crisis and the slow thawing of credit in the recovery that followed affected small business banking deeply. But there were troubling signs for small business lending in the U.S. economy long before the crisis hit. The number of community banks, which have always been more likely to lend to small firms, had been declining since the 1980s. The Federal Reserve Bank of Cleveland summarized the problem: "The factors unleashed by the financial crisis and Great Recession added to a longer-term trend. Banks have been shifting activity away from the small business credit market since the late 1990s, as they have consolidated and sought out more profitable sectors of the credit market."[2]

We saw in Chapter 3, that the increase in post-crisis regulation caused a disproportionate burden to small banks, which affected small businesses' access to capital. Some had believed that if these regulations were reversed, small community banks would flourish again as they returned to their roles as the providers of smaller loans to local small businesses with whom they had relationships. But Trump-era rollbacks of some of the Dodd-Frank requirements did not slow the underlying trends. As we will discuss further in this chapter, structural changes in the banking industry were the root cause of

© The Author(s), under exclusive license to Springer Nature Switzerland AG 2024
K. G. Mills, *Fintech, Small Business & The American Dream*,
https://doi.org/10.1007/978-3-031-55612-8_4

the decline in small businesses' ability to rely on community banks for their credit needs.

Small Businesses Rely on Community Banks

Community banks are an important thread in our story because they provide a disproportionate share of loans to small businesses. In 2021, small business loan approval rates were 67% at small banks versus 48% at larger banks.[3] Thus, it is not surprising that, when compared with large banks, community banks dedicate a higher share of their assets to small business lending. In 2021, the smallest community banks held just 5% of the assets in the banking industry but made 16% of the loans to small businesses.[4] (Figure 4.1). Mid-sized community banks (with assets $1 billion to $10 billion) held 9% of the assets and made 19% of small business loans.

What is it about community banks, their local presence, and the relationships they build that is so important in small business lending?

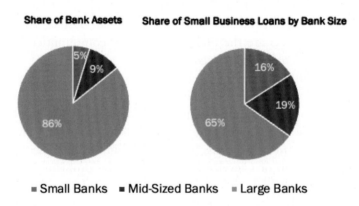

Figure 4.1   Community banks Provide a Disproportionate Share of Small Business Loans
Note: Small banks are defined as those with $1 billion in assets or less, and mid-sized banks as those between $1 billion and $10 billion in assets. The large banks are those with assets over $10 billion. Small business loans consist of commercial and industrial loans of $1 million or less.
Source: Author's analysis of FDIC Statistics on Depository Institutions Report, vol. 16, no. 4, "Availability of Credit to Small Businesses," Federal Reserve Banks Publications, October 2022.

Defining Community Banks

It's helpful to be explicit about what a community bank is. As with small businesses, there is no universally agreed-upon definition. The term most often refers to banks that are small—generally with less than $1 billion in assets, but sometimes going up to $10 billion—do business within a limited geographical area, and are focused on traditional lending and deposit taking. These banks do not have the resources, geographic footprint, or diverse product offerings that larger banks often possess, but they tend to know the communities they serve more intimately.

To understand the advantage a community bank might have in making loans, imagine that Michelle owns an ice cream parlor and wants to open a second one across town. She runs into problems securing the financing she needs because three years ago, she was late on several loan payments, a red flag for lenders. However, a local banker who knows Michelle personally may understand that the reason for the late payments was a family medical emergency, that other locals vouch for Michelle's character and ability, and that her credit is otherwise spotless. That banker will likely consider Michelle a better credit risk than she would appear if her numbers were run through a standardized formula.

Small firms tend to be more "informationally opaque"—that is, they don't have as much publicly available, transparent information for lenders to review Local banks are more able to invest the time and personnel to build closer relationships with borrowers, which then makes it easier for them to assess a borrower's creditworthiness.[5] The economic literature indicates that larger banks are more likely to rely on standardized, quantitative criteria when deciding whether to make a loan to a small firm, while smaller banks are more likely to use qualitative criteria that look beyond the numbers to the applicants' personal qualities.[6,7]

Focusing on local markets and having more insights into the borrower may be an advantage for community banks. One study found that loans performed better when borrowers were located closer to their lenders. Borrowers 25 to 50 miles from the lending bank were 10.8% more likely to default on a loan, while those located 50 or more miles away were 22.1% more likely to default.[8]

Relationship lending can have additional benefits, including providing the added function of counseling small businesses while monitoring the loans. About three-quarters of borrowers ask bankers for financial advice, making these sustained relationships valuable for the borrowers, who can run more successful businesses as a result, and for the lenders, who can provide more

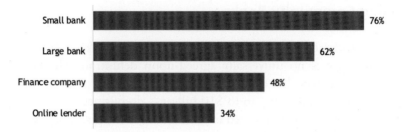

Figure 4.2   Borrower Satisfaction by Institution Type. Percentage of Borrowers Satisfied
Source: "2022 Small Business Credit Survey: Report on Employer Firms," Federal Reserve Banks, May 2022.

credit and other financial services to those businesses over time.[9] Research found that firms with longer-term banking relationships experienced stronger credit growth and lower interest rates during a financial crisis, and maintained greater investment and employment growth than firms that did not have such relationships.[10]

With higher approval rates and a focus on relationship banking, small businesses are more likely to hear a "yes" in response to their application at local banks than they are at larger banks. Thus, it is no surprise that community banks are more highly rated when it comes to customer satisfaction. In 2021, small banks had a satisfaction rate of 76%. Meanwhile, satisfaction for large banks sat at just 62% and online lenders trailed the pack at only 34% (Figure 4.2).

The Decline of Community Banks

Not every country has a large ecosystem of community banks serving small businesses locally. In order to understand how this came about in America, we need to go back 200 years to the early days of the Republic. Since the time of our Founding Fathers, many Americans have been skeptical of an energetic government and a powerful financial system, such as the one Alexander Hamilton advocated, and have more or less sided with Thomas Jefferson, who favored decentralized and relatively weak government. The history of U.S. central banking is a microcosm of this ongoing conflict. Congress created two central banks, in 1791 and 1816, only to see both charters expire under Presidents Jefferson and Jackson. The creation of the third central bank, the Federal Reserve, only happened after a difficult and acrimonious political battle in the early 1900s.

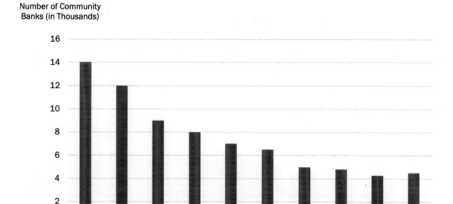

Figure 4.3   Banks have been Declining, 1984–2023
Note: FDIC Call Report data as of Q1 2023.
Source: FRED Economic Data, Federal Reserve Bank of St. Louis, Federal Financial Institutions Examination Council (FFIEC); FDIC Call Reports.

As a result, the U.S. banking system was often chaotic, with state-chartered "wildcat" banks proliferating between 1816 and the Civil War, along with more frequent banking crises than in many other Western countries. The number of U.S. banks boomed with more than 10,000 commercial banks operating by the mid-1890s. By 1921, there were more than 30,000 banks in the country, an all-time high.[11] The vast majority were small and focused on serving their local communities.

After a series of failures in the 1920s and 1930s largely due to the agricultural depression of the 1920s and the Great Depression that followed, the number of U.S. banks dropped to about 15,000 and stayed roughly around that level until the 1980s. But by 2023, only about 4,600 commercial banks remained. Through failure, consolidation, and mergers, the number of U.S. banks had dwindled, even while the banking sector had grown much larger[12] (Figure 4.3).

The Banking System Has Become More Concentrated

As the number of lenders decreased, assets in the U.S. banking system became increasingly concentrated in a small number of larger banks. From 1984 to 2017, while the number of banks declined by 66%, the total assets in the

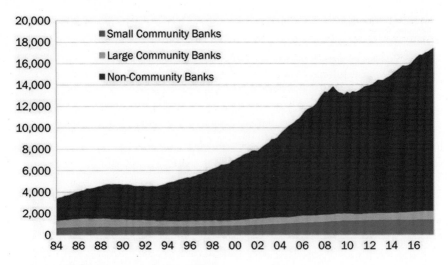

Figure 4.4 Total Assets by Type of Bank
Note: For the FDIC definition of large and small community banks, as well as non-community banks, see: https://www.fdic.gov/regulations/resources/cbi/report/cbsi-1.pdf.
Source: *Adapted from FDIC community banking research project, "Community Banking by the Numbers," February 16, 2012.*

industry grew from $3.7 trillion to $17.4 trillion.[13] Almost all of that growth occurred in non-community banks (Figure 4.4).

The largest banks have seen the lion's share of this growth. The assets of the four largest banks grew from $228 billion (6% of total banking assets) in 1984 to $6.1 trillion (44% of total banking assets) in 2011.[14] Another way to express the widening gap between the smallest and largest banks is that, in 1984, the average non-community bank was 12 times as large as the average community bank. By 2011, the multiple had grown to 74 times as large. By 2019, the multiple had grown to 82 times as large.[15]

The size of the average community bank also grew significantly during that time. Banks with assets less than $100 million accounted for essentially the entire decline in the number of bank charters from 1984 to 2011. Meanwhile, the number of community banks holding between $100 million and $1 billion in assets increased modestly during this period.

Wave of Consolidation

Until the early 1990s, most states limited or prohibited banks from acquiring or opening branches across state lines, while a few states even restricted branching within the state itself. These rules were put into place because poli-cymakers worried that larger, multi-state financial firms would be too hard to supervise. As a result, the number of U.S. banks was kept artificially high.

After large numbers of small banks and thrifts failed during the 1970s and 1980s, Congress decided that the banking system was not concentrated enough.[16] They came to believe that small, local banks were too susceptible to local economic conditions, and consolidation would help them diversify their geographic risk. The Riegle-Neal Act of 1994 eliminated most of the restric-tions on interstate branching and contributed to a wave of consolidations in the banking sector.

From 1995 to 1998, about 5.7% of banks consolidated each year. One analysis suggested that this was almost entirely due to mergers and acqui-sitions, which Riegle-Neal made easier.[17] The rate gradually declined, but between 2004 and 2007—prior to the financial crisis and in good economic times—3.7% of banks were still merging or consolidating every year. Finan-cial crises also precipitated a decline in the number of community banks. Between 1984 and 2011, 2,555 banks and thrifts failed, mostly during the savings and loan crisis of the early 1990s, and during the 2008 crisis.[18]

Few New Bank Charters

Of course, bank failures and consolidations are nothing new. In the past, however, new banks would step in to fill some or all of the market gaps left when incumbent banks retreated. In recent years, that has not been the case. From 2000 to 2008, the Federal Deposit Insurance Corporation (FDIC) approved more than 1,000 de novo, or new bank, charter applications.[19] Before that, the fewest number of de novo charters approved in any single year was 15 in 1942.[20] This activity ground to a halt after the 2008–9 financial crisis. From 2010 to 2018, only 8 new charters opened. Activity improved slightly in the following years, with 45 new charters that opened between 2019 and 2023, but remained low compared to the pre-2008 trend (Figure 4.5).[21]

One reason for the slow pace of applications and approvals was that the FDIC and other regulatory agencies became more cautious after the 2008–2009 crisis. De novo banks chartered between 2000 and 2008 were more "financially fragile and failed at a higher rates" than more established small banks.[22] In addition, after the 2008 crisis, regulators required a higher level of capital at banks to make them safer, and many would-be bankers saw the application process as too difficult and the level of regulation as too onerous. In 2016, the FDIC took steps to make the process easier, and higher interest

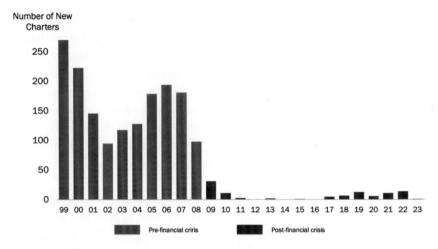

Figure 4.5   Rate of New Bank Formation Declines
Source: "Commercial Banks in the U.S.," FRED Economic Data [Federal Reserve Bank of St. Louis]; "Statistics at a Glance, Historical Trends," FDIC Quarterly Banking Profile, June 30, 2023.

rates in 2022 sparked a slight increase, but the number of applications for new banks remained historically low. The failure of Silicon Valley Bank in March 2023 added to concerns of regulators about approving new bank applications.

Consolidation Is Problematic for Small Business Lending

Bank consolidation and the disappearance of local community banks have been a problem for many small business owners. Tommy Davis, the North Carolina small business owner mentioned earlier, closed his Nationwide Insurance office in Colerain and moved to Windsor, a larger town 25 miles away, after the local community bank closed. For Tommy, it was "like a death sentence for a small town because the bank is the center of all activity."[23] Economists have found that community bank closings have historically had a prolonged negative impact on the credit supply available to local small businesses.[24]

Interestingly, this decline in credit persisted even when a new bank from another location opened a branch in the market. These results underscore the importance of lender-specific relationships and local information for small business lending. This information is often held within local bank branch personnel and lending systems and can disappear or become less relevant if large banks bring in different personnel or more automated lending systems. Of particular concern are the findings showing that the negative effect on small business lending was concentrated in low-income and high-minority neighborhoods, where local relationships may be a more significant factor in lending decisions.[25]

The Impact of Bank Mergers on Small Business Lending

While bank consolidation is generally a threat to small business lending, some research found that certain bank mergers had a postive impact on small business lending. One study by National Bureau of Economic Research (NBER) economists suggested that acquisition of a local bank by a small bank led to increased small business lending in the region.[26] This is likely due to the acquiring small bank's interest in increasing small business lending in a geographic area where it already possesses a comparative advantage. These findings underscore the importance of not only the size of the acquirer, but also its location and strategy with regard to small business lending.

Relationship Lending and Large Banks

As banks get larger, they typically have more branches, are more geographically dispersed than community banks, and have more employees to coordinate. Because of this, large banks need explicit rules and underwriting guidelines to keep loan officers rowing in the same direction and producing consistent outcomes.[27]

Larger banks, especially those with more than $10 billion in assets, are more likely to use a "cookie cutter" approach to lending, relying on standardized data such as a borrower's FICO (Fair Isaac Corporation) credit score and financial statements. They find it hard to manage a relationship approach to lending and include "soft" or subjective information, such as a borrower's character, in their loan decisions.[28] In addition, larger banks tend to be less creative in developing customized loan structures tailored to a small business's needs. According to the 2017 FDIC Small Business Lending Survey, large banks use standardized small business loan products 65% of the time versus 9% at smaller banks.[29]

As the number of community banks declines and as larger banks create even more automated and standardized lending decisions, there is a concern that market barriers and frictions will proliferate. The smallest and newest businesses, especially those that lack historical financial information or have weathered financial issues, will likely have a harder time accessing capital from traditional sources. More borrowers will find themselves judged only by rigid formulas, unable to make a case for themselves to a banker with an open ear, increasing the possibility that creditworthy borrowers will slip through the cracks, opening up further gaps in small business lending markets.

In the inevitable automated future, bankers will face a significant challenge: how to continue to capture soft factors while also increasing efficiency and reducing costs. Relationship lending is expensive and its costs tend to affect the smallest loans the most. One solution is to "harden" soft information by finding new types of data that provide additional insights to traditional automated lending formulas. Another is to automate data gathering, but reserve a place for a human loan officer to tailor the final loan size, duration, and pricing to best meet the needs of the particular small business. We will explore how technology offers a myriad of possibilities for new data sources and insights in later chapters. However, amidst these promising advancements is the risk that automated systems will completely displace relationship lending, leading to the loss of important benefits from local relationships and ongoing counseling during loan monitoring.

Small Business Loans Are Less Profitable

Another serious structural issue is that small business loans are less profitable for banks than many other lines of business. The chief obstacles are the difficulties and costs of the traditional methods of underwriting small business loans, and the lack of ways for banks to offload small loans from their balance sheets, as the secondary market for small business loans is not robust.

Information about small business borrowers is important because small business lending is riskier than large business lending. Small businesses are more sensitive to swings in the economy, have higher failure rates, and generally have fewer assets to use as collateral for loans. But, as we have discussed, reliable information on small businesses is difficult to obtain because the operating performance, financials, and growth prospects of small businesses are hard to see and predict. There is little public information about the performance of most small businesses because they rarely issue publicly traded equity or debt securities.[30] Many small businesses are run by inexperienced or busy owners who may lack detailed balance sheets, understate their tax returns, or keep inadequate income statements. This information opacity makes it more difficult for lenders to tell creditworthy and noncreditworthy borrowers apart.

Another factor working against small business lending is that the cost of loan underwriting does not scale with the size of the loan. In other words, it costs about as much for a bank to process a $100,000 loan as a $1 million loan. That means that smaller-dollar loans are less profitable for banks. As a result, banks are less likely to lend at lower dollar amounts.

One response for a bank is to move away from small business lending and focus on more profitable activities. Some banks have reduced or eliminated loans below a certain threshold, typically $100,000, and some will not lend to small businesses with annual revenues of less than $2 million. Often, the largest banks will refer businesses below a certain size to their small business credit card products, which are usually more expensive for borrowers.

Most Small Business Loans Cannot Be Easily Sold

One way for banks to reduce their risk exposure and increase the funds they have available to lend is to sell off some of their loan portfolio. They often do this by securitizing loans, which involves bundling loans they have made into a single security that can be sold on a secondary market. This is common with mortgage loans, which can be easily bundled because most of them are underwritten using standardized formats.

Until recent years, essentially no secondary market existed for small business loans. Loans to small firms are not easy to standardize, since they vary in documentation and terms. In addition, there is a general lack of data available on how these loans perform. One exception is loans made through the Small Business Administration's (SBA's) 7(a) program, which are sold with a government guarantee. Historically, about 40 to 45% of SBA loans have been securitized.

Creating a secondary market for small business loans is not a new idea. In the 1990s, Congress considered creating a government agency similar to Fannie Mae and Freddie Mac to sponsor securitization transactions.[31] In 1994, Congress took a different approach by reducing barriers to securitizing small business loans, but those changes ultimately had little effect.[32]

If accurate data on small businesses' credit were standardized and widely available, the securitization of small business loans would be more widespread. This may be on the horizon. As metrics-driven lending develops, the ability to eventually identify and describe risk pools should improve the packaging and pricing of small business loans and allow them to trade more seamlessly.

Searching for Small Business Financing Is Costly and Frustrating

As a result of these structural issues, even qualified small business borrowers can struggle to find willing lenders. Research from the Federal Reserve Bank of New York found that in 2013, the average small business borrower spent more than 25 hours on paperwork for bank loans and approached multiple banks during the application process.[33] Some banks have even refused to lend to businesses within specific industries that they considered particularly risky, such as restaurants.

The reduction in the number and role of community banks has made searching for and securing a bank loan even more time-consuming and costly. Meanwhile, the low relative profitability of small business lending combined with a lack of accurate data on small business borrowers has meant that larger banks have not stepped in to fill the role traditionally played by local lenders. In this environment, everyone is frustrated. Small businesses often feel that banks don't know them anymore and don't care about their business. Bankers rail against the regulatory regimes and feel oppressed by the costly and confusing morass of compliance requirements.

* * *

The solution is to look forward rather than backward. The structural changes in U.S. banking are not likely to reverse themselves, even if the regulatory environment is optimized (Chapters 13 and 14 take on the flaws in the current regulatory environment and propose principles for a "smarter" regulatory structure). We will not return to an environment of 15,000 banks, most of which are owned and operated in local communities, anytime soon.

But there are other ways to solve the problem. We know that small businesses need access to capital to grow and operate their businesses, and that banks are increasingly finding these loans less appealing to make. But just because banks have not been making these loans does not mean that there are no profitable loans to be made. Part II of this book focuses on how technology is changing the dynamics of lending. But first, it's important to ask, what exactly is the problem we are trying to solve? The next chapter examines what small businesses want, including what size and type of loans they need, and identifies gaps where the current lending market is failing to deliver.

5

What Small Businesses Want

Financial crises reminded us that capital is the fuel that small businesses rely on to grow and create jobs. The most common sources of funding for small firms are retained earnings and the owners' personal resources. However, bank credit is a vital source of external funding for many, especially the economy's Main Street businesses. The 2008–2009 recession made bank funding more difficult to obtain, and in its aftermath, there was a robust public debate about whether banks were ramping up small business lending fast enough. In 2014, this debate was in full swing—was there really a gap in small business financing? The same question occurred in 2023 as small businesses emerged from the pressures of the Covid-19 pandemic and faced tightening capital markets. Were lenders and policymakers being responsive enough to this important but often overlooked segment of the economy?

This question is not an easy one to answer because of the lack of good data on U.S. small business lending. Until recent regulatory changes, no government entity tracked loan originations to small businesses in the aggregate, much less in detail. Banks, of course, have the raw data about their own loan businesses, but it has not historically been collected as part of the Federal Deposit Insurance Corporation (FDIC) call reports or other required activity. The FDIC does collect data on the stock of loans on the balance sheets of banks, but since that number is a net of the additions and pay downs of loans, the flow of new loans can be obscured. Survey results, particularly from the Federal Reserve (Fed), are helpful resources, as are loan numbers from the Small Business Administration (SBA) and from reporting required under the Community Reinvestment Act (CRA). However, these sources of data don't tell the whole story.

© The Author(s), under exclusive license to Springer Nature Switzerland AG 2024
K. G. Mills, *Fintech, Small Business & The American Dream*, https://doi.org/10.1007/978-3-031-55612-8_5

Good policy requires real-time information on loan originations to small businesses so that the gaps can be identified. Other countries, such as the United Kingdom, have taken on this data collection challenge successfully, viewing it as vital to small business policy. An important provision of the Dodd-Frank Act, Sect. 1071, required the collection of this data and delegated that responsibility to the Consumer Financial Protection Bureau (CFPB). However, due to resistance from the banking lobby, rulemaking around the provision was only implemented in 2023, more than 10 years after it became law. Even then, challenges in the courts and resistance from industry continued including a vote in Congress designed to repeal the legislation. This is unfortunate since data from this rule is critical to bring real-time clarity to small business credit gaps and ensure they are addressed with timely policy solutions.

As the country slowly emerged from the 2008–2009 credit crisis, the best available data showed a worrisome picture. There was a gap in small business lending in smaller size loans. Banks generally define small loans as those under $250,000, but the most severe gap was for loans under $100,000.[1] For loans above those thresholds, and even more so above $1 million, there was robust competition. Regional banks such as Zions, Regions, and Key Bank had targeted loans between $500,000 and $5 million to fuel their growth. They saw that it would be profitable to give larger small business loans to well-run small businesses recovering from the recession or looking to buy equipment or fuel expansion. For loans of this size, the traditional model worked, with bankers cultivating a relationship and providing advice and additional banking services.

But what about the creditworthy Main Street business who wanted a small line of credit, or $20,000 to buy a van? Banks pushed these customers toward business credit cards or declined to serve them at all. This was a serious concern because small-dollar loans were what most small businesses wanted. Thus, for many years during the recovery, the smallest firms were having more trouble obtaining bank funding, in part because they were the ones seeking the smallest loans. This unmet need made the industry ripe for disruption by the new fintechs, as we will see in Chapter 6.

The Small-Dollar Loan Gap

How many small businesses seek outside financing and how many want small loans? The Federal Reserve's 2021 Small Business Credit Survey indicated that 34% of small businesses had applied for credit in the past 12 months.[2]

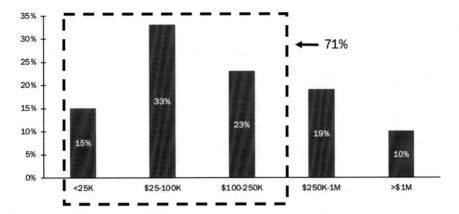

Figure 5.1 Small Businesses Want Small-Dollar Loans. Percentage of Applications From Small Businesses by Loan Size
Source: "2021 Small Business Credit Survey: Report on Employer Firms," Federal Reserve Banks, March 2022.

In terms of the size of loans small businesses want: almost three-quarters of small business loan applications from employer firms were for small-dollar loans—loans under $250,000—and almost half of the loan applications were for amounts under $100,000 (Figure 5.1).

This means that 71% of the small business owners approaching a bank for a loan want a product that the bank would, in many cases, prefer not to provide or cannot provide profitably. As we saw earlier, it takes as much time and effort, if not more, to make a small loan as it does to make a large one. The revenue from the fees and interest is lower and the risk is often higher. Banks do make money providing credit cards for these small-dollar needs, as the fees tend to be higher and the credit process is automated. But credit cards are usually more expensive to the small business owner than loans, and not all expenses can be paid using a card, making them a less than optimal solution in many cases.

The Smallest Businesses Struggle the Most

Access to capital is the most difficult for the smallest businesses. In 2021, loan approval rates for firms with fewer than 5 employees were the lowest of any cohort of businesses. Micro-firms applying for loans faced a funding shortfall more than three-quarters of the time, while companies with 50 to 499 employees experience a shortfall about 45% of the time. The situation deteriorated for all groups in the post-pandemic market, with approval levels for 2021 significantly lower than those for 2019 (Figure 5.2).

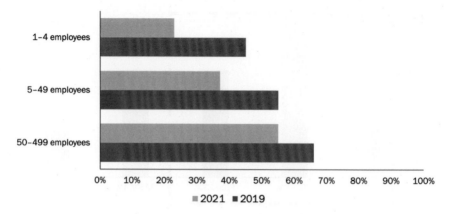

Figure 5.2   Share of Firms That Received All Financing Sought
Source: "2021 Small Business Credit Survey: Report on Employer Firms," Federal Reserve Banks, March 2022.

It is not surprising that the smallest firms have more trouble with financing. In general, the smaller the firm, the riskier it is, the more likely it is to fail, and the fewer assets it has to offer as collateral for a loan. The smallest firms are also the most informationally opaque. They often don't have complete financial statements and their taxes can understate their profits. Gathering a bank package to apply for a loan can be a long and tortuous process. And once it is completed, it is often not as compelling as it could be—the business owner may well be good at their business, but inexperienced in financial analysis and presentation.

Even controlling for credit scores, Fed data shows that smaller businesses have a harder time getting loans. In 2016, firms in the "low credit risk" category with revenues of less than $1 million had an approval rate 28 percentage points lower than low credit risk firms with more than $1 million in revenue. In the "high credit risk" category, the approval rate was 10 percentage points lower for small firms.[3]

With this knowledge we return to the question: how large is the gap in access to capital for small-dollar loans for the smallest firms? Eighty percent of firms with annual revenues under $250,000 want a loan of less than $100,000.[4] Thus, this large group of very small businesses—the same ones that are more informationally opaque and often riskier—wants the smallest, least appealing loans for banks to provide.

Start-Ups Versus Ongoing Businesses

Access to capital is also an issue for younger firms. In 2019, about half of firms more than five years old received all of the financing for which they applied, while this was true for only about one-third of the firms less than five years old (Figure 5.3).

Banks rely on the creditworthiness of small business owners themselves in their lending decisions, which is even more of an issue for start-ups. According to the Fed survey, 92% of small firms less than two years old rely on the credit score of the owner to acquire outside financing, compared to 84% of firms more than five years old.[5]

Why Small Businesses Seek Financing

We have analyzed the supply forces at work in the small business lending market, but what about the demand side? What do small businesses want, why are they seeking financing, and what kinds of products will meet their needs? Recall that there are four main types of small businesses and that, for example, Main Street firms have different growth objectives than new tech start-ups. Even within a category, small business needs can differ. In Chapter 2, we introduced Gelato Fiasco, an ice cream shop with big expansion plans, and Tony from the next door Big Top Deli, who was satisfied with his single location. As a result, their business plans required different types of capital, in different amounts, with different durations, and for different purposes.

One reason to take out a small business loan might be to start a business. Because of lenders' resistance, new entrepreneurs who get loans rely heavily on leveraging personal assets often in the form of a home equity loan. They also draw down savings, take on credit card debt, or ask for money from friends

Figure 5.3 Share of Firms With Financing Shortfalls When Applying For $250,000 or Less, by Age of Firm
Source: "2019 Small Business Credit Survey: Report on Employer Firms," Federal Reserve Banks, December 2019.

and family.[6] More than two-thirds of businesses less than two years old were started using funds from one or more personal sources.[7] Venture capital is important for a certain segment of start-ups with high-growth potential that need larger sums of money and high-risk investors, but it is barely on the radar as a source of funding for most other types of new firms.

As discussed earlier, this book focuses on small businesses that are seeking loans rather than equity capital. We look primarily at the needs of the Main Street firms, suppliers, and sole proprietors. Among these businesses seeking loans, a significant number, 42% are seeking funding to expand— whether that means opening a new location, hiring more people at an existing location, or perhaps buying a new machine to expand production (Figure 5.4).

However, the most common reason small businesses seek loans is for operating expenses. Recall that small businesses have bumpy cash flows and often do not have a clear picture of their future cash needs. They also have cash buffers of, on average, less than one month. Therefore, many small businesses rely on a loan or line of credit to weather the uneven monthly or seasonal fluctuations. Linda Pagan, the owner of a successful millinery shop in Manhattan, found the slow periods in her business dramatically challenging, calling them the "trifecta of terror."[8] (see Box). Linda and her hat shop are not alone in facing the anxiety associated with cash fluctuations. The small business owner's need for liquidity and capital to survive rough patches is fertile ground for the game-changing breakthroughs in cashflow forecasting that technology can provide. In Chapter 10, we will explore some of these possibilities.

Use of Proceeds	Percent of Small Businesses
Operating Expenses	62%
Expand Business/New Opportunity	42%
Refinance / Pay Debt	30%
Replace Capital Assets / Make Repairs	29%

Figure 5.4 Small Businesses Use Loans to Operate and Grow Their Businesses. Percentage of Small Businesses Who Applied for a Loan
Note: These percentages add up to more than 100%, as many small businesses state more than one use for the loan proceeds.
Source: "2021 Small Business Credit Survey: Report on Employer Firms," Federal Reserve Banks, May 2022.

Small Village Shop in the Big City

Linda Pagan has owned The Hat Shop in New York City for more than 25 years. Based in SoHo in lower Manhattan, she provides specialty made-to-order hats for grand occasions, and for the everyday purpose of keeping the head warm in winter and protected from the sun in the summer. Linda believes in using local suppliers, usually other small businesses. Her feather provider is based in Queens, the fourth-generation company that makes her hats' ribbons and silk flowers is on 37th Street, and a basement studio on Grand Street blocks the hats.

Linda is a champion of the small businesses in her community. In 2009, the influx of large stores in SoHo spurred her to organize her block to form an association of independent business owners. In 2016, the area was designated the Sullivan-Thompson Historic District by the Greenwich Village Society of Historic Preservation, focused on maintaining the block's unique owner-operated small businesses and historic flavor.

But despite Linda's knack for building a loyal customer base and the high quality of her hats, she dreads the slow months, usually January through March, when cash flow can get tight. She dubs this slow period the "trifecta of terror." After Christmas, her shop experiences a seasonal drop in sales. At the same time, sales tax is due from the holiday season and by March, she has to buy inventory for the busy upcoming Kentucky Derby sales season.

2016 was a particularly rough year for Linda. Money was tight and sales were down. Instead of dipping into her savings, Linda took out a loan from an online lender, OnDeck. The process was simple: Linda provided OnDeck with her bank statements and business documents, and quickly received a $30,000 loan. She ended up having the best Kentucky Derby sales in shop history, and promptly paid back the loan with $2,000 in interest.

Customer-Product Fit—What Loan Is Right?

More than simply getting access to capital, it is also important to make sure that small businesses get financing that fits their needs. This means accessing the right product at the right price and duration. This customer-product fit is critical to a healthy small business credit market.

For example, short-term loans that are repaid in a few months work well for seasonal businesses or for firms that need to purchase unusually large amounts of inventory for holidays or certain times of the year (such as The Hat Shop described above). Longer, multi-year, term loans are a better fit to finance equipment or real estate purchases, since the purchase is typically made to increase long-term revenue, which will then be used to pay off the loan. If a short-term loan is used for an equipment purchase, it may come due before the business has increased its revenues enough to be able to pay it off. This could lead to a default on the loan, or a cycle of refinancing, each time paying additional fees. Ensuring that each small business gets the right kind of loan is a win–win for both the borrower and the lender, increasing the probability that the business will succeed and that the loan will be repaid.

The main types of financing available to small businesses today fall into a few distinct categories:

Term loans are paid back on a set schedule. They are often used by small firms to buy equipment or real estate.

Bank lines of credit are liquidity available for a business to draw down on an immediate basis to smooth out uneven cash flows.

Merchant cash advances (MCAs) let businesses—usually retailers who take debit and credit card payments—get a lump sum cash advance. The lender is repaid by taking a percentage of the businesses' future sales.

Receivables financing allows a small business to sell or pledge some of its accounts receivable to a third party. In return, it gets immediate cash in an amount which represents a discount on the total receivable. This discount compensates the third party for taking on the risk that it may not be able to collect the full amount of the receivable that was purchased.

Business credit cards are often the most accessible forms of financing, but they carry high interest rates and are not permanent financing, making them less than ideal for ongoing working capital needs or for large, one-time investments that will not immediately generate revenue.

SBA loans are an option for some applicants who cannot get financing from lenders without credit support. In these cases, the SBA partially guarantees a loan made by an authorized lender. The guarantee makes the loan less risky, since there is a smaller level of exposure for the bank if the borrower defaults. This incentivizes lenders to provide financing. Since women and minority-owned businesses have a harder time than others do when it comes to accessing credit, it is not surprising that the SBA over-indexes in these kinds of loans.[9]

How does a small business owner know what loan is right? In the past, the local banker who knew the small business owner helped make sure that there was customer-product fit. In the process of discussing the small business's plans and prospects, the banker saw the financials, assessed the use of the loan proceeds, and made a judgment as to whether the endeavor would be a success. This interaction allowed the banker to make an informed credit decision and the customer got advice and counsel about the right loan product.

As the presence of community bankers declines, who will take the responsibility for making sure there is customer-product fit? In a borrower-lender relationship, the interests of the parties should be aligned. It is not a good idea for a lender to give someone a loan that is so expensive that they can never pay it back, or one that has a timing mismatch. Maintaining optimal matching of the borrower to the loan that meets their needs is an important challenge for the more recently developed automated small business lending products.

Filling the Gap

With a better sense of what small businesses want, we turn to the question of who will deliver it. As banks moved away from small-dollar loans and lending to small firms, entrepreneurs stepped in to fill at least some of the gap with creative solutions. Around 2010, new fintech entrants emerged in the small business lending segment, bringing a technology-driven approach to solving some of the market's issues.

The most visible initial innovation was a "digital first" approach where the process was done online, not in banks. The new lenders introduced a simpler credit application process and used algorithms to make quick and low-cost lending decisions. The new credit processes used more relevant and timely data from a small business's own bank account and other financial activities to make more nuanced decisions about whether to offer credit.

Most importantly, they created a better customer experience for the small business. Instead of Xeroxing a pile of paperwork, walking from bank to bank trying to get a loan, and waiting weeks for a response, small businesses could now apply online in minutes, have a response within minutes or hours, and have the money in their account within a day. These changes addressed some of the more painful frictions that had been plaguing the small business lending market.

The innovators were met with an early positive response from small businesses. The Federal Reserve's 2015 Small Business Credit Survey found that more than half of small businesses surveyed were dissatisfied with a difficult application process at their bank, while only one-fifth said the same about their online lender. Nearly half also expressed dissatisfaction with a long wait time for a credit decision from their bank, while again, only about one-fifth said the same about their online lender (Figure 5.5).

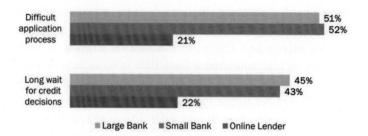

Figure 5.5   Borrower Dissatisfaction by Lender Type
Source: "2015 Small Business Credit Survey: Report on Employer Firms," Federal Reserve Banks, March 2016.

Based on their ability to provide a better customer experience, online lenders grew and took share from banks until 2020 when the Covid-19 pandemic hit (Figure 5.6).

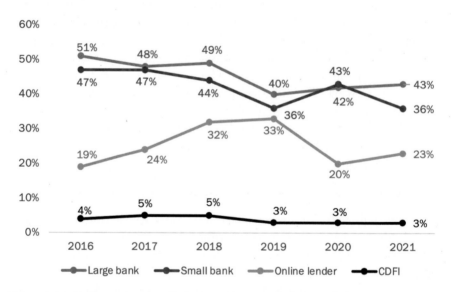

Figure 5.6   Credit Sources Applied to by Small Businesses
Source: Author's compilation based on "2022 Small Business Credit Survey: Report on Employer Firms," Federal Reserve Banks, March 2023 and "2019 Small Business Credit Survey: Report on Employer Firms," Federal Reserve Banks, December 2019.

* * *

By 2023, the landscape was full of new innovations, and a large array of potential winners and losers. Technology was demostrating the power to solve many of the market frictions we identified in Part I of this book and enabling more lending to creditworthy borrowers at a lower cost and with a better customer experience.

Part II details how the cycle of fintech innovation has transformed the small business lending market. After some early success, new fintech entrepreneurs faced powerful competition including from banks and other traditional lenders who refused to be counted out (see Chapters 6 and 7). Then, when the Covid-19 Pandemic hit, the required shift to online interactions increased the willingness of both borrowers and banks to engage in digital solutions (see Chapters 8 and 9).

Part III lays out how advances in technology can bring about a positive state, "Small Business Utopia," where lending solutions significantly improve, and explores what players or combinations might be well positioned for future success. With the increased availability of data, lenders should be better able to identify the financial prospects of smaller companies, and through process automation of their systems, make small loans profitably. The resulting more efficient market should mean better matching of creditworthy small businesses with willing lenders, closing the small-dollar loan gap. Yet, we will see in the chapters that follow, that like many cycles of disruption, the story is not as simple as "they all lived happily ever after."

Part II

The New World of Fintech Innovation

6

The Fintech Innovation Cycle

In 1947, Bell Labs developed a small device known as the transistor. This miniature piece of hardware could control the flow of electricity, either amplifying or switching it. Using the transistor, electronic devices like radios and computers could be built more cheaply and reliably—and smaller—than their predecessors that relied on vacuum tubes. The transistor formed the basis for the electronics industry, perhaps the most economically and culturally important sector in the world. Most often built using silicon, the transistor created Silicon Valley in both substance and name.

But as important as the invention later became, it received little notice at first. Design and production problems had to be resolved. Potential had to be translated into concrete products. It was unclear how the innovation would go to market, and how large the market would be for it once it did. Ten years later, after a slow start, transistors had reached mainstream product markets and could be found in radios, hearing aids, clocks, phonographs, and more.[1] In the late 1950s, another transformative event occurred. Jack Kilby at Texas Instruments patented the integrated circuit, which placed transistors and other components onto a single chip. Engineers worked to cram more and more transistors onto a chip, boosting their functionality along the way. This led to further innovations through miniaturization, plummeting costs, and ever more powerful chips that enabled the creation of personal computers in the 1970s, and led to everything from iPhones to pet tracking devices.

Today, we rely on chips that can hold hundreds of millions of transistors every time we pick up our smartphones or drive our cars. What began as a simple invention to direct electric currents eventually gave us the modern-day products and services that transform how we conduct many facets of our

K. G. Mills, *Fintech, Small Business & The American Dream*, https://doi.org/10.1007/978-3-031-55612-8_6

daily lives. Yet, in 1947 and in the early years after the initial discovery, the transformative nature of the transistor was unclear.

While we are not necessarily predicting that innovations in fintech will be as transformative as the transistor or integrated circuit, the change from in-person bank lending to digital, data-driven options heralds the start of a significant cycle of innovation in a market that has not, up until recent years, seen much change. Fintech covers a broad array of new technologies, from crypto currencies to online insurance, of which the changes in small business lending are just one part. The path of innovation in small business lending will be influenced by activity in other parts of financial services, including consumer lending and payments. But it will ultimately follow its own distinct course. The chapters that follow explore the early days of fintech lending, delineate role of fintech during the Covid-19 pandemic, and outline the forces that will shape the future state of small business lending. Who will be the winners and losers? What will the transformation lead to in terms of products and options that will impact the vitality and growth of small businesses?

We are at the beginning of the fintech innovation cycle. The early innovations in digital lending were like the initial phase of the transistor, foundational changes which opened the door to a new future in the way that small businesses access capital. Progress with transistors was initially slow as the market waited for infrastructure and products to develop. The same lag has been observed in the early days of online lending. What will be the "chip" that unleashes the full potential of fintech and creates transformational change in the small business lending market?

The Innovation Life Cycle

The creation of the transistor and its integration into the now ubiquitous chip is an example of how the innovation cycle works in action. An invention or fundamental change occurs in a market and is at first adopted by just a few "first movers." The use cases for the innovation are unclear and the players who go to market often take on substantial risk, with the potential for large market share if the innovation is commercially successful. As more entrepreneurs understand the innovation's potential and translate it into new products and industries, the innovation becomes more widespread. Eventually, products become standardized, and the market reaches a large scale with strong acceptance and usage. Then, new innovations come into play that compete with the current products, and thus begins the next innovation cycle.

These innovation cycles create economic progress. Joseph Schumpeter, one of the most influential economists of the twentieth century, was known for his work on innovation and business cycle theory. Schumpeter did not see economic growth as a gradual, steady climb like many economists did. Instead, he believed growth came from innovation, which was, in his words, "more like a series of explosions than a gentle, though incessant, continual transformation."[2] These discontinuous innovations overturned old ways of doing things and destroyed incumbent firms, and even entire industries.

Schumpeter cast the entrepreneur as the hero of his economic story, leading what he described as a "process of industrial mutation ... that incessantly revolutionizes the economic structure from within, incessantly destroying the old one, incessantly creating a new one. This process of Creative Destruction is the essential fact about capitalism."[3] For Schumpeter, innovation was not invention per se, but rather the application of inventions in economically useful ways. Innovation could mean a new product, a new production process, opening up a new market, securing a new source of supply for production, or designing a new market structure for an industry, such as by creating or breaking up a monopoly.[4]

Later in the twentieth century, several scholars built on Schumpeter's work, including Everett Rogers, who popularized the innovation S-curve in his 1962 book on the diffusion of innovations. Others have since adapted Rogers' S-curve to include a four-stage life cycle for innovations: Ferment, Takeoff, Maturity, and Discontinuity.[5] Ferment describes the early stages of an innovation when the products and uses are not fully understood, and new avenues are being explored. Takeoff is the growth phase in which new companies, new products, and new customers fuel a rapid increase in adoption and usage. Eventually, sometimes after many years, a market reaches the maturity phase. Finally, discontinuity occurs when the market is overtaken by another innovation.

Our story of the transistor was just one example of how innovation follows the S-curve pattern, but there are plenty of other cases as well. Think, for example, about videocassette recorders (VCRs). The forerunners of VCRs were massive and expensive magnetic tape recorders, first invented in the 1950s. It was not until the 1970s that the VCR format was standardized and made affordable enough for mass consumer adoption. By the 1980s, two major formats had shaped the market: JVC's VHS and Sony's Betamax. VHS won the format war largely because its cassettes allowed for longer recording times—a major selling point for consumers. By the late 1980s, the VCR was maturing, growing primarily from movie rentals and making VCR ownership widespread.[6] Finally, in 1995, DVDs were introduced, disrupting the market quickly due to the smaller size and superior capabilities of the disks.

Financial Services and the Innovation Life Cycle

In banking, the automated teller machine (ATM) was a visible example of the innovation cycle. First introduced in the late 1960s purely to dispense cash, it caught on in the 1970s as banks added functionality that allowed customers to conduct other banking services such as deposits. By 1980, shared networks proliferated, and banks began to view ATMs as necessities, and finally, as replacements for branches. From the late 1990s to the present, ATMs have remained common, but new innovations have moved customers toward mobile banking, and cards have made cash less important for transactions.

The evolution of banking services reflects the changes that have occurred in payment technologies, beginning over four centuries ago. This evolution can be envisioned as a series of S-curves (Figure 6.1). In Europe, physical currency and checks were gradually accepted as payment starting in the 1600s. They were disrupted by a series of innovations—credit and debit cards, electronic payments, and ATMs in the 1960s to 1980s—which caused the number of checks written to peak in 1995 and decline ever since. In more recent years online banking has proliferated as well as methods such as direct transactions (e.g., Venmo) and mobile payments such as ApplePay. Contemporary innovations such as digital currencies and direct payments through Open Banking represent the next innovation discontinuity.

However, apart from changes in payments, the banking sector has generally been slower to adopt innovation than many other industries. When innovation has occurred, small business products have often been the last ones affected. Until the small business fintech innovation cycle began in about 2010, small business lending was still a tedious process and decisions about whether to extend credit were generally made slowly, using personal underwriting and methods of assessment that had not changed in many decades. Small business lending was long overdue for innovation.

Why Did Innovation Lag in Small Business Lending?

With the advent of the Internet, entrepreneurs began challenging old-line industries in earnest. The technology to move lending completely online

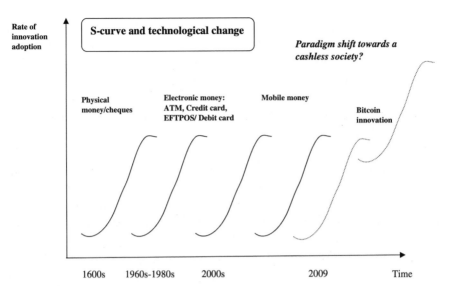

Figure 6.1   Evolution of Payment Technologies
Source: Jarunee Wonglimpiyarat, "S-curve Trajectories of Electronic Money," The Journal of High Technology Management Research 27, no. 1 [2016].

existed before 2005. Why had marketing, underwriting, and servicing of loans—particularly small business loans—largely taken a back seat?

There are several possible explanations for the slow pace of innovation in lending, and in small business lending in particular. First, the banking sector is heavily regulated. With so many industries and markets ripe for innovation in the age of the Internet, many entrepreneurs may have seen the financial sector, with its heavy overlay of rules, as an unappealing market. Second, the high level of regulation and supervision engendered a risk-avoidance culture at many banks. Banks employ armies of people whose job it is to ensure that they accurately assess and manage their risks. It can be difficult for an organization with a risk-averse culture to accomplish innovative internal change.

An example of the regulatory drag on innovation in banking is the ability to deposit and handle checks electronically. Traditionally, banks were required to transfer original paper checks among themselves to make payments, and depositors received their paper checks in their monthly bank statements. In 2003, Congress passed a law known as Check 21, which allowed deposits to be made with electronic photos of checks, and for banks to transfer checks electronically as well.[7] Although the technology to do this existed well before, it required a new law to provide the convenience and cost reduction of electronic check deposits that we now expect.

A third barrier to innovation is the fact that the small business loan market is more heterogeneous than the consumer market. Mortgages, for example, are largely standardized and simple for the market to understand and securitize. Small business loans involve more risk in part because each business is different, and their credit needs vary according to their industry, age, financial history, and other factors. Each business has a different credit profile and many loans have non-standard terms.

A final possibility is the relative size of the small business lending market. According to the Federal Reserve, U.S. banks held $365 billion in Commercial and Industrial (C&I) loans of less than $1 million in 2019—a good proxy for the stock of small business loans.[8] In addition, there was $578 billion in spending on small business credit cards in the same year.[9] These numbers add up to just $943 billion in small business credit, which is large in absolute terms, but small relative to the consumer market. Banks held about $1.8 trillion in consumer loans on their balance sheets in the same period.[10] In addition, the Federal Reserve Bank of St. Louis estimated the total consumer credit owned and securitized as more than twice as large, or about $4.2 trillion, plus another $2.3 trillion in residential real estate loans.[11,12]

Although small business lending was clearly an important segment for many banks, it is often not the largest source of activity or profit, and not the priority for innovation. For JPMorgan Chase, although small business has been mentioned often in the CEO's speeches and in the company's annual report, the small business lending segment constituted just $33 billion compared to $262 billion of credit for consumers.[13] The voices of small business customers were not loud enough to demand more convenience and better service. Until faced with a real threat of disruption by fintech innovators, the traditional industry players felt little pressure to change the way they provided services to small businesses.

The Small Business Lending Innovation Curve

The first phase of innovation in small business lending emerged as the recovery from the 2008 credit crisis took hold. Fintech lenders had been around before then, most notably CAN Capital, which was founded in 1998 and pioneered the merchant cash advance (MCA).[14] But OnDeck really provided the first noteworthy small business-focused innovative lending approach. Why not, asked OnDeck founder Mitch Jacobs, use the actual data from a business's bank account—including the record of what bills they had recently paid—to help determine their creditworthiness? This information was more current than the traditional measures used in small business credit, primarily the business owner's personal FICO (Fair Isaac Corporation) score. As Jacobs put it, "The time is right, the adoption of software by businesses is high, and there's an opportunity for businesses to quickly create a full data profile that minimizes risk for lenders and opens up a vast sum of capital for the small business owner."[15]

In the 2008–9 recession, FICO scores had indeed proven unreliable predictors of default risk, and many like Bank of America, which had relied on them extensively in 2005 to 2007 to make automated loans, had withdrawn from the small business lending market with heavy losses.[16] And, as we discussed in Chapter 3, banks' slow return to small business lending in the aftermath of the recession, particularly to the less profitable small-dollar loan segment, left a gap in the market that innovators like Jacobs began to fill.

Ferment

The first, or ferment, phase of the online small business lending innovation cycle relied on available technology to rethink two long-standing frictions in the small business lending market: the speed and ease of the customer experience and the visibility of small business finances to lenders for credit underwriting. These pain points were not new, and the technology being used was not groundbreaking, but early fintechs such as OnDeck, LendingClub, and Kabbage gained momentum by creating experiences that were simpler and faster for small business customers. The applications were easy to complete, taking about half an hour at the time, and money could be in the business's bank account within days.

For small businesses, this time frame was unheard of, and for many it was the decision driver. Despite higher pricing, borrowers flocked to the new offerings, drawn by this superior and attractive customer experience. The first concrete analysis of the appeal of the new online products came in the 2015 Federal Reserve (Fed) Small Business Credit Survey. A shocking 20% of small business applicants reported applying for online loans, even more than were applying to credit unions (Figure 6.2).

While the initial belief was that these respondents were applying to fintech companies, it later became clear that many were actually using their bank's online application, so the number applying to fintechs was likely lower. Nonetheless, the real or perceived speed of adoption put fintech lenders on the radar of venture capitalists and other early-stage investors, and spurred competition.

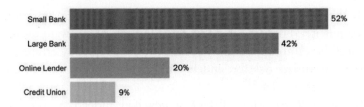

Figure 6.2   Twenty Percent of Applicants Applied to Online Lenders in 2015
Credit sources applied to (percentage of loan/line of credit applicants)
Source: "2015 Small Business Credit Survey," Federal Reserve Banks, March 2016.

At the time, we dubbed this period the "wild west," as literally hundreds of new firms—including online lenders, online loan marketplaces, and data analysis firms—entered the market. From 2013 to 2015, many argued that online lending would fundamentally disrupt the marketplace and push traditional banks out of business. Data that already existed, from Yelp reviews to a small business's bank and credit card files to utility bill payment histories could now be accessed through application programming interfaces (APIs), a major development in computer software that allowed for easier and more efficient data sharing. Automated underwriting algorithms offered a lower cost (and potentially higher quality) innovative replacement for expensive personal underwriting activities. The combination of access to new data and novel underwriting formulas enabled online lenders to start taking market share. In Schumpeterian terms, it appeared that creative destruction would occur as the "takeoff" phase gained steam.

"Takeoff" Aborted

Despite this momentum, the small business lending innovation cycle took a surprise blow in the summer of 2016. An internal probe at LendingClub, one of the leading online lenders, revealed that the company had failed to disclose information to an investor regarding a loan pool. The LendingClub board responded by firing the charismatic CEO and founder, Renaud Laplanche.[17] OnDeck, which had gone public with a valuation of over $1 billion and a share price of $20, saw its stock price plummet by 42% between December 2015 and July 2016.[18] Concerned industry observers also began to question whether the new entrants had truly brought disruptive innovation to the market, or had simply made the application experience faster and more pleasant for borrowers. Were online lenders offering new products or were they just offering the same loans and lines of credit processed more quickly and at a higher cost to the borrower?

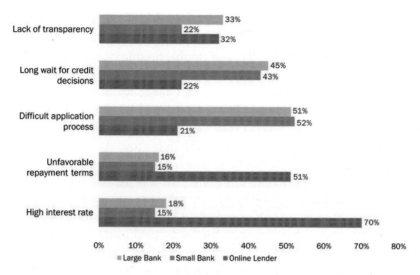

Figure 6.3 Borrowers' Reasons for Dissatisfaction by Lender Type
Percentage of employer firms dissatisfied with their lender in 2015
Source: "2015 Small Business Credit Survey," Federal Reserve Banks, March 2016.

In the 2015 Fed credit survey, some troubling information about the price of those online loans also emerged. While borrowers generally expressed satisfaction with the ease of the online lending experience, they complained about the high costs and hidden fees (Figure 6.3).

Anecdotes about small businesses falling into debt traps began to appear in the media, and concerns about "bad actors" found their way into the halls of Congress and the offices of regulators. More questions arose: were the new algorithms actually better predictors of small business credit than the bank underwriting models? Were they even as good? And, if the innovation was just in the customer experience, why couldn't banks replicate these processes? Were they just a bunch of "dinosaurs," unable to adapt to change or would they respond vigorously? Who held the competitive advantage?

Ferment—Part II

Thus began a second phase of the small business innovation cycle, or perhaps a mini-cycle of further fermentation. The original development of a technology and Internet-enabled front-end application process was so appealing to the small business owner that it jolted the industry into a new era. But, at this point, there was little innovation in the loan products that were delivered. In fact, the products were arguably worse—at least in terms of their cost to borrowers—primarily due to the competitive disadvantages of the new players.

For one, the new online lenders had trouble finding customers. Small business owners are busy and, despite the appeal of a faster experience, online lenders found that placing targeted ads on Google was not enough to reach this fragmented customer base. Beyond just reaching small businesses, the online lenders also needed to get their ads in front of the borrower at almost exactly the moment when they were ready to borrow. As a result, acquiring customers was like finding a needle in a haystack. Customer acquisition costs reached about 15% of revenue, some of which was passed back to borrowers in the cost of the loans.

In addition, the new fintech entrants had little track record of performance and no access to the cheap capital that banks held in the form of deposits. Many were using high-cost money from hedge funds to finance their loans. Peer-to-peer lenders played matchmaker, for a fee, between eager borrowers and individuals and institutions that wanted returns. The unit economics of the innovators, that is, their ability to make profit on a per loan basis, were proving to be a challenge.

At the same time as the early players were stumbling, the dinosaurs were waking up. The established banks and other lenders saw their customers enjoying the ease of the faster and friendlier customer experience, and decided they needed to respond. At first, many just tightened their timelines for responding to loan applications. Turnaround times went from weeks or even months to 10 to 14 days. Processes were still partly manual, but banks worked on incremental improvements to create fewer burdens for the applicant. This alone made a difference to many small businesses, who finally found more responsive loan officers with a sense of urgency at the other end of the phone. In the months that followed, many banks, even some of those least prone to embracing change, came to realize that they too could use technology to automate small business lending, either by partnering with the new fintech challengers or by beating them at their own game.

Each bank had its own strategy for testing the fintech waters. JPMorgan Chase took early action, partnering with OnDeck in 2015 to deliver an automated small business loan product "white-labeled" under the Chase brand. Wells Fargo developed its own product, called FastFlex, an online fast-decisioned option for small business loans under $100,000 launched in May 2016. Between 2012 and 2017, Citibank invested in more than 20 fintechs to keep an eye on the developing sector and see what innovations might prove worth incorporating. Even community banks engaged, defying the initial view that they would be too small and too technologically backward to explore the new frontiers. Eastern Bank in New England hired a team of fintech entrepreneurs to create Eastern Labs and develop their own in-house small business lending product. After successfully launching Eastern Labs internally, they spun out the technology into its own company, with the purpose of selling the software to other community banks.

In this second period of ferment, as the innovation cycle continued to evolve, banks focused on reasserting their leadership in small business lending. Banks realized that they could remain major players because they had at least two important advantages over their fintech competitors. The first advantage was that banks had a pool of customers with whom they already had relationships—and they had access to insights that come from these customers' bank accounts, credit cards, and other bank activities. If a fintech lender like OnDeck could build a company based on data from small business bank accounts, why couldn't the banks that actually held those accounts use that same data to rebuild their lending processes? The second advantage was that banks had access to lower cost capital in the form of customer deposits. The greatest challenge for the banks would, of course, be how to change—how to bring new ideas and technologies into a traditional culture in order to better serve their small business customers.

By 2019, J.P. Morgan was investing $9 billion annually in technology and Bank of America had a full team focused on data-centric analysis of small business customers. Fintech infrastructure players were developing applications that community banks could use to bolt onto their existing core systems to provide automated solutions for smaller-dollar loans. Banks were investing in fintechs and even making acquisitions. Then the world shut down in response to a dangerous pandemic virus: Covid-19.

The Role of the Pandemic

In March 2020, the United States responded to the spreading threat of Covid-19 by mandating the closure of venues where the public gathered including restaurants and other non-essential retail locations. Most of these were small businesses that then faced an existential crisis. With low cash reserves and no money coming in the door, how long could they survive? Fortunately, the federal government acted quickly. Within weeks, programs were developed and funded that would ultimately funnel over $1.2 trillion of relief to impacted small businesses.

Chapters 8 and 9 will explore those programs in depth, particularly the Paycheck Protection Program which deployed over $800 million in forgivable loans in several tranches. Banks were the initial distribution channel for those loans. However, it quickly became apparent that there were large gaps in the ability or willingness of banks to serve the smallest businesses and underserved businesses, particularly those that were Black-owned. In response, the federal government authorized non-banks, including many fintechs to get the loans into the hands of as many eligible businesses as possible. This effort ultimately proved highly successful. Over 13 million small businesses received federal aid that helped avert massive failures and ensure a more rapid economic recovery from the pandemic shock than had been experienced in the 2008–2009 financial crisis. Despite worrisome pockets of fraud, post-pandemic economic research showed that fintechs were effective at reaching small businesses that traditional lenders could not or would not serve.[19]

The mainstreaming of fintech during the pandemic is an important inflection point in the small business lending innovation cycle. Although fintech solutions had multiplied in the period from 2015 to 2019 the trajectory of growth was only linear. With some exceptions, such as Square, fintechs had little broad public exposure and were viewed in policy circles as largely fringe and second tier competitors. Banks were accelerating their efforts to use technology to better serve both consumer and small business clients. None of the large tech players had decided to enter the market in a robust way, leaving the field to the trusted banking brands. However, in the early days of the pandemic response, as the banks either declined or were unable to broadly serve the needs of small business customers, they left the door open for a step change in the participation of fintechs in the market.

Data and Its Impact on the Innovation Cycle

The pace of change in technology also had a significant impact on the timing of the fintech innovation cycle. We might ask why did innovation of this kind occur and accelerate in the period beginning in 2010—and not five or ten years earlier or later. The key breakthrough that enabled the first phase of small business lending innovation was access to data through Application Programing Interfaces or APIs. Data and the ability to analyze large amounts of information rapidly were the big drivers behind the transformations in small business lending. Relevant data became increasingly available on small businesses through a wide variety of sources. In fact, there was so much additional data available that the question changed from "how do I access information on a small business?" to "how will better data improve my ability to do effective small business lending?".

The availability of data changes many parts of loan processing and monitoring activities. One area of great impact is in the credit decision—can the business repay the loan? Additional data to drive better risk assessment is particularly valuable, since small business creditworthiness is difficult to calibrate, due to the heterogeneity and information opacity of small businesses that we discussed earlier. With the newly available sources of data, lenders from banks to new fintech players could get a more timely and holistic picture of the small business's financial health and ability to repay.

Making the data useful requires developing algorithms that consistently and accurately predict risk. Although greater availability and multiple sources of data certainly helps, businesses are so different, and their profitability so volatile, that it is a challenge to create algorithms that work well for all the various sizes and industries and ensure that these formulas are predictive through the ups and downs of business cycles. The evolution of data acquisition and credit algorithms will be discussed further in Chapter 10, as confidence in the ability of technology to better predict risk has proven to be key factor in the acceleration of the fintech innovation cycle.

Takeoff: Small Business Lending of the Future

The earliest fintech innovators responsible for pushing the small business lending market to a more automated, easy-to-use process have not been the ones to benefit the most from their innovations. This is not unusual. Henry Ford did not invent the automobile, but he dramatically improved the processes by which they were made, and reaped profits and fame as a result. Once told that the Velvet Underground, the seminal 1960s rock band, had only sold 30,000 copies of their debut album, famed musician and producer Brian Eno retorted that "everyone who bought one of those 30,000 copies started a band."[20] Those who change the world do not always profit most from their actions.

The early innovations in small business lending, enabled by entrepreneurs using new sources of data and rethinking the customer experience, proved not to be the end of the road, but rather, an early stage. As in the story of the transistor and the chip, another set of transformative inventions was required to push the market forward and develop the solutions that change the game for small businesses.

What is the "chip" of the small business lending story? As we examine the next phase of the innovation cycle, we begin to see what determines the winners. The first stages of innovation came from entrepreneurs who saw and understood the pain points of the small business customer. Making the loan experience faster and easier was a breakthrough that got the attention of small businesses and started the chain reaction of industry response. The next phase of innovation includes solutions to another critical small business pain point: today, there is no tool, no platform, or set of services that provides a small business with a central place to conduct *all* of its financial activity in an integrated, easy-to-use way.

Small businesses often get in trouble because of unexpected cash flow shortfalls. A late customer payment or an unusual inventory need can cause a sudden demand for financing. Most small business owners have low cash buffers. But what if they could see and understand their financial situation and needs more easily? And what if they could borrow the right amount with the right terms at the press of a button? What if they had one dashboard from which to conduct all of their financial activities? Such a platform would include integration of banking activity, cash flow insights and management, and payments processing. It would allow accounting software and tax planning tools to communicate seamlessly with bill paying and retirement planning functions. Artificial intelligence—or even personal advisors—could provide insights and options, based on a holistic picture of the small business.

We call this future state "Small Business Utopia," a technology-enabled environment where small businesses can run their operations with greater success and longevity. The best lenders of the future will operate in an ecosystem which enables small business owners to better understand what their financing needs are and allows them to access capital quickly and at a competitive and transparent cost. This future may sound distant and difficult to achieve, but the technology required to make it a reality exists today.

Getting to Small Business Utopia will not be easy, in part because many innovations have unintended consequences. Lead was added to paint to make it more water resistant, maintain its color, and dry faster, and added to gasoline to reduce engine knock and boost octane. However, after it became increasingly clear that lead in the environment was a major health hazard, the government began phasing out leaded gasoline in 1974 and banned lead in paint for consumer use in 1978. Even the technological innovations that have allowed us to connect with anyone in the world, get groceries delivered right to our doorstep, and search the web for any information we desire, have also brought with them new issues.

There is abundant evidence that innovation in finance can have negative, or even disastrous, outcomes. The market for over-the-counter derivatives—financial products often used to manage risk that were designed and sold in customized transactions rather than on publicly traded exchanges—grew exponentially in the decade prior to the financial crisis. Many financial firms reaped huge profits through the creation of ever-more-complex products that, in some cases, made the financial system more fragile and vulnerable to collapse. In the fintech innovation cycle, decisions that are rational to individual lenders and borrowers may, at the same time, prove collectively destabilizing to the broader financial system. Unfortunately, we have seen the consequences to the economy—and particularly to small businesses—of operating without a well-functioning regulatory structure.

On the other hand, we also have seen that too much or the wrong kind of regulation can impede innovation, particularly in the heavily regulated banking sector. Thus, to achieve the best outcomes, we must develop government policy that promotes innovation while protecting consumers, small businesses, and the financial system. We will discuss regulatory gaps and the potential for "smarter" regulation that addresses the risks that technological change will bring in Chapters 13 and 14.

Reaching "Small Business Utopia"

In Small Business Utopia, a truly efficient market, operating under appropriate regulatory oversight, will ensure that every creditworthy small business has customer-friendly access to the capital they need to start and grow their business and create jobs. This optimal small business environment will give business owners an integrated view of the cash needs of their businesses. These insights will allow them to be able to take on the right type of capital, at the right time, at the right price, with the right duration, and use it in a way that maximizes their operating potential. This future state will also benefit lenders in a virtuous cycle, as the costs to make a small business loan will be lower, the risk of default will decrease, and the successful borrower will then likely be a repeat customer for a future loan as their business continues to grow and succeed.

* * *

The innovation cycle in small business lending has gathered steam because technology has delivered new breakthroughs that reduce the long-standing frictions in the ability of new and old lenders to serve the market. The remainder of Part II describes the path of change in small business lending to date. Chapter 7 documents the activities of the early fintech lenders and Chapter 8 and 9 describe the impact of the Covid-19 pandemic on small businesses and on fintechs who participated in the massive delivery of government aid funding. Part III takes a further look at technology and the future of small business lending. Chapter 10 returns to how a unified platform like "Small Business Utopia" might look in the not-too-distant future. Chapter 11 explores who will be the winners and losers in the new landscape and Chapter 12 outlines some strategic options for banks. Finally, Part IV outlines the state of the regulatory system that governs small business lending in the United States and suggests principles for regulatory reform to increase the likelihood of successfully and safely achieving the heights of the small business lending innovation cycle that these early stages have promised.

The cycle of Schumpeter's creative destruction is only partway through its course. The best results for small businesses lie ahead.

7

The Early Days of Fintech Lending

In June 2013, about 350 people gathered in the Empire Room at Convene Innovation Center in New York to take part in the first ever LendIt (now Fintech Nexus) conference. Co-founded by Peter Renton, the head of Lend Academy, the one-day event featured a keynote by LendingClub founder and then-CEO Renaud Laplanche. His speech, entitled "Transforming the Banking System," told participants that they had the opportunity to emulate disruptive companies such as Netflix and Amazon, and to reshape financial services. Later panel discussions focused on direct and peer-to-peer small business lending models, using better data to make lending safer and more profitable, and exploring why venture capitalists were funding online lending companies. The day ended with a cocktail reception, and the entire event concluded by 7:30 PM.[1,2] Almost all of the small family of fintech lending players attended, but banks and other traditional lenders were notably absent.

The response to this first conference was so positive that Renton and his team turned it into an annual event. In May 2014, the second LendIt conference was a two-day affair that took place at the San Francisco Hilton. Interest had exploded to around 950 in-person attendees and nearly 2,000 watching online. The substance became more specialized, with sessions on small business and short-term lending, loan securitization, peer-to-peer lending in other countries, crowdfunding, and even a Q&A on legal and accounting issues. Significant attention was paid to longer-term industry trends regarding credit underwriting models and the use of big data. Some international fintech issues were touched upon, but most of those were saved for the LendIt conferences in Europe and China that started in 2014 and 2015, and also

K. G. Mills, *Fintech, Small Business & The American Dream*, https://doi.org/10.1007/978-3-031-55612-8_7

became annual events.[3] By 2015, the conference had grown to 2,500 attendees, including banks and credit unions. It featured sessions on "Borrower Acquisition at Scale" and "Partnering with Banks."[4,5] Former U.S. Treasury Secretary and LendingClub board member, Larry Summers, predicted in his keynote that fintechs would take over 70% of the small business lending market.[6] The fintech disruption had been launched.

The Frictions of Small Business Lending

Lending to small businesses has always been much more difficult than lending to consumers for two reasons that we have discussed at some length in Part I: the heterogeneity and the information opacity of small firms. Each small business has different characteristics based on industry, location, size, and business goals. Additionally, it has been hard to see what is going on inside these firms. Even small business owners themselves are often unsure about what their future cash flows and revenues will look like. As a result, it is difficult to develop a full and nuanced picture of a small business's credit-related metrics: the size of their revenues, when they incur large expenses, how quickly they pay, and how their business is trending. This kind of information makes up what one investor called a "truth file"—a way of capturing the essence of the business's future prospects.[7] For small businesses, developing a truth file has always been notoriously difficult, particularly for smaller and newer firms.

Around 2000, the development of new information interfaces, known as open APIs (application programming interfaces), helped trigger important changes in the quantity and quality of available information on small businesses. An open API is a connection that allows third-party developers to access selected data from a company's site, which can be used to create new applications.[8] In 2000, eBay became one of the first e-commerce companies to use an open API to make extensive information available on small businesses that were selling products on the website. This created a data pipe for online lenders to access information about a small business's eBay sales. The entry of Plaid in 2012 provided a unified API for banking data, which allowed new and existing players to access valuable bank account transaction information and use it to build applications for the lending ecosystem.[9]

This new backend infrastructure altered some of the long-standing frictions in the small business lending market. With these breakthroughs in data access, lenders could make better-informed underwriting decisions. In the past, underwriting largely depended on FICO (Fair Isaac Corporation) scores and tax returns, which were not a timely reflection of a business's activity. With new data sources, real-time information once hidden from view or perhaps reported inaccurately by a small business became more visible to underwriters who could use it to better identify creditworthy borrowers.

The First Movers

The fundamental innovation was harnessing the power of the data and new analytic engines, but the incidental innovations were almost as powerful. Enabled by technology and inspired by market need, fintech start-ups brought a new "digital first" approach to online small business lending starting in the late 2000s. This early period lasted through roughly 2013 and was dominated by a few first movers—including CAN Capital, Lending-Club, Kabbage, and OnDeck—that each broke new ground in their own way. One common hallmark of the early players was the automated turnaround of online applications that were easy to fill out and created a much better customer experience. These fintechs also brought other new approaches to the market including risk-based pricing, different sources of capital, and twists to traditional products and services.

Risk-Based Pricing

Many credit CAN (Credit Access Network) Capital, founded in 1998, with inventing the merchant cash advance (MCA). The original MCA products relied on a patented technology that allowed credit card receipts to be split between multiple parties.[10] For a small business, this meant that a percentage of its credit card sales could automatically be sent to the MCA provider in order to pay down the advance.

CAN tapped into a market that banks often found too risky: small businesses with urgent cash needs. Since many small businesses experience frequent cash flow fluctuations and have low cash buffers, quick and responsive lenders, even expensive ones, were in high demand. CAN and other MCA lenders were able to extend credit to riskier borrowers using two approaches that traditional banks avoided. First, they used true risk-based pricing, adjusting the interest rate they charged for the perceived risk. Banks have generally had narrow interest rate ranges, pricing loans largely based on what other banks are charging and assessing risk primarily to make binary decisions about whether or not to lend, as opposed to the rate at which to lend. This has been due in part to the regulatory requirements that govern banks' capital levels. Particularly after the 2008–2009 recession, regulatory audits could classify a loan as too risky, and force it to be "qualified" or offset against the banks' capital, making banks reluctant to take on a risky loan asset even if they could theoretically charge a high rate.

The second reason MCA lenders were willing to take on riskier loans was that the structure of the product provided a new and valuable type of collateral. Small business lenders, including those lending through the Small Business Administration (SBA) programs, often rely on a personal guarantee from the business owner to provide greater certainty of repayment. In such a case, the bank uses the borrower's personal assets, often their home, as collateral. Technology allowed MCA lenders to extract loan payments directly from the borrower's bank account or credit card receipts. This technique gave the lender a new kind of collateral—immediate access to customer receipts—rather than waiting for the borrower to make a payment. Being first in line for incoming cash, even before it hit the bank account of the business made the loan much more secure.

Many online lenders followed this structure and the pricing levels set by CAN to create a framework for the making riskiest loans. The new products were generally priced at a fixed amount. A borrower might receive $10,000 and repay $12,000 by remitting a set percentage of their daily receipts to the lender as they came in. This was appealing to some small business owners, as their repayment schedule would vary based on actual sales. Business owners also liked knowing the total cost of the loan. But because the schedule to repay the loan was based on sales and not a fixed time frame, it was nearly impossible to calculate an annual percentage rate (APR) or interest rate before knowing when the loan would be paid back, creating difficulties for small business owners trying to compare the cost of an MCA to that of a traditional loan.[11] With a standard repayment time frame, APR prices could be well north of 30%, and even reach 100% or more.

New Sources of Capital

Another early fintech was LendingClub, which began as a consumer lending company in 2007. LendingClub was a pioneer of peer-to-peer lending, using technology to bring one of the oldest and most basic forms of consumer lending into the modern world. Like Prosper, another early entrant in consumer loans, peer-to-peer lenders did not make the loans themselves. Instead, they matched individuals and institutional investors willing to provide funding to borrowers seeking capital. By 2010, LendingClub owned 80% of the U.S. peer-to-peer lending market.

During its first few years of operation, LendingClub mostly provided consumer loans, reaching $1 billion in loan volume in 2012. The company went public in 2014 with an $8.5 billion valuation, one of the largest IPOs for a consumer-facing Internet company at the time.[12] In 2015, LendingClub began to extend credit by matching investors with small business borrowers, providing small-dollar loans between $15,000 and $100,000, with "fixed interest rates starting at 5.9% with terms of one to five years, no hidden fees and no prepayment penalties."[13] LendingClub aimed for ease and simplicity in the loan application process, specifically targeting the painful customer experience that borrowers were getting at banks. In order to sell more of these loans, LendingClub partnered with BancAlliance to gain access to a referral network of hundreds of community banks.[14]

New Data

Another fintech first mover was Kabbage, which launched in 2010. Unlike LendingClub, which began with consumer loans, Kabbage focused on small businesses from the start. Their early business model was to provide working capital loans to eBay merchants, using eBay's newly developed open API to access data on potential small business borrowers and make underwriting decisions.

Kabbage engaged with several partners, including Celtic Bank, using that relationship to scale lending products from the Kabbage platform. Partnerships with Intuit and UPS provided access to customer data to assess creditworthiness, and a partnership with online payment processor Stripe opened up access to more small business customers. Co-founder Kathryn Petralia noted that while Kabbage had started as a niche e-commerce lender, by 2018, a full 90% of its business borrowers were offline businesses, and the company had originated a total of $5 billion in loans to more than 130,000 small businesses.[15,16]

Founded in 2006, OnDeck also set out to provide small business credit using a proprietary credit scoring system, known as OnDeck Score. This system integrated public records, accounting, and social network data in addition to personal credit scores.[17] In 2012, at a small business lending conference held by the SBA and the U.S. Department of the Treasury (Treasury), OnDeck told the gathering that it was using bank account data to obtain real-time information on small business transactions. This announcement sent a signal to lenders: why use historical data if one could determine creditworthiness in real time? OnDeck went public in 2014 with a $1.3 billion valuation, and in 2015 they began offering credit lines and long-term loan products.[18] By 2018, OnDeck touted itself as the largest online small business lender in the United States, having issued over $8 billion in small business loans.[19]

As with LendingClub and Kabbage, OnDeck's proprietary creditworthiness score could only have been created through APIs that provided access to data from non-traditional sources. In a 2018 interview, LendIt co-founder Peter Renton remarked on how the first movers had set the stage for the fintech revolution. "The data that Kabbage was getting from UPS, eBay, etc., and how they were using it to make predictions—this had never been done before," said Renton. "This was brand new intelligence. There has always been data available, but no one knew how to use it until Kabbage and OnDeck came in and pulled it together."[20]

The Small Business Lending Ecosystem—Circa 2015

The success of the early entrants did not go unnoticed. From 2013 to 2015, dozens of new firms entered the small business online lending ecosystem. The space changed so rapidly that it didn't even have a fixed name. Sometimes the sector was called marketplace lending, reflecting the early success of Prosper, LendingClub, and other peer-to-peer lenders, while at other times, it was called online, alternative, or fintech lending.

The entrants active in this period fell into six categories. There were four types of lenders: balance sheet, peer-to-peer, platform players, and invoice and payables financers. In addition, there were multi-lender marketplaces where small businesses could shop for and compare lenders and their products, and firms that provided data to the other players in the ecosystem (Figure 7.1).

Balance Sheet and Peer-to-Peer Lenders

Balance sheet lenders included those offering MCA products and one- to two-year term loans. These companies held the loans on their firm's balance sheet. Peer-to-peer lenders, by contrast, matched interested investors with potential borrowers. They dominated the early fintech landscape, particularly in the United Kingdom, where government support for new lenders increased following the 2008–2009 financial crisis. One particularly strong U.K. entrant was Funding Circle, a small business-focused peer-to-peer lender that entered the U.S. market in 2013 through a merger.[21]

	LENDERS		MULTI-LENDER MARKETPLACES	DATA PROVIDERS
Balance Sheet Lenders	○ ApplePie Capital ○ CAN Capital ○ Credibly	○ Fundation ○ Kabbage ○ OnDeck	○ Biz2Credit ○ Fundera	○ Dun & Bradstreet ○ Equifax
Peer-to-Peer Lenders	○ Credibility Capital ○ Funding Circle	○ Lending Club ○ StreetShares	○ Intuit QuickBooks ○ Lendio	○ Experian ○ FICO ○ FreshBooks
Platforms	○ Amazon Lending ○ PayPal ○ Square			○ Intuit ○ PayNet
Invoice and Payables Financing	○ American Express ○ BlueVine ○ C2FO	○ Fundbox ○ NOWAccount ○ Taulia		○ TransUnion ○ Xero

Figure 7.1 Small Business Fintech Lending Ecosystem in 2015
Source: Author's analysis based on Jackson Mueller, "U.S. Online, Non-Bank Finance Landscape," Milken Institute Center for Financial Markets, curated through May 2016.

Platform Players

Although they grew to be critical players in online lending, platform lenders did not enter the emerging market until 2011 and their efforts did not gain momentum until a couple of years later. The most visible platform, Amazon, launched Amazon Lending in 2011 and, by the summer of 2017, they were lending $1 billion annually to small businesses with loans ranging from $1,000 to $750,000.[22,23] With the clear potential to expand into other products and services, they became the player to watch. PayPal launched PayPal Working Capital in 2013 and, by 2017, they had lent a total of $3 billion to small businesses.[24]

Square had a built-in base of small businesses using their card payment processing device that could be easily attached to a smartphone. Jack Dorsey, Square's founder (and co-founder and later CEO of Twitter), saw that customers needed small amounts of capital to meet their fluctuating cash needs. He also saw the value of the insights that Square could glean from using their proprietary data on businesses' daily cash receipts and the advantage of having first access to the receipts for debt repayment. In 2014, he formed Square Capital and, in 2015, he hired Jacqueline Reses from Yahoo to lead the effort. By 2016, Square had lent $1 billion, with an average loan size of $6,000.[25] By 2018, Square Capital was originating almost $400 million in loans per quarter, largely to the underserved segment of extremely small businesses seeking very small loans.[26]

Another important platform player was American Express, which already had a customer base of thousands of small business credit card users and had built visibility and goodwill through its Small Business Saturday initiative and the OPEN small business brand. American Express began utilizing its access to sales and payments information to provide capital to qualified American Express credit card users, allowing these small businesses to access short-term financing at a lower interest rate.

Invoice and Payables Financing

Several new companies began providing invoice financing to help businesses with late-paying customers or seasonal cash flow fluctuations. While factoring—a form of lending that allows a business to sell its invoices to a provider and get immediate cash in exchange for a fee—had long existed, the automation of that process allowed it to occur more seamlessly.

Invoice financing solutions are particularly important for small supply chain companies, which play an underappreciated role in the U.S. economy.[27] Recall our example from Chapter 2 of Transportation and Logistical Services (TLS), a trucking company with 30 employees outside of Birmingham, Alabama. Now imagine that Coca-Cola, one of its biggest customers, decides to delay their payment terms from 30 to 60 days. This would create an unexpected cash crunch for TLS. Online invoice financing provides a solution for small suppliers like TLS to get paid more quickly if they need to.

On the other side of this equation, a second set of products such as Working Capital Terms created by American Express allowed companies to delay a payment by having the platform pay the vendor, with the company taking on the obligation to pay back the money in 30, 60, or 90 days. This product acted like a business credit card, but provided more flexibility in that payments could be made to entities that did not accept cards, and terms and pricing were more like those of a short-term loan.

Many fintechs and platforms developed innovative invoice and payments solutions including Fundbox, BlueVine, NOWAccount, and C2FO. Some products were classified as loans, while others were not. All of the providers of these products, however, recognized the reduced risk of lending when they had access to a small business's invoices, a strong piece of collateral to back up the advance.

From the perspective of small businesses, for whom late customer payments have long been a potentially life-threatening nightmare, the new innovations provided a large range of more cost-effective and accessible options. Traditional factoring companies such as CIT, once the industry leader, were never inclined to create this kind of innovation, and their products were notoriously expensive and difficult to obtain. As we saw with the government's QuickPay program in Chapter 3, timely payments improve cash buffers and small business performance. Thus, the availability of these fintech products might save thousands of small businesses from untimely demise as a result of cash timing gaps.

Marketplaces

Another group of entrants that emerged during this time were the online lending marketplaces. Companies such as Fundera and Lendio offered small businesses the ability to comparison shop for loan products from both banks and alternative lenders. Marketplaces took a referral fee for each loan originated through their site, which proved worthwhile to many fintechs struggling with customer acquisition. Consumer marketplaces for loans and mortgages have long existed, but small business loan comparisons are more difficult as the products have more variability and small business owners often have less clarity about what kind of loan they need. Thus, online small business marketplaces are a much needed vehicle to create a more transparent, easier to navigate credit experience.

Data Providers

Data providers became an important part of the new technology-enabled lending ecosystem. Xero and FreshBooks began competing with QuickBooks as a software through which small businesses could manage their finances. Yodlee, a data aggregator, provided software to help businesses predict future cash flows and expenses.

Others collected information on the lending industry itself. PayNet gathered data from banks and commercial finance companies to provide insights and credit ratings to the lenders on their platform. Enigma mined the entire range of publicly available small business data, from business registrations to health inspections of New York City restaurants, and organized it into accessible information available by individual entity. Meanwhile, Orchard collected and shared data about the new fintech players, tracking the number of companies and loan originations, and providing advanced analytics on the nascent industry.[28] These providers developed important information streams for both banks and online lenders, as well as policymakers and regulators.

Small Business Online Lending Appeared Poised for Takeoff

By 2015, online lenders were originating around $5 billion annually in small business loans.[29] The new entrants would have plenty of room to grow by addressing the market gap in small business lending, particularly the small-dollar loans that banks did not want to make.[30] During this time, venture capital investment in fintech skyrocketed, growing by almost 140% between 2013 and 2014 and by over 50% between the two following years, reaching nearly $9 billion across 578 deals in 2015 (Figure 7.2).[31]

The new fintech small business lending market seemed poised for takeoff—the phase of the innovation cycle in which volume accelerates and new customers jump into the marketplace, leaving behind old products and companies. Yet, despite the investment and the hype, this expected jump did not occur. What happened instead was another cycle of innovation. Organizational theorist Geoffrey Moore described discontinuous innovations as those that force us to "change our current mode of behavior or to modify other products and services we rely on."[32] But, he added, "truly discontinuous innovations are new products or services that require the end user and the marketplace to dramatically change their past behavior, with the promise of gaining equally dramatic new benefits."[33] During this period, fintech innovations changed the markets for established financial products but, for several reasons, were not yet able to change the lending process in a way that was "truly discontinuous."

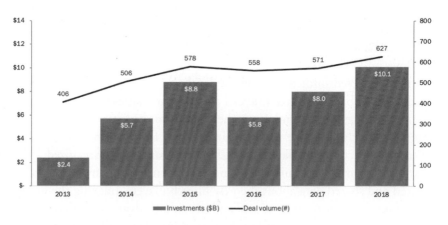

Figure 7.2   Fintech-Related Funding in the U.S. by Year
Source: "MoneyTree™ Report Q4 2018," PwC/CB Insights, 2019.

The early movers in the fintech space had shaken up the industry by using new information sources and technology to deliver lending products in a way that was highly automated. From the perspective of the small business owner, the customer experience was significantly better, particularly in terms of speed. But in other important ways, there had been little real innovation in the actual products. With many of the offerings characterized by high prices and low transparency, small businesses began raising concerns about bad actors in the market. Cracks in the fintech success story began to appear.

Challenges to Online Small Business Lenders

By 2017, the industry's underlying issues had caught up to the nascent fintech companies. Rosy predictions about the future of online small business lending were on the decline. This was due, in large part, to a growing realization that many of the innovations brought by the new fintechs could be imitated by incumbent banks, as well as concerns over the advantages that large platform players could exercise if they chose to enter the market.

It started to become clear that both incumbents and disruptors had advantages and disadvantages, and that the winners would be the group that could most quickly and effectively address their shortcomings. Comparing the incumbent players (large banks like JPMorgan Chase and Wells Fargo and smaller community banks) with the new fintech entrants, it became apparent that no one was the clear winner. Instead, it was a pretty mixed picture (Figure 7.3).

Existing banks had the large pools of customers that fintechs were struggling to find. The 2015 annual reports of OnDeck and LendingClub showed that sales and marketing efforts were among the largest operating expenses for both lenders, at about 24% and 40% of gross revenue, respectively.[34] On a per loan basis, average costs to acquire a customer were estimated to be $2,500–$3,500 per loan.[35] By comparison, in 2017, regional New England lender Eastern Bank reported an average marketing cost of $500 per small business loan under $100,000.[36]

Banks also had access to low-cost deposits, while online lenders were largely forced to rely on capital markets to fund loans. Yield-seeking individuals and hedge funds were early sources of capital, but they were expensive and soon dried up as the Federal Reserve began to raise interest rates and the real level of risk in some fintech loans became apparent.

In the early days, the lack of federal regulatory oversight of non-bank lenders was perceived to be an advantage. Banks were reeling from increased compliance costs caused by Dodd-Frank, leading many to predict that the

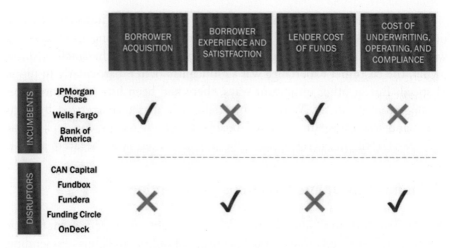

Figure 7.3   Incumbents and Disruptors: Advantages and Disadvantages
Source: Author's analysis based on "The Brave 100: The Battle of Supremacy in Small Business Lending," QED Investors and Oliver Wyman, 2015.

disruptors would see large benefits from "regulatory arbitrage." However, the lack of federal oversight was a double-edged sword. The inability of non-banks to obtain a federal charter may have actually inhibited the national growth of online lenders, as they were forced to charter themselves state by state, use a bank partner, or create products that did not qualify as loans.

The early fintechs had clearly initiated innovations that reduced some of the barriers to a smoother matching of borrowers and lenders in the small business marketplace. They created an advantage by using technology to deliver an easier, faster digital customer experience, but it was unclear whether that advantage was sustainable. Although fintechs were the first to catch on, there was nothing preventing incumbent banks or even Big Tech companies from imitating or even beating them at their own game.

By 2018, the market was consolidating, as peer-to-peer lending stopped growing, and traditional banks increasingly incorporated fintech innovations via acquisition, imitation, or partnership. Perhaps that is why the mood at LendIt 2018 was less exuberant than when it started in 2013, and why the conference had diversified by adding an entire track dedicated to blockchain technology.[37]

* * *

Despite the stops and starts, the fintech innovation cycle was underway. The early movers had shown that it was no longer acceptable for banks and other lenders to provide the same small business products and service levels they had for the past several decades. Small businesses had gotten a taste of a new level of service and were in search of more. The stage was set to see how technology might change the game—how additional innovations from current players or future entities might serve the financial needs of small businesses in novel ways that were affordable, integrated, and intelligent.

Then in March 2020, the unthinkable happened—the world shut down in response to the Covid-19 Pandemic. In the United States, fintechs rose to the occasion and were crucial players in delivering government aid to small businesses, especially the smallest and underserved businesses that banks refused to rescue. The fintechs' quick action proved to many that technology could extend the reach of small business lenders, delivering access to capital to segments poorly served by banks alone.

8

Small Business and the Covid-19 Pandemic

In March 2020, the world as small business owners knew it stopped. In a matter of weeks, the Covid-19 pandemic had reached a terrifying level with hospitals overcrowded and deaths mounting. Governments across the world took radical measures for the health and safety of their people, instituting lockdowns which shut the doors for most small businesses. In the U.S., Congress quickly instituted small business relief programs, including hundreds of billions in funding for the Paycheck Protection Program. Small businesses desperately called their bank—if they had one—to get in the queue before the money ran out.

Ocrolus CEO, Sam Bobley, and newly hired Senior Vice President, David Snitkof, immediately saw a need in the chaotic PPP application process and knew they had the technology to help. Ocrolus, founded in 2014 in New York, focused on document automation, serving lender and bank clients. They had developed the capacity to have machines read and understand financial documents such as payroll reports, bank statements, and tax forms, the very information needed to fill out the required PPP applications. At first some of the documents—such as the IRS 941 (Employer's Quarterly Federal Tax Return)—were new to both banks and Ocrolus. Banks hired armies of people, but Ocrolus was able to tune its machine learning and automation algorithms to process documents for PPP loans at a massive scale.

Both banks and fintechs turned to Ocrolus technology for help. Several smaller lenders were able to issue as many or more PPP loans than the nation's largest financial institutions, thanks to this type of automation. By the end of 2021, Ocrolus had processed over 13 million documents for PPP, helping millions of small businesses quickly gain access to funds they wouldn't otherwise have received.

In fact, the Covid-19 pandemic proved to be a real turning point for technology's journey in small business lending, including the engagement of small business owners who had never used digital access. "I think the PPP was an eye-opening experience for folks that were only used to in-branch interactions. PPP required folks to go through an online process, whether they wanted to or not, because the banks were literally shut down," David Snitkof observed.[1] Many banks moved to automated processes faster than they might have otherwise due to the pressures of the crisis. For some this opened the door to a wider acceptance of data-driven lending tools to augment loan underwriting in the post-pandemic era.

In any case, in the spring of 2020, technology proved a game changer for the pandemic relief effort. Snitkof commented, "I think of PPP as a case of 'fintech to the rescue'. Our country wouldn't have been able to get this level of funding to small businesses of all sizes and types without the automation that fintech contributed."[2]

The Covid-19 Pandemic

On March 11, 2020, the World Health Organization declared Covid-19 a global pandemic.[3] In the United States, the Covid-19 virus had exploded in several cities, with infections and deaths skyrocketing from New York City to Sioux City, Iowa. At a White House press briefing on March 31, leaders of the Coronavirus Task Force estimated the virus could cause between 100,000 and 240,000 deaths.[4] This turned out to vastly underestimate the more than one million deaths over the next three years. Yet it was clear from the early days that this virus would have grave consequences. Given the highly contagious nature of Covid-19, the obvious solution was to limit interpersonal interaction. With masks and other personal protective equipment in short supply, schools and offices began to close and public officials took steps to limit economic activity to essential services.

By April 7, 46 states representing 97.8% of U.S. GDP had implemented some kind of partial or full lockdown.[5] Businesses of all kinds ceased operations. Particularly hard hit were retail and customer-facing businesses, who saw traffic come to a complete halt in a matter of days. The sudden stop in economic activity led to historic drops in GDP and employment in the United States and in almost all major economies. America suffered its largest quarter contraction in over 70 years, as GDP fell by 8.9% in the second quarter of 2020. Countries around the globe experienced similar or worse drops in output, as GDP fell by more than 21% in the United Kingdom and 19% in Mexico.[6]

Impact on Small Businesses

Small and medium-sized businesses were disproportionally affected by the lockdowns. As we saw in Chapter 2, the United States has over 4 million Main Street small businesses and 27 million sole proprietorships many of which are focused on in-person customer service.[7] Hairdressers, Uber drivers, restaurants, and local shops had to close their doors, at least temporarily. (Retail, including both physical storefronts and e-commerce, makes up the largest small business industry segment at 15.1%, followed by food and restaurants at 13.7%, and health, beauty, and fitness services at 9.7%).[8] The more than 1 million supply chain small businesses also felt the impact as factories and larger businesses—their main customers—shut down. Thus, for an estimated 21 million small business owners and employees, their entire world and livelihood changed almost overnight as they faced financial instability and tremendous uncertainty about the future.

Small businesses underpin the economic well-being of the country, and the crisis that followed the Covid-19 pandemic was not the first time small businesses faced economic adversity. As we saw in Chapter 3, in the financial crisis of 2008–2009, small businesses employed 50% of the private sector workforce but accounted for over 60% of the net job losses in the economy. In the first months of the pandemic, small businesses were again disproportionately affected. The number of "working business owners plummeted from 15 million in February 2020 to 11.7 million in April" due to public health mandates and demand shifts.[9]

By April 3, over 60% of small businesses surveyed by Alignable, a small business community with over 5 million members, reported significant impacts on their businesses and expressed serious concerns that their businesses would close within the next month.[10]

Uneven Pandemic Effects

If small businesses were hit hard, women- and Black-owned businesses were hit even harder. The count of women actively running businesses decreased 16% from 5.4 million to 4.0 million during a two-month period at the start of the crisis. During the same two months of 2020, Black business ownership declined more than 40%, the largest drop across any ethnic group according to the work of Robert Fairlie of the University of California, Santa Cruz.[11] The study also showed that Black-owned businesses were more likely to be located in areas with high volumes of Covid-19 cases and had less access to relief.

In the face of this crisis, local and state governments correctly prioritized individual health and safety imperatives. As hospitals became overwhelmed and the death toll continued to rise, mayors and governors mandated business closures. For small businesses, forced to flip their open signs to "closed" for the foreseeable future, there was a desperate need for economic assistance from the federal government.

U.S. Government Response

In early March 2020, there was great uncertainty about the severity and length of the pandemic and the related need for business closures. Most believed that a bridge program until June or July would be required, after which Covid-19 cases would decline. Even with this optimistic time horizon, the impact would be severe. As we saw in Chapter 3, most businesses have very little liquidity, with the average business holding only 27 days of operating cash. Certain industries such as restaurants were even more cash constrained, with an average of only 16 days of cash on hand, making them particularly vulnerable to the pandemic closures.[12] Given the sudden halt on incoming cash, with a full expense load, these businesses would soon be forced to close permanently.

Federal Aid for a Global Crisis

The magnitude of the support required and the speed with which it needed to be delivered to save small businesses was daunting. Yet the government was able to act quickly. The first non-travel case of Covid-19 was confirmed in California on February 26 and the first U.S. death was reported on February 29.[13,14] By the end of March, New York City alone had over 30,000 cases and almost 1,000 deaths.[15,16] Yet on March 6, just a week after the first death was reported, Congress issued the first legislative response to the virus enacting an $8.3 billion emergency coronavirus spending package, shortly followed by a second Act on March 14, which passed with bipartisan support. Aid to small business was included in the third and largest bill, the CARES act, that passed on March 27.

$1.2 Trillion Dollars for Small Businesses

Between March 2020 and September 2022, 15 federal government agencies, the Federal Reserve (Fed), and governors and mayors across the country acted to implement dozens of small business relief programs. The efforts centered around the over $1.2 trillion dollars that were allocated to small businesses primarily through four programs lead by the Small Business Administration (SBA): the Paycheck Protection Program ($792 billion), the Covid-19 Economic Injury Disaster Loans ($405 billion), the Shuttered Venue Operators Grants ($15 billion), and the Restaurant Revitalization Fund ($29 billion).[17] Other notable efforts included: Treasury's State Small Business Credit Initiative ($10 billion) and the Federal Reserve's Paycheck Protection Program Liquidity Facility. The total dollars allocated far exceeded any past relief efforts. For example, the largest spending for a recent disaster occurred after Hurricane Katrina in 2005, totaling $110 billion across multiple federal programs.[18] The SBA also had mechanisms in place to regularly support annual disaster spending in the $25–$30 billion range.

The goals of the pandemic federal aid were twofold: keep employment levels high to prevent the hardship and disruption of massive layoffs and prevent large-scale failures in the small business sector. Given the lack of liquidity, some worried that 20–30% of small businesses in the country could be lost.[19] Since some of the most vulnerable small businesses maintained a local presence, this could mean shuttered locations on Main Streets for months or years to come. Job loss was clearly a great concern. Small restaurant, accommodation, and retail establishments alone employed 14 million people.[20] Thus, on March 27 as part of the Coronavirus Aid, Relief and Economic Security (CARES) Act, the Paycheck Protection Program was born (Figure 8.1).

The Paycheck Protection Program

The Paycheck Protection Program (PPP) focused on helping small businesses maintain their payroll and keep their employees on the job during the crisis. Across three rounds of PPP funding, over 11 million loans to 8.5 million businesses were approved and distributed from 5,500 lenders across the country.[21] Ultimately, $792 billion of relief was extended to small businesses, making it one of the largest public finance programs in U.S. history.[22]

Small businesses, independent contractors, and self-employed individuals were eligible to apply for PPP loans through a very short application of

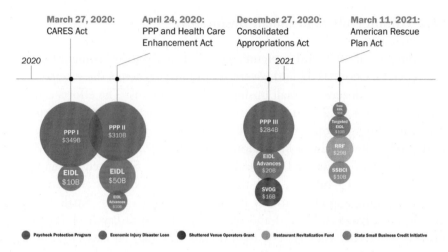

Figure 8.1   Timeline of Federal Aid for Small Businesses
Source: Author's analysis based on Small Business Administration data.

about five pages.[23] The maximum loan amount was calculated based on 2.5 times the borrower's average monthly payroll costs, up to a maximum of $10 million. Borrowers could use the loan proceeds to cover payroll costs, including salaries, wages, and benefits, as well as rent, mortgage interest, and utilities. The interest rate on PPP loans was set at 1% with a duration of five years. However, PPP loans would be forgiven if two conditions were met. First, proceeds had to be used to cover payroll costs, mortgage interest, rent, and utility costs over the eight-week period following the provision of the loan, but not more than 25% of the loan forgiveness amount could be used for non-payroll costs. Second, small business recipients were required to maintain employee counts and compensation levels.[24] These conditions reflected the initial goal of the PPP funding: to keep people employed.

CARES Act Provides Funding

Fueled by the urgency of the pandemic shutdowns, implementation of the Paycheck Protection Program was unusually rapid. The small business provisions were on the very first page of the CARES Act, symbolizing that lawmakers understood the grave threat to small businesses and were making relief a priority. The Act was signed into law on March 27, approving an unprecedented $349 billion of funding. By April 2, authorized banks took the first applications, deploying funds within days. A mere two weeks later, on April 16, over 1.5 million loans had been approved and the entire $349 billion pool was exhausted.[25] During this first round of funding, traditional banks administered almost all of the loans (91%) and mostly served their existing customers.[26]

The Federal Reserve Injects Essential Liquidity

While Congress had passed the bills appropriating the funds and the banking system was chosen as the fastest way to get money to small businesses, the issue of liquidity still needed to be addressed. PPP was going to distribute $349 billion to American small businesses in a matter of days. Who had the money to do that? The answer was the Federal Reserve (Fed). On March 15, even before the final CARES Act funding was approved, the Fed announced that it would support participating financial institutions with the liquidity needed for the program and encouraged banks to borrow from the Fed's discount window, a central bank lending facility, to manage short-term liquidity needs.[27]

The Fed authorized a special Paycheck Protection Program Lending Facility (PPPLF) program which provided liquidity to lenders facing high demand for PPP for no additional fees. The facility was available to any authorized PPP lender including non-bank lenders such as fintechs, who generally did not have access to the Fed discount window. At its peak in June 2021, advances reached $90.6 billion. Over 850 lenders used the facility, most of which were small, community banks but about 70 non-banks also availed themselves of the access.[28] The support from the Fed was critical because of the choice to run PPP through private sector institutions who did not have the liquidity on their balance sheets to cover the unprecedented levels of funding that the pandemic crisis required. Without this piece in place the program would have failed.

Round 1: The SBA and the Banks

The Small Business Administration (SBA) faced enormous challenges in implementing pandemic relief due to the large volumes and quick timetable required. The first phase of PPP at $349 billion was ten times the average annual SBA lending level, and all the money needed to be put out in a matter of weeks. To be sure the PPP loans were fully guaranteed and did not require underwriting efforts, but all the applications still needed to be received and processed. The SBA technology relied on a relatively old system called E-Tran. As soon as the program launched, the E-Tran platform was quickly overwhelmed by the volume of requests made by the banks. For instance, in the opening hours of the program, Bank of America submitted 10,000 applications.[29]

The SBA allocated funds on a first-come, first-served basis. Initially, as demand choked the system, small businesses and bankers alike bemoaned seemingly endless technology crashes and long queues. In addition, it quickly became evident that the demand from small businesses was much larger than the Round 1 allocation and even more funding would need to be provided.

Banking Relationships and Firm Size Mattered

Even more worrisome, serious inequities in the allocation of funds soon became apparent in the first round of PPP. Banks had prioritized their existing customers and larger loans, leaving out the smallest businesses and those without a banking relationship. The average loan size in the first round for employer businesses was over $200,000, much larger than the size required by most small Main Street businesses. Larger businesses grabbed the lion's share of the available funds. Over 60,000 loans were over $1 million, totaling about 42% of the dollars allocated in the first round.[30]

The inequities were glaring, even in that moment. Underserved businesses and sole proprietorships were at the end of the line. Black-owned businesses in particular were only able to access 2.1% of the loans in the first tranche of the PPP funding.[31] Sole proprietorships accounted for 4.3% of the loans and only 0.003% of the total loan value.[32] An online survey commissioned by two equal rights organizations found that only 38% of African American and Hispanic small business applicants had received some or all of the federal funds they had requested.[33]

These patterns are consistent with historical gaps in small business lending. However, they are even more concerning given the lack of risk taken by the lender in the PPP lending process. Since the loans were guaranteed by the federal government, the lender did not take on the perceived added risks of lending to a very small business or a minority-owned business. If the inequities were not risk-based, what was causing them? As we will explore in the next sections, multiple issues appear to have been at play, including a lack of relationships and a lack of trust among various communities with regard to the banking system and frictions related to bias and access to information. PPP then becomes a critical area for insights as we explore the barriers to full access to small business capital—and the impact of technology on removing those constraints.

Round 2: Fintechs Can Play Too

On April 24, just as the Round 1 funding ran out, Treasury and SBA green-lighted the involvement of additional lenders, many of whom were fintechs. Simultaneously, Congress passed a second PPP round of $310 billion, much to the relief of small business owners in the queue. The second round of PPP showed a dramatically different story. The average loan dropped from $200,000 to $70,000 and then to $33,289 in the third round.[34] The addition of the new lenders was immediately successful in enabling smaller businesses to take advantage of the program. The amount of loans under $50,000 dollars went from less than 750,000 in the first round, to over 2.75 million in the second round. Over 800,000 sole proprietors accessed the funding, compared to 67,000 in the first round.[35]

Many economists have examined the impact of banks and banking relationships on the ability of small businesses to access PPP funds.[36] Most banks, particularly the larger ones, prioritized lending to existing customers. For the top four banks, 68% of the total PPP loans they made went to businesses that had checking accounts with the bank. For medium banks the number was 39%, still higher than the overall program average of 28%.

The strength of the U.S. banking system, particularly its large number of community banks, has long been an important asset. The importance of this banking network is likely one reason why policymakers chose it to distribute PPP loans. In many ways, this was a good decision. Over three thousand banks participated and distributed 74.3% of the loans. Research found that in locations with more banks and more relationship banks, businesses not only received more PPP overall, but also accessed funding earlier.[37] Another study found that half of banks' PPP loans went to borrowers within two miles of a branch.[38] However, as described in Chapter 4, some communities are underserved by the banking system. Thus, the distribution of PPP through banks disadvantaged many businesses without local banks and those without banking relationships.

The choice to augment the PPP distribution by using fintechs was critical to the eventual success of the program. Fintechs relied mostly on online and automated processes that were able to extend the program's reach to previously underserved regions and communities. Research shows that fintechs disproportionately served communities in lower income zip codes with fewer bank branches and industries with lower small business lending.[39] Importantly, researchers also found that fintechs mostly extended the supply, rather than substituted for banks in providing loans.[40]

Figure 8.2   Share of Loan Count by Loan Size
Source: Author's analysis based on tabulations by Sabrina T. Howell of the NYU Stern School of Business.

Fintechs Reach Smaller Businesses

Unlike banks, fintech lenders were accustomed to coding first to solve problems and immediately automated the application process. These consumer-centric processes made it easier for smaller businesses with limited capacity to access the PPP program. As fintechs expanded their reach in the second round, the proportion of loans under $25,000 dollars went from 28 to 63% and rose to 80% in the third round (Figure 8.2). As the program evolved, banks also started partnering with fintechs as technology providers to increase their reach on small-dollar loans.

Impact on Minorities

The involvement of fintech lenders and their use of automation to fuel the application process made a big difference in getting Black-owned businesses better access to relief funding. This was critical because many of these businesses faced greater hurdles to survive the crisis. Over 67% of Black-owned businesses reported being either unprepared or very unprepared to respond to the challenges brought by the pandemic compared to only 43% of white-owned businesses.[41] And in the early days of the crisis, Black-owned businesses experienced particular difficulty accessing government support. One reason for the heightened difficulties was that these business owners lacked relationships with traditional bankers who could process their applications. They turned to other sources, including Community Development Financial Institutions (CDFIs), but a critical key to unlocking significantly broader access to the pandemic aid programs turned out to be easy-to-use application processes developed by fintechs. By the end of the program, fintech lenders were responsible for an extraordinary share (53.6%) of PPP loans to Black-owned businesses, while only accounting for 17.4% of all PPP loans (Figure 8.3a)[42]

Reaching these communities ended up being a prime role of the fintech lenders in PPP. More than a quarter of the loans made by fintechs went to Black-owned businesses (Figure 8.3b). This is a very high concentration compared to banks who made between 3 and 8%.

The economists who published this research found two underlying reasons for the findings: first, online loan origination allowed lenders to reach

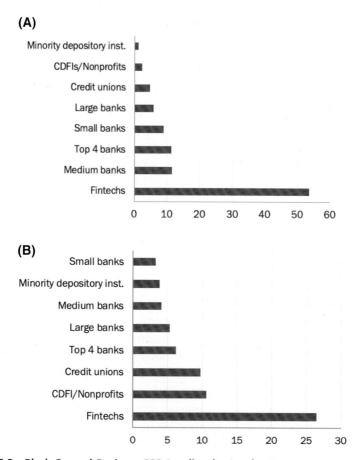

Figure 8.3 Black-Owned Business PPP Lending by Lender Type
(A) Share of Loans to Black-Owned Businesses Made by Lender Type. (B) Share of All Loans Made by Lender Type to Black-Owned Businesses
Source: Sabrina T. Howell, Theresa Kuchler, David Snitkof, Johannes Stroebel and Jun Wong, "Lender Automation and Racial Disparities in Credit Access," The Journal of Finance, 2023.

borrowers in regions with higher minority shares that are traditionally under-served by banks. Second, by studying the differences in loan activity in banks before and after they implemented automation, they concluded that the automated processes reduced human influence on decisions and could thus mitigate racial discrimination in lending. They noted: "while there are legitimate concerns that the use of algorithms may lead to discriminatory effects, for example because these algorithms are trained on biased data, our results suggest that there may be substantial equity benefits from automation. Specifically, by eliminating the manual review conducted by biased humans, automation could reduce the incidence of taste-based discrimination."[43] These findings are critical, indicating the potential for technology to improve the large and persistent gaps in small business lending to underserved small businesses.

Round 3: How Long Is This Going to Last?

On December 27, 2020, a third round of PPP was made possible through the Consolidated Appropriations Act, which delineated $284 billion in additional funding. This was welcome news as the pandemic was far from over. New Covid-19 cases had risen from 1.2 million in September 2020 to 6.4 million in December 2020 and lockdowns that had been easing were reinstated in many locations.[44]

Anti-Fraud Updates

The third round of PPP involved multiple regulatory changes designed to continue to reach the smallest of businesses, target fraud, and allow small businesses to take out a second loan. The anti-fraud changes were particularly important. As Associate Administrator for the Office of Capital Access at the SBA, Patrick Kelley, testified in Congress: "unlike in the first rounds of PPP, the 2021 guaranty process eliminated instant approval of applications. Instead, funding for loans was contingent on passing front-end SBA compliance checks such as verifying income with IRS and cross-checking Treasury's Do Not Pay list."[45]

Unemployment Insurance Benefits

At the same time PPP was being deployed, the U.S. Departments of Labor and Treasury worked on enhanced unemployment insurance programs to provide financial assistance to millions of workers who had lost their jobs or had their hours reduced due to the economic impact of the pandemic. This was good news for small businesses that were forced to lay off some employees and particularly for 26 million sole proprietors and independent contractors who now found themselves unable to work due to lockdown restrictions. The unemployment insurance expansion was implemented through the CARES Act's temporary Pandemic Unemployment Assistance.

The new program had two key incremental benefits: it provided unemployment insurance benefits to workers who were not normally eligible, such as self-employed workers, independent contractors, and gig workers, and it included an additional $600 per week for 13 weeks (April 5 through July 31, 2020) for all eligible workers, on top of their regular unemployment insurance benefits.[46]

Many businesses were now facing a new dilemma: should they have their employees go on unemployment or keep them on the books and seek payroll support through PPP? In the midst of the chaos between public health restrictions, uncertainty about the length of the pandemic, and the complexity of the various relief efforts, the decision-making process for small business owners was incredibly challenging. Many had to completely reinvent their businesses, pivoting to online sales or no-contact home delivery. As they rethought their business models, they had to estimate their future cash inflows and expenses. Could they afford to keep their employees while their in-store activities were closed? What expertise would they need to adjust to online sales and marketing and distanced deliveries, and how much would that cost? What could they just do themselves? On the employees' side, those who were earning lower wages found the new unemployment benefits highly attractive because many could earn the same or higher income while staying safely at home.

In addition, in the early days of the PPP program there was considerable uncertainty about how the program would work. What expenses qualified and how did they need to be calculated and documented? Would the application get funded and how long would it take? And would the loan actually be forgiven? Business owners uncertain about their new business needs and the PPP loan process might lean toward laying off employees and encouraging staff to use the enhanced unemployment insurance benefits.

A Round for Sole Proprietors

In terms of number of loans disbursed, Round 3 was dominated by sole proprietors. Over 3 million sole proprietors were able to access the PPP,

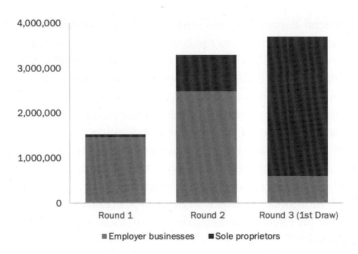

Figure 8.4   Number of Loans to Employer Businesses Versus Sole Proprietors
Source: Robert W. Fairlie and Frank M. Fossen, "The 2021 Paycheck Protection Program Reboot: Loan Disbursement to Employer and Nonemployer Businesses in Minority Communities," AEA Papers and Proceedings, Vol. 112, May 2022.

with an average loan of $14,186, in stark contrast to the first two round (Figure 8.4). Since Round 3 also allowed for second draw loans, a million sole proprietors were able to get a second loan during that same year. Economic research showed that the changes made in the third round of PPP successfully increased access by minorities and the smallest of businesses to government relief funds.[47]

The Aftermath: Forgiveness

PPP loans were forgivable on three main conditions: employee and compensation levels were maintained, the loan proceeds were spent on payroll costs and other eligible expenses, and at least 60% of the proceeds were spent on payroll costs.[48] If these conditions were met, borrowers were not required to repay the loans, which effectively became a grant.

To request forgiveness, borrowers applied directly through the SBA's website by filling out a one-page form with basic information about the borrowers' business, the loan amount, the usage of the loan, and the lender. The borrower had 10 months after the last day of the covered period to apply for forgiveness. As of October 2022, 93% of all PPP loans had submitted forgiveness applications representing 96% of the total loan value, and the SBA had already officially forgiven 99.6% of those applications.[49]

The Covid-19 Economic Injury Disaster Loan

Simultaneously, the CARES Act allowed the SBA to radically expand a long-standing but infrequently used program called Economic Injury Disaster Loans (EIDL). These loans were meant for businesses that may not have sustained physical damage in a natural disaster but did suffer negative economic consequences. The program had been deployed to great effect in the Gulf region in May 2010 to help fishing communities impacted by the Deepwater BP Oil Spill.[50] In 2020, the government saw that the EIDL program was the right vehicle to provide financial support to businesses and nonprofits who suffered economic injury from Covid-19.[51]

EIDL and EIDL Advances

One main difference between PPP and the EIDL loans was that the latter were not forgivable. However, EIDL loans possessed low interest rates of 3.75% for small businesses and 2.75% for nonprofit organizations and could be repaid over a long period of up to 30 years. Loans were meant to support a variety of expenses, such as payroll costs, rent, and even debt. Loan applicants could also request an EIDL Advance to supplement their loan. EIDL Advances were immediate grants of up to $15,000 and did not need to be repaid, even if the organization was later determined to be ineligible for an EIDL loan. Advances were generally granted within three days of applying, helping to compensate for the slower loan application processing time. Businesses could get an EIDL loan or advance in addition to their PPP grant, with certain offsets.[52]

SBA Operational Response

The sudden high volumes in the EIDL program created a massive operational challenge for the SBA. As opposed to PPP, Covid-19 EIDL loans were processed directly by the SBA and did not rely on external financial institutions. The disaster loan division was accustomed to gearing up from a steady-state employment level of 800 people to over 3,000 loan processors in the event of a large-scale regional disaster such as Hurricane Sandy in 2012. Due to the spike in pandemic demand, SBA operations expanded their workforce, but they still struggled to keep up. The turnaround time for the application review process rose to over 38 days in the summer of 2020.

Backlogs grew until September 2021, when a reorganized management team implemented new processes and performance management. As a result, the SBA increased its daily loan processing rate from around 2,000 applications to more than 37,000. By the end of the program in 2021, the SBA had disbursed approximately $390 billion in EIDL loans to almost 4 million small businesses and nonprofits.[53]

Although only about half the size of the PPP program, EIDL had the advantage of being a direct government program, so it was effective at reaching businesses uncomfortable accessing pandemic relief from a financial institution. However, given the massive operational requirements, there was no way that the SBA could have scaled to meet the extraordinary level of national demand in the earliest days of the pandemic. Thus, initially tapping into the existing private sector infrastructure—banks and other lenders—and then supplementing with direct EIDL loans and grants proved to be an effective combination.

The Restaurant Revitalization Fund

By fall 2020 it was clear that the pandemic was not going away any time soon and that business closures would continue in many regions. On March 11, 2021, the American Rescue Plan Act established the Restaurant Revitalization Fund (RRF) to help restaurants and other eligible businesses keep their doors open. This program provided restaurants with funding equal to their pandemic-related revenue loss up to $10 million per business with a limit of $5 million per physical location. Recipients were exempt from repayment as long as they utilized the funds for qualified expenses by March 11, 2023.[54]

The RRF was viewed as a great success. It was well understood and easy to access and was particularly effective in reaching underserved businesses. During the first two weeks of the program, applications from women and minority-owned businesses received priority. This was important because demand for the program was strong even from the beginning and eventually reached $72 billion, more than twice the available funding level. Of the 101,000 businesses awarded money, over 70% were owned by veterans, women, and minorities. The program, also run by the SBA, was praised for fraud detection and for the efficiency of the SBA application process.[55]

The Shuttered Venue Operators Grants

A second targeted program also passed in December 2020, recognizing that the pandemic would continue to prevent large gatherings for some time to come. The Shuttered Venue Operators Grant (SVOG) program provided up to $10 million to live venues, independent movie theaters, and cultural institutions forced to close or significantly reduce their operations because of the pandemic.[56,57]

Grants were made relatively slowly due in part to the way the program was structured. As opposed to EIDL loans and PPP which were awarded on a first-come, first-served basis, Congress structured the SVOG to prioritize the hardest hit venues. For example, the initial two weeks of SVOG awards were designated for organizations that experienced a revenue decline of 90% or more between April and December 2020 as a result of the COVID-19 Pandemic.[58] Though it took some time, the program eventually distributed $14.57 billion from the $16 billion available.

These two programs, targeting some of the hardest hit industry segments, benefited from lessons learned by federal administrators earlier in the crisis. Implemented almost a year after the pandemic began, they had much more seamless rollouts without system crashes, better reach, and more effective fraud prevention. But the complexities of the programs and the staggered timing of their funding probably would not have worked in the early panicked days of the crisis, when the federal response correctly kept the initial programs as simple as possible.

Additional Programs

The SBA was not the only federal entity that allocated significant resources to small businesses during the pandemic. The U.S. Treasury Department also played a key role in prioritizing small business in the pandemic funding and in making the decision to include fintechs in the ranks of eligible lenders early in the PPP process. As mentioned earlier, the Fed also played a critical role in providing liquidity to PPP lenders. In addition, in April 2020, the Fed established the Main Street Lending Program to lend to small- and medium-sized businesses and nonprofit organizations, though in practice the facility focused on larger small business segments, mostly supporting loans above $500,000. Although well intended, this program largely went unused, as larger businesses had other liquidity options that did not dry up in the pandemic.

In contrast, one complementary program from the U.S. Treasury was well received and deserves particular mention: the State Small Business Credit Initiative (SSBCI). The SSBCI was a repeat of a 2010 Treasury initiative to provide funding to states to support their own credit support programs. SSBCI totaled $10 billion and was focused not on the onset of the crisis, but on the recovery. Although it took about a year to design and implement, it allowed local entities from each state to design their own programs which ranged from venture to credit support and other guarantee initiatives. Over 39 states, territories, and Tribal governments participated.

* * *

In total over $1.2 trillion in federal funds found their way into the hands of about 13 million American small business owners in an unprecedented effort that engaged almost five thousand lenders, including banks, CDFIs, credit unions, and fintechs.[59] Was the whole effort worth it? Did this extraordinary set of actions save millions of small businesses that would have otherwise shut their doors and plunged the nation into a prolonged economic downturn and increased inequality? In the next chapter, we assess the impact of the pandemic aid programs for small businesses, with particular attention to the issue of fraud, and draw conclusions about the efficacy of the program's deployment and the economic impact.

9

Did the Pandemic Small Business Aid Work?

The Paycheck Protection Program (PPP) was well utilized by small businesses and a lifeline for many, but the program also attracted many bad actors who saw a way to fraudulently access the unprecedented level of federal funds being disbursed. The level of fraud was exacerbated by how quickly the program was implemented and the admirable desire to keep the application simple to encourage access, especially by smaller, less sophisticated entities. Many types of fraud, some preventable, led to the loss of billions of dollars in federal funds. However, by most analyses, the final numbers appear to be well under 10% of the total funding, arguably an acceptable trade-off for rapid deployment and wide reach.

This chapter will describe several different types of documented PPP fraud, including problematic actions by borrowers and certain fintech lenders. It also explores what could have been done to prevent the issues. Two underlying themes emerge: first, the lack of a federal registry for small businesses, something that exists in many other developed nations, led to difficulties in quickly establishing who was, in fact, eligible for benefits. Creating such a registry would be beneficial not only in preventing fraud, but in a wide range of small business policymaking and programs, though such an effort would likely encounter resistance. Second, creating the ability to check information against accurate, automated, and available small business databases is a key to a better fraud detection infrastructure for the future.

© The Author(s), under exclusive license to Springer Nature
Switzerland AG 2024
K. G. Mills, *Fintech, Small Business & The American Dream*,
https://doi.org/10.1007/978-3-031-55612-8_9

Public Backlash and Early Fraud

On April 20, 2020, Shake Shack announced that it was returning the $10 million PPP award it had received just 10 days earlier. Media outlets reported that several large businesses like Ruth's Chris Steak House had gotten significant PPP allocations, while smaller businesses watched helplessly as funding ran out. Shake Shack's CEO explained that instead of PPP they would use other sources of capital, such as raising $75 million from stock sales to investors. Smaller businesses didn't have access to that kind of equity capital, so he believed the $10 million should "go back in the pot" and more money should be added.[1] In other high-profile cases, the Los Angeles Lakers basketball team received $4.6 million and AutoNation, a Fortune 500 auto retailer, received $77 million.[2]

In fact, over 200 public companies received PPP loans.[3] Given that the program was designed for small businesses, how could this have happened? In the face of the media backlash, many—but not all—returned the funds. The controversy shed light on the many ways that PPP could be misinterpreted or misused. While Shake Shack had more than 6,000 employees across the country, it qualified for PPP because it fell into the category of business with a NAICS code beginning with 72 (Accommodations and Food Services), possessing more than one physical location and employing less than 500 people per location. Shake Shack employed 42 people per location on average. Similarly, the Lakers were eligible because the company was in fact definitionally a "small business," employing around 300 people, below the 500 employee threshold.

Multiple Types of Misuse and Fraud

These high-profile early stories and subsequent discoveries of fraud and misuse have led to a narrative in some quarters that PPP and other pandemic programs were riddled with fraud, waste, and abuse, perhaps at levels that called into question the effectiveness of the whole effort. However, as time progressed, and more cases of potential fraud were fully investigated, the numbers have come down. A 2023 report from the Small Business Administration (SBA) suggests that of the $1.2 trillion of total pandemic relief funding an estimated $36 billion across 744,000 loans will prove in the end to have been fraudulently obtained.[4] This is a large amount of money and many loans, but in the end reflects only 3% of the total federal pandemic aid.

Of the 11.5 million PPP loans, 3.7 million (32%) generated alerts or red flags as "potentially fraudulent." However, after review and investigation, the final number of loans sent to law enforcement was projected to be 223,000, totaling $7.4 billion and equaling less than 1% of the final $792 billion PPP amount. In the Covid EIDL program, the default rate was higher and the SBA charged-off about $52 billion by the end of 2023, totaling about 14% of the approved dollars.[5] Due to additional anti-fraud measures implemented in 2021, the other two major pandemic programs involving restaurants and shuttered venues were each only projected to have under 1% of fraud. While we may never have full clarity on the final numbers, there are lessons to be learned from layers and types of fraud and misuse that have been documented.

Eligibility Versus Ethics

As noted above, the highly publicized instances of Shake Shack and similar large companies describe a category of businesses that were technically qualified to receive funding, but perhaps should not have taken it, or at least not stood at the head of the line in a program with limited resources. Larger businesses have access to capital markets for both debt and equity funds that small businesses simply cannot use. PPP funding was clearly intended to reach that vast majority of the smallest businesses that had no other options. To be fair, in the dire moments of April 2020, it was not clear if the debt and equity capital markets would function, so many larger companies grabbed the liquidity the federal government was offering. The initial funding of $349 billion in PPP Round 1 was 30 times larger than annual SBA lending levels, so it was hard to fathom that unprecedented demand would cause the funds to run out in less than two weeks. Nonetheless, when it became evident that the money would be gone before smaller businesses in the queue had been served, it was clear that the distribution mechanism had not worked equitably. If no other PPP funding had been allocated, the result would have been disastrous for millions of American businesses.

Fake Businesses

Most of the concern about fraud revolved around applications which falsely claimed to be small businesses. PPP attracted a large number of fraudulent actors, both organized and individual, who saw a way to access the large pot of federal funds. According to researchers at the University of Texas at

Austin, about 10% of fintech loans and 4% of bank loans were flagged as potential unregistered businesses.[6] The Congressional Subcommittee report suggested that 800,000 businesses that did not exist before February 15, 2020, and 240,000 inactive businesses received funds.[7] On further investigation, however, a large proportion of these businesses were identified as legitimate and the red flags were removed.[8]

Real Businesses with Fake Numbers

The next category of fraud related to real small business owners with real businesses that might have manipulated their numbers to get a larger PPP loan. If the lender processing the PPP application had access to payroll records, this fraudulent behavior would have been flagged and avoided. Thus, banks who served customers with whom they already had relationships were better able to avoid this type of intentional or even accidental misrepresentation. There were some attempts during PPP to link existing payroll data to applications, but they were not seamless, and the smallest businesses tended to have only manual payroll systems.

Real Businesses with Bad Accounting Skills

Even with the relative simplicity of the PPP forms, many small businesses did not have proper payroll records, and some may have used inconsistent or incorrect information based on a genuine misunderstanding, leading lenders or the SBA to "flag" their application. The full extent of issues in the category of valid applicants with incomplete or incorrect submissions is likely large. In fact, those who made up numbers can be hard to distinguish from real businesses that, in the chaos of the crisis, might have made genuine mistakes when filling out the various applications.

Lender Oversight and Lender Fraud

On the lender side, the urgency of the program led to confusion and inconsistency in the processes used to verify loan applications. Calls went back and forth daily between lenders, SBA officials, and U.S. Treasury representatives to try to clarify the appropriate level of scrutiny that should be given to applications. Usual credit processes were clearly not relevant given the 100% government guarantee and the speed required by the situation. But what verification was possible or appropriate? Many lenders from the time recall pressure from Treasury to process PPP loans as fast as possible. This was perhaps the right priority, given the stresses of the moment, but the Treasury also suspended access to its screening resources including IRS data and its "Do Not Pay" list. The concern was that these gates would slow the process, creating anxiety and even panic among loan applicants. There was no automated way to process the massive volume of verification checks quickly.

Fearing eventual blame for high fraud levels, traditional lenders limited their involvement. In subsequent rounds of funding, as the new fintech lenders stepped in to fill the gap, the reach of the program improved, but the fraud issues became more severe. The combination of the urgency of the situation and inefficient systems and databases unequipped for automated vetting led to the inability to properly identify the fraudulent activity before it was too late.

Unfortunately, it appears there was also massive fraud perpetrated by at least two new fintech agents. The PPP paid lenders reasonably high fees to induce them to participate. The fees were larger for small loans: lenders earned a five percent fee on loans of $350,000 or less, a three percent fee on loans of more than $350,000 and less than $2 million, and a one percent fee on loans of $2 million and above. Two firms—Blueacorn and Womply—saw an opportunity to profit from the program. Evidence from a 2022 congressional inquiry revealed internal emails describing the firms' strategy to minimize oversight and target the most profitable customers to maximize fee revenue.[9]

Solutions

We can certainly learn much from these episodes to determine what measures would comprise an optimum anti-fraud infrastructure for future federal programs. In particular, the four step verification measures implemented by the SBA in 2021 seem to have improved the controls, as over 86% of the likely fraud occurred before they were in place.

A Central Database

An important object of controls is to prevent people from trying to access funds by pretending they owned a small business when they did not. This type of fraud was prevalent in PPP because the United States lacks a national business registry that can be used to verify the existence of a business and the identity of its owner.

A central business registry is not some farfetched concept. Many countries have public business registries, making the existence of a private company or association easy to confirm. Almost all European countries have such databases, such as Denmark's Central Business Register (CVR) and Switzerland's Central Business Name Index. Although these databases are public, private solutions can be easily built on the wealth of centralized business information, using APIs to connect the databases to authorized agencies and lending institutions for restricted purposes.

Some centralized data does exist in the U.S., but it was hard to access during the early days of the pandemic. The Department of the Treasury's Do Not Pay list enables federal agencies to check multiple data sources to verify a recipient's eligibility to receive federal payments.[10] Beginning in early 2021, Treasury granted the SBA access to the Do Not Pay list to screen every new loan application in Round 3 of PPP in order to verify each applicant's eligibility. Establishing this federal coordination earlier would clearly have been beneficial, as 57,000 PPP loans worth $3.7 billion were disbursed to businesses on the Do Not Pay list in 2020.

In 2021, the SBA also received permission to use IRS data including tax transcripts to both verify a business's authenticity and confirm revenue levels. A key recommendation of the SBA 2023 Fraud Report is to insist on real-time "yes/no" entity verification for all future federal programs.[11]

Use of Third-Party Data and Multiple Layers of Information

In the absence of a central federal database, what private sources of information can be leveraged to prevent fraud? One area for development is to broaden the data sources and the methods for business entity verification. Extensive data exists in multiple places including registries kept by secretaries of state, marketplace listings, credit reporting agencies, crowdsourced review sites, social media websites, and payment processors.[12] Some data is public while other sets are proprietary and need to be purchased. Creating valuable information from these data sets is complicated and requires nontrivial analytics. The same business can appear in multiple places under different names. Who can say if "Pete's Pizza" is the same business as "Pete's Family Pizza"? Enigma, a data aggregation company for small business information, markets a product designed to facilitate entity verification. This is useful for fraud prevention and can become the base for building more intelligence about a customer or potential borrower.

Data providers like Enigma and others have also discovered ways to negotiate access to additional data streams such as payroll, credit card revenue, growth, and industry classification. As more small businesses use digital services, the reach and validity of these data sources are growing. As we will discuss in later chapters, there are large and complicated issues around data privacy and ownership for these third-party data providers. But in the future, access to this information is essential to transform fraud detection and reduce the pain and frictions in accurately establishing eligibility for government programs.

Disclosure

When the SBA started issuing PPP loans in April, detailed data on recipients was not available. By July 2020, a limited data set was released, excluding specific information on loans under $150,000 and exact amounts for larger loans. The SBA cited privacy concerns for the limited transparency. However, following a court's approval of a Freedom of Information Act request in December 2020, full details of all recipients were disclosed and were regularly updated until the end of the pandemic.[13] This publicly accessible data clearly played a role in reducing the number of bad actors or firms inappropriately accessing public funds. As Justice Louis Brandeis once stated, "Sunshine is the best disinfectant."

Was PPP Successful After All?

By 2023, the U.S. economy had largely put the Covid-19 pandemic in the rear-view mirror. The U.S. stock market, which had plummeted in the early days of the pandemic, began a strong climb, with the S&P 500 gaining over 26% by the end of 2021. Employment also recovered quickly, though labor market participation lagged as many groups declined to reenter the workforce.

Economic activity was also deeply impacted at the beginning of the pandemic but had mostly recovered by the end of 2021. The Census Bureau Index of Economic Activity (IDEA), an aggregation of 15 of the Census Bureau's primary economic data points, showed that activity plunged at the onset of the pandemic but surged as the economy reopened (Figure 9.1).

It seemed that the policies enacted, and the resilience of citizens and business owners had granted the wish of all—a V-shaped versus a U-shaped recovery from the pandemic stresses. Unemployment rates dropped to 6.1%

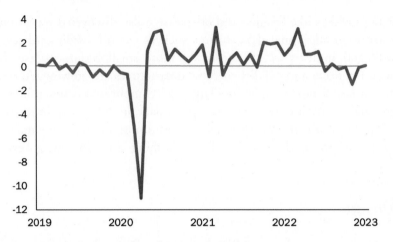

Figure 9.1   Census Bureau Index of Economic Activity
Source: Author's analysis of U.S. Census Bureau Data, accessed June 2023.
Note: An index of 0 indicates that the index is in line with its long-term average since 2004, a period of generally modest economic growth.

in April 2021 and 3.1% in April 2022, after a high of 14.7% in April 2020, leaving employers, particularly small businesses, struggling to find workers (Figure 9.2).

Alignable surveys from March 2022 showed that 65% of all small business employers reported being unable to fill open positions. This challenge was especially pronounced in the restaurant and manufacturing industries, where

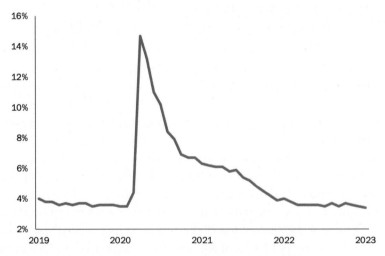

Figure 9.2   Unemployment Rate, January 2019 to January 2023
Source: Author's analysis of U.S. Census Bureau Data, accessed June 2023.

more than 85% of small businesses could not find workers.[14] The shortage of workers caused wages to rise, contributing to inflationary pressures.

Demand for many items surged as consumers spent the savings accumulated from staying at home and receiving stimulus payments during the pandemic lockdown. Supply chain disruptions from Covid-19 shutdowns caused prices to rise in everything from used cars to semiconductors. On top of those pressures, the Russian invasion of Ukraine (one of the world's largest producers of wheat and corn) fueled spikes in food and energy costs. By the beginning of 2022, inflation became more of an economic concern than pandemic-related survival. As businesses entered 2023, one in three small business owners ranked inflation as their highest concern.[15]

In the face of this economic bounce back, how do we assess the effectiveness of the federal policies such as PPP on small businesses? Clearly, any evaluation of these efforts needs to be made taking full account of the pressures of the crisis and the objectives of the programs. In time, the level of urgency of the moment of March and April 2020 may fade in the collective memory. But to any who experienced the uncertainty of the early pandemic lockdowns, amidst the stress and fear, there was a pressing small business imperative: get a vast amount of financial help distributed as widely as possible to ensure small business owners and their employees could weather the storm.

With this lens we use four major criteria to evaluate the pandemic-related federal policy efforts, focusing particularly the largest program, PPP: (1) the impact on small business employment; (2) effectiveness in helping businesses to survive; (3) equity in terms of the availability of the funds to all the various types of small businesses; and (4) speed of deployment and uptake by small businesses. We will assess each of these in turn.

Small Business Employment

Because PPP was designed in March and April 2020, its primary goal was to preserve employment. After all, it was called the *Paycheck* Protection Program. In light of the broad economic impact of the pandemic, it is critical to consider whether the program successfully preserved employment, as it was designed to do.

Many who had lived through the 2008–2009 financial crisis believed it had been the most difficult period they would ever see for small business. Yet the impact of the Covid-19 pandemic in the spring of 2020 was even more severe. Small businesses lost over 8 million jobs in the second quarter of 2020 compared to 1.8 million in the first quarter of 2009. However, the two crises

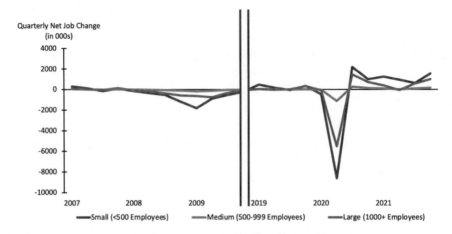

Figure 9.3 Small Businesses (<500 Employees) Bore the Brunt of the Pandemic's Impact
Source: Author's analysis of Bureau of Labor Statistics, Business Employment Dynamics data.

were similar in that small businesses lost more jobs than larger businesses (Figure 9.3). Compared to large businesses, small businesses lost 2.8 times more jobs in 2009 and 1.6 times more jobs in 2020.

The small business recovery from the 2008–2009 financial crisis was painfully slow. Small businesses did not log net quarterly employment gains for 8 quarters, and those gains lagged the recovery for larger businesses until April 2014. In contrast, small business recovery in the pandemic crisis was much faster. By the following quarter, small businesses had reached positive hiring levels and even surpassed larger businesses in their hiring recovery. As discussed in earlier chapters, the 2008–2009 financial crisis and the painfully slow recovery for small business had deep costs. The extraordinarily large, rapid federal interventions directly targeting small businesses early in the pandemic clearly had a role in the faster recovery during from 2020 to 2021.

Economic Research Findings

Many of the foremost economic papers looking at early data during the pandemic saw the PPP program as performing very poorly in terms of its original employment objectives. They estimated only 2–3 million jobs were saved, making the cost of the program $170,000–$257,000 per job saved.[16] Later studies took issue with both the methodology and the results of these works. A particular concern was the focus in the early studies on the largest small businesses (those with greater than 250 employees) and the strategy of making comparisons between firms below 500 employees and above 500 employees (which corresponds to the eligibility cutoff for the program). According to one economist, "a finding of modest effects in large firms does not entail the same modest impact at firms with 5 or 10 employees. Since small firms are more financially fragile, these firms stood to gain the most from a PPP loan. As such, evaluations using the employee size cutoff likely underestimate the true impact of PPP by a significant margin."[17] Additionally, larger firms were more likely to have alternative sources of funding and more established financial planning strategies. The same researcher, using a broader set of firms which incorporated smaller firms on the spectrum, found a positive employment effect of 18.6 million jobs.[18]

Another important nuance in the assessment of PPP comes from the heterogeneity of small businesses both in size and industries. Barlett and Morse found that small businesses had varying survival capabilities and resilience strategies depending on their labor flexibility and committed costs. In their study of small firms in Oakland, they compared a pizza shop which employed 20 staff members and had a greater ability to lay off employees and survive, with a bakery owner with only one cook, without whom the business would not survive. They found that for the smallest businesses, the sole proprietors and businesses with few employees, PPP was a critical lifeline.[19] Additional research found that PPP was more effective at retaining employment in industries with greater remote work capabilities.[20] This heterogeneity may help explain the wide variance in estimates of jobs saved by the program, which ranged from 3 to 18 million, with some upper estimates as high as 55 million.[21] However, there is general agreement in the research that PPP funding played an important role in improving small business employment outcomes, as the program intended.

Business Failures and Survival

A second important criterion to evaluate the pandemic era government programs is their impact on business survival. A critical concern in the dark days of March 2020 was the prospect of empty storefronts for months and years in towns across America based on how vulnerable small businesses were due to their low cash buffers. Given the sudden and brutal impact of lockdowns, preventing small business failures was a key objective of federal aid. Research published between 2021 and 2023 estimates significant positive effects of PPP on preventing permanent business closures. Early work by Bartik and colleagues which looked at survival rates of firms using Alignable data showed that closures were projected to create 35.1 million in job losses

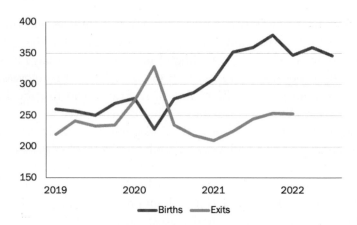

Figure 9.4   Firm Births and Exits Between 2019 and 2022
Source: Author's analysis based on the Bureau of Labor Statistics, Business Employ-ment Dynamics, accessed October 2023.

if the crisis lasted for 6 months.[22] The impact of such broad business failures would have been devastating. Later studies began to differentiate between temporary and permanent closures, finding that aid may have helped some businesses survive mandatory shutdowns long enough to reopen as pandemic restrictions were lifted.[23] The PPP money also provided capital for many owners to pivot their business models—for example from dine-in to delivery. Overall, estimates of PPP's impact on business survival range from 5 to 20%.[24] Oddly, after the initial six months of the crisis, exit rates of small business began to stabilize and surprisingly, new business starts accelerated (Figure 9.4).

In the second quarter of 2020, over 700,000 establishments closed according to the Federal Reserve (Fed), but soon after there was a robust increase in new entrants, showing perhaps the great resilience of entrepreneurs, and their ability to pivot and find opportunity out of a crisis.[25]

Equity in Access

The federal response delivered over a trillion dollars to 13 million small busi-nesses, with the vast majority being in the form of small-dollar loans. PPP, despite a rocky start, was a program for the smallest businesses: Eight million of the 11.4 million loans granted were smaller than $25,000. America's banking industry was the most important conduit for PPP loans to get into the hands of small businesses. However, banks tended to serve existing customers and focused on applications for larger loans, which were easier for

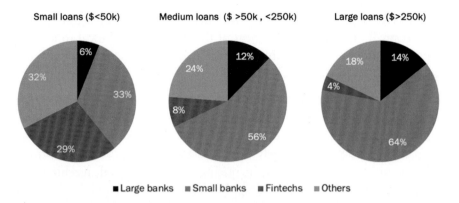

Figure 9.5   **Share of PPP Loans by Size and Lender Type**
Source: Author's analysis based on tabulations by Sabrina T. Howell of the NYU Stern School of Business.

them to process (Figure 9.5).[26] The inclusion of fintechs as designated distributors of PPP loans dramatically increased the effectiveness of the program in reaching the smallest businesses, and as we saw in Chapter 8, played a definitive role in reaching Black-owned businesses. In the end, the programs were a lifesaver for a wide range of diverse small businesses in every corner of the nation, many of whom would not have survived without this massive intervention.

Program Speed and Reach

The Paycheck Protection Program was the product of an early and formative decision to prioritize speed and reach, perhaps at the expense of fraud oversight. In hindsight, this decision has proved controversial, with many accusing the program of wasting taxpayer dollars. However, in terms of speed, PPP was extraordinarily successful. Despite some early bottlenecks, $1.2 trillion dollars reached an astonishing 13 million businesses in just 18 months. Thanks to the efforts of many bankers and programmers who worked night and day to implement the program and push applications through, the United States successfully delivered one of the largest and most far-reaching aid programs in the world.

In hindsight, some of the fraud could have been prevented if government agencies had been able to securely share IRS business identifiers or if they had had access to a robust source of entity verification data on small businesses. Yet, even with its faults, it is widely acknowledged in the literature that policymakers made a defensible trade-off between speed and other considerations in the PPP's design.[27] Complexity is the enemy of successful program deployment to small businesses. In the heat of the crisis, it was critical to keep the program as simple and accessible as possible and doing so contributed to its high national reach and penetration.

* * *

Given the intense and urgent nature of the crisis, the federal small business pandemic response is largely viewed as a success. In each of its primary goals: maintaining employment, increasing business survival, reaching all of America's small businesses, including the most vulnerable, and doing it all in a timely way, the results of PPP are positive. And amidst the chaos of getting money out as quickly as possible, one critical lesson emerged: where traditional banks were limited in their ability to reach the small businesses most in need, technology was the linchpin in ensuring that funds got into the hands of even the smallest businesses. Covid-19 was a wakeup call for financial institutions on how technology must be a central part of their future service solutions. The pandemic also changed the game for fintechs who established more robust relationships with millions of small businesses and created partnerships with banks and other lending institutions.

In Part IV, we will explore how technology will continue to change the game for small business owners and the impact of new financial and platform players on the small business lending landscape. But before we go on, it is worth taking a moment to be grateful for the efforts of so many to make saving small businesses a priority during the Covid-19 pandemic. Without the work of these government officials, bankers and fintech entrepreneurs, many small businesses, who make up such a significant part of the U.S. economy would have had to close their doors forever. Thankfully, with the help of the programs described here, the small business economy weathered the storm and can look to a brighter future of innovation and change.

Part III

Technology Changes the Game

10

Small Business Utopia

On a Thursday morning at 5:30 AM, Alex sipped her latte, her elbows atop the service counter. Each day at this time, the sunlight through the front window blanketed her coffee shop and she enjoyed a few moments of peace and quiet before the morning rush began. With 30 minutes to spare before she corralled her baristas for their morning pep talk (and shot of espresso), she unlocked her iPad and up popped her most valuable assistant: her small business dashboard. A graph on the upper right predicted her cash position at the end of the week. After payroll expenses, she would have $5,000 left over. In seconds, Alex's supply advisor scoured her accounts, sales and expense histories, local weather forecasts, event information, and past tourism data and told her she would need five new sets of filters and 1,000 plastic cups for the coming week. She ordered them from her distributor with a single touch. She also knew the shop needed a new espresso machine, but she had been putting it off for over a month. With the savings in her account, she could either order the new machine now or make a payment on the term loan she had taken out two years ago to start the business. If she continued to put off a replacement, the machine could break at any moment, and espresso was the second-best selling item on the menu after iced coffee. On the other hand, she was almost done paying off her loan, and procrastinating another month would add interest.

Alex asked her business bot for advice. "You can do both," it reported. "Given your expected sales for the month, it looks like you'll be able to use your savings to pay down the loan and put the espresso machine on your credit card, which has available credit of $3,500. When the credit card payment comes due in 30 days, you will have the cash to pay it off, based on current sales projections."

Alex ordered the espresso machine and paid down the loan, and for good measure, she delayed paying herself for a week, knowing she had enough money in her savings and that sales would jump the next week, when the school year ended and summer vacation began. Just to make sure there were no mistakes, she ran an instant credit check and confirmed she had $3,500 of available credit, and then she double-checked her projected sales based on prior years. Remembering that Dunkin' Donuts had recently opened down the street, Alex asked her bot for sales ideas to ensure they met their goals for the first week of summer vacation.

"It is going to be above 75 degrees next week, so iced coffee, which has a profit margin of 53% will likely sell more than usual. Dunkin' Donuts is running a sale on iced coffee next week. When they have run similar promotions in the past, you have lost an average of seven of your daily customers. If you send your regular customers a coupon for $1 off iced coffee, I estimate you will increase your margin for next week by 3%. Would you like me to send an e-coupon to your regular customers now?" With one tap, the coupons were sent. After the morning pep talk with her staff, Alex opened the doors for the day, confident in where her small business was headed.

At the end of the day, as Alex was closing up, her bot reminded her that it was June 1, and that quarterly taxes would soon be due. She momentarily worried that she had overlooked her tax payments when buying the new espresso machine, but then the bot said, "Don't worry. Your estimated tax payments have already been accounted for in your cash projections for June." Finally, with a few more taps and swipes, Friday's payroll was set, healthcare deductions were taken from her employees' paychecks, and taxes were ready to file.

Small Business Utopia

Alex's story allows us to visualize a golden age of financial services that fintech innovations are poised to deliver for small business owners. We call this state "Small Business Utopia." Alex has access to the capital she needs to operate and grow her business, she can easily understand her cash flow, and she has real-time insight into customer acquisition and sales techniques that can help her business prosper. In this story, a machine augments Alex's ability to run her business through artificial intelligence that collects a range of data, knows how to assess and learn from it, and can answer our protagonist's questions about her business's financial situation.

Consumers have financial apps and bot advisors that analyze spending, suggest investments, and give updates on credit scores. But solutions for small businesses are more difficult because the small business data picture and decision array are more complex. Small business owners have access to accounting software, bank balances, credit cards, tax payments, and bank loans digitally but each exists in their own information stream. The owner of a local craft brewery told me she goes home and, sitting on her bed, opens up her QuickBooks ledger on her computer, her bank account on her iPad and her Square payments on her iPhone and tries to pull them together manually to understand her future cash availability.

A "smart" environment for small business is one that integrates these and other data sources and draws out the implications for cash balances and business decisions. This environment would include timely financial offers and lending options that are useful and relevant to the business owner. The optimal platform would allow small businesses to conduct their financial life in one convenient place and incorporate an intelligent advisor. Such a high functioning portal could have significant outcomes: fewer good businesses might fail and more businesses would have the confidence and financial resources to grow successfully.

Reaching this state of Small Business Utopia involves getting three factors right. First, technology needs to make information streams about small businesses more readily accessible and integrate them in ways that illuminate the small business's financial health and future needs. Second, credit or other appropriate loan products need to be more easily available to the small business borrower through an embedded format. This automation will require lenders to refine their expertise in determining who is creditworthy. Third, to be successful, the new environment must be built around the needs of small businesses, rather than a consumer concept that is simply modified for small business use. In the past, all three conditions were hard to meet. Today, they are within our reach.

A Platform to Rule All Others

In the story of Alex and her coffee shop, she comes to work and logs into one system, her small business dashboard. This dashboard already exists in many forms but has not been perfected or widely deployed. Instead, today's business owner generally has one system, perhaps QuickBooks or Xero, for their accounting software, a portal for bank transactions, another like HubSpot or

Salesforce for marketing and sales, and a separate payroll system such as ADP or Gusto. A payments system records credit card receipts, but those tools are often not integrated into any other management software. In addition, there might be a healthcare or benefits portal, and taxes are often paid separately, offline.

Ask small businesses about their concerns and they often mention their worries about forgetting to make a quarterly payroll tax payment or coming up short because they neglected to put away the cash that they will owe. They fear that they have not planned well for fluctuating cash needs and might run into trouble when they have to pay for a big order of inventory, or if a large customer pays late. In bigger businesses, enterprise resource planning (ERP) systems take care of cash forecasting based on an integrated platform that draws on sales information, supply chain systems, and manufacturing and production data. But these enterprise platforms don't work for small businesses. Instead, the small business owners themselves must put together in their heads, or on a spreadsheet, their forecast of future cash levels.

This manual process requires that a business owner actively desires to know their cash position and has a nontrivial level of analytic ability. And the process is prone to error or incorrect judgments. With technology, it is easy to imagine a much better solution. At the simplest level, an automated dashboard or bot needs access to the various data streams related to the business that may now exist digitally but in separate silos. Such a platform will also require a sophisticated overlay of intelligence, with the capacity to comfortably interact with the user and take in new information to improve the usefulness of its responses. Finally, the dashboard solution must be provided in a way that is embedded in a business owner's normal routines.

The basic technology to create such a connected dashboard exists, and the concept has been discussed for over 5 years, including in the first edition of this book. Why, if it is what small businesses need, has it not been perfected and already adopted widely? There appear to be two basic reasons for the slower than expected trajectory: greater difficulty in the ability to aggregate clean streams of predictive data and more complexity in the fit of these tools with the needs of the small business owner.

Every data stream lives within the purview of a different provider, each of which may or may not be inclined to provide access. Some of the data, such as banking information, has not historically been controlled by the business owner. This is why Open Banking initiatives in Europe and the United Kingdom, and the rulemaking around Dodd-Frank Section 1033 which gave ownership of banking data to U.S. consumers, were so momentous. (Open Banking and its implications are discussed further in Chapter 14). Even if data is available, it is seldom in a standardized format and is often riddled with inaccuracies. This has given rise to a whole category of fintech companies whose sole focus is providing clean streams of relevant information, (see below for more on data aggregators).

If a cash flow tool or dashboard were available to small businesses, one would think it would be quickly adopted because the benefits would be obvious. However, early providers of stand-alone cash forecasting tools did not see wide acceptance. Greater traction appeared as platforms developed solutions that were integrated into the daily financial activities of the business. Business owners might not open a tool just to do cash analysis, but they would check their cash and projected liquidity when they went to their bank account to pay a bill. Experience with new offers such as embedded lending has shown that credit options are most appealing when provided in a relevant context and as part of a business owner's normal routine.

The slower than expected progression of the dashboard's development is also likely related to the heterogeneity of the small business market. Business owners vary greatly in their comfort with and use of technology, and in the complexity of their businesses. Some have little need for a cash projection tool as their businesses are steady and predictable, and their years of experience allow them to essentially know their cash model in their head. Others have manual systems in their businesses that would need to be automated before the dashboard could be accurate. Even within an industry category, the motivations of business owners, the way they run their businesses, and the decisions before them vary greatly. One cafe may want to expand its business and purchase the cheapest supplies available; another may desire to stay tiny and focus on only high-quality locally sourced products.

Today's models don't understand these nuances and are therefore not robust enough to be trusted for critical decisions. But advances in artificial intelligence show how a model might be trained to be far more attuned to the goals and working environment of the individual business. Alex's bot converses with her about business issues and goals and is able to translate that into intelligent advice, based on data analysis beyond the capacity of the typical owner.

In 2023, the rapid adoption of ChatGPT showed the vast appeal of natural language conversations with artificial intelligence. That same year, Shopify previewed a new bot called "Sidekick," an intelligent advisor available 24/7 who is at your side and on your side.[1] Small business owners might move more quickly to embrace a tool like this, if it is built for their needs and works for them.

Artificial Intelligence and Fintech

Fintech solutions are clearly poised to make a large leap forward in terms of accessibility and ease of use due to recent advances in artificial intelligence (AI). John McCarthy first coined the term artificial intelligence in 1956, but it had its roots in ancient history, where philosophers mused about thinking machines. In 1950, Alan Turing laid the foundation for AI research asking, "Can machines think?" The first AI programs were written in the late 1950s and early 1960s, followed by rule-based systems in the 1970s and 1980s, machine learning in the 1990s and 2000s, and then deep learning, a subfield of machine learning, in the 2010s.[2]

The field of AI today is vast, encompassing a wide range of technologies and applications. These include machine learning, deep learning, robotics, computer vision, natural language processing, neural networks, expert systems, reinforcement learning, and many others. But most of these activities were unknown to the public until the appearance of the surprisingly realistic and adaptive conversational generative AI application, ChatGPT, in 2023.

AI and Small Businesses

How will AI impact small business lending? Machine learning has already transformed the accuracy of the big data building blocks for assessing small business financial risk. For example, it has allowed Plaid to develop highly accurate data on the bank accounts of small businesses in a standardized format with high coverage. Codat, a financial data API provider, spent six years building models that clean and correctly categorize the data in QuickBooks and other small business accounting software.

AI has shown that (with proper training) it can understand the nuances of the world of small businesses and account for financial data correctly. In addition, information is available on more and more businesses as cash usage declines and even sole proprietorships have a way to take digital payments. These improved digital data resources directly address the first friction we have described in small business lending: information opacity. For the first time, it is possible to see inside a small business quickly and accurately.

Machine learning and other AI techniques have also made some progress on the second friction: heterogeneity. Because of the wide coverage it is possible to compare a small business to thousands of others in the same industry, of a similar size, or in the same geography. In the past, a lender was underwriting a dry cleaner one day and a parts supplier the next. It was very hard to get a sense of the "truth file" on how a dry cleaner, for example, was performing versus its peers or its potential. With the advances in AI and big data, the lender (or the automation) can assess 1,000 similar dry cleaners and determine if the one under consideration is near the top or the bottom in terms of performance. This helps with one part of the heterogeneity issue. However, more complex challenges remain.

Small business owners are so unique and their motivations and operations are so individualized that it is hard to create an algorithm that takes into account all the peculiarities of each business. How can the lender deliver a product that has the right customer-product fit—the right size, duration cost, and terms that give the business owner the best chance of achieving their goals and paying down the loan successfully? In the future, one could imagine asking an AI-enabled bot who is deeply familiar with the small business owner and their preferences to help. For example, the bot could be asked to write a program to predict cash shortages under a variety of possible scenarios, and then assess different loan options or perhaps design an optimal solution.

Apart from financial questions, AI technology can already accomplish many useful tasks to assist a small business, such as building a website or suggesting copy for new products that might be offered in an online store. This is quite different from technology solutions of the past where a small business owner might buy a one-size-fits-all software that required set up before use. With AI, instead of doing the work using software as a tool, the owner can just ask a trained automated assistant for what they need. The AI bot is able to respond to a command in the business owner's preferred language, understand what is required, and take the necessary next steps. This is a game changer.

To be sure, existing AI assistants need improvement. The current standard is most effective for cookie cutter solutions with less operational variability, such as in franchises. However, if AI bots evolve as predicted, they will soon be able to handle more complicated tasks and provide valuable individualized advice that is directly relevant to the business owner.

The Role of Big Data in Establishing Creditworthiness

The dashboard we have described would not just benefit the small business owner. It would also create valuable insights for a lender. Lenders such as Amazon, Shopify, and Square already rely on transaction data from their platforms as inputs in credit decisions. But for small businesses that do not sell at retail, lenders do not yet have the equivalent data on their prospects. A platform that provides an intelligent overview of revenue, receipts, orders, payments to suppliers, and other expenses would help a lender make a real-time credit decision and offer loans at the push of a button. Businesses could proceed more securely, knowing they had access to greater cash buffers, and lenders would have the benefits that cash flow transparency provides to the underwriting and risk assessment process.

The use of new data in underwriting started slowly as fintechs emerged. One of the most important breakthroughs was fairly mundane: the idea that OnDeck pioneered in 2010 of using current activity from a business's bank account as a more timely indicator of whether a business was credit-worthy. A business that was paying its rent and suppliers on time was likely a better loan prospect than one who was behind and missing payments. Other data streams, such as Yelp reviews, looked interesting, but initial algorithms struggled to find good results with these novel indicators.

Indeed, the development of new data-rich algorithms and predictive small business credit scoring proved more complicated than was originally antic-ipated. However, after some work, many lenders have found formulas that predict risk well using cash flow indicators.[3] Most rely on information from bank statements and payment flows as the core information sources, but the exact formula varies widely depending on the industry, the type of loan, and the objectives of the lender. For example, when making merchant cash advances, several providers rely almost solely on the transaction history (six months minimum) of the business's credit card receipts, in part because they are paid back first from that precise payment stream. For a bank trying to serve a community where many businesses have thin credit files, access to real-time bank information and accounting records have proven valuable for filling in the gaps. Each lender must experiment with a variety of informa-tion sources and algorithms to find the formulas that fit with their products and goals.

To add to the difficulties, large, accurate third-party data sets on U.S. small businesses have historically been hard to obtain. Bank accounts could initially be accessed only by permission of the user who had to release their usernames and passwords. The resulting process, known as "screen scraping," created enormous security risks for loan applicants. Over time, there has been great progress on these initial frictions. Plaid and similar infrastructure firms have built APIs that allow access to bank account data. And a number of fintech firms have built entire businesses around being data aggregators, focused on the acquisition and cleaning of small business information.

The Data Aggregators

Data aggregators like Enigma (see box), Codat, and Ocrolus have reset the ability of small business lenders to access and utilize information. These platforms collate, clean, and standardize financial signals including bank accounts, accounting records, payment streams, and dozens of other information flows. Each signal is a piece of raw data which may indicate an important event or behavior, such as a dip in monthly revenue or an overdue payment. These insights are valuable, but the critical question is how all these data points come together to provide a view on the creditworthiness of the small business.

The resulting intelligence is sometimes referred to as "scoring." Scoring is a derived metric, typically resulting from the analysis of multiple signals. It gives a summarized perspective on creditworthiness—like a credit score. Some lenders will always prefer to create their own credit models using raw data feeds or signals, and will benefit from the larger pools of clean and timely data available from data aggregators through APIs. Others may find that new small business scores developed as products from credit bureaus and data companies are highly predictive and valuable for underwriting. Research has shown that it is even possible to create data from soft information, such as the owners' motivations for entrepreneurship and the constraints they face, that is more predictive than administrative data (such as age or business sector).[4] Though the code has not yet been fully cracked, the ability to predict risk in small business loans has already been dramatically improved by using available signals and scoring.[5]

Data aggregators also have products that can transform banks' activities beyond credit assessments for lending. One of the most powerful is the ability to find small businesses and speak to them about their credit needs on a personalized basis. Lenders can reduce sales and marketing costs by reaching businesses at the right time with loan products that are prescreened to fit their needs. Other products include ways to automate compliance such as Know Your Business (KYB) and Sanctions screening, helping lenders stay up to date with changing regulations without having to use manual processes.

Small Business Data Aggregator: Enigma

Founded in 2011 by Marc DaCosta and Hicham Oudghiri, Enigma emerged in response to a clear challenge: vast swaths of public data relating to small businesses remained largely inaccessible and underutilized. Extracting insights from hundreds of sources ranging from public government data, a large crawl of the web, and merchant transaction data coming from a consortium of top issuing banks, Enigma provided identity, firmographic, and financial health data about millions of U.S. small and medium businesses. As data sources grew and new use cases arose, its ability to create an integrated picture of companies increased. "Enigma has grown up in the era Big Data, which was really a story about applying open source technologies to large quantities of highly structured data," Oudghiri commented.[6] The data can serve both ends of the small business landscape: on the one hand, a small business owner who wants accessible insights about the business and on the other hand, marketing and risk assessment teams at larger institutions who want to understand and better serve SMB clients.

Data Usage Outside the United States

Usage of new data sources in the United States lags activity in the rest of the world. In many parts of the developing world, fintech has revolutionized small business lending by using technology to expand access to capital. For example, Tala, a fintech founded in 2011, offers micro-loans between $10 and $500 to over 7 million consumers and small businesses across four emerging markets: Kenya, India, the Philippines, and Mexico. Tala's primary source of information comes from a mobile phone application.[7]

Kenyan fintech M-Pesa started as an innovative concept by Vodafone's Safaricom in March 2007. It is now the largest fintech platform in the region with over 51 million customers, including 465,000 businesses. M-Pesa allows users to send and receive money, pay bills, and get short-term loans.[8] Such networks have been particularly beneficial for the underbanked. Research has shown that access to digital credit in Kenya, even at high interest rates, improved the financial well-being of borrowers who were otherwise credit constrained.[9]

In India, a digital identification system called Aadhaar became the largest of its kind in the world with over 1.2 billion Indian residents registered. The digital ID is assigned at birth and is required to access railway tickets and many government and healthcare services. The government also introduced the concept of linking Aadhaar with bank accounts, although after a Supreme Court ruling in 2018, some of these linkages were made optional.[10] Nonetheless, the digital system has transformed life for many small businesses that find they can now transact safely and securely across geographies without handling cash. "Earlier, when I used to go home to my village, I had to hide all the cash—literally all my savings for months—in my socks, so as to not be robbed on the train," reported Tej Pal, a 44-year-old who sells fruits near Delhi.[11]

Even in largely cash economies like Morocco (see box), innovation is reshaping the landscape of small business lending, illustrating the potential of fintech to bridge financial gaps and foster economic growth.

Chari: Fintech in Morocco

Ismael Belkhayat and Sophia Alj were discussing the new fintech product they were about to launch through the distribution company, Chari that they had founded in 2020 to serve small mom and pop shops. In rural Morocco, many consumers rely on these small businesses for their daily purchases with the large majority of transactions being conducted in cash.[12] Through their relationships with the small business shop owners, Ismael and Sophia realized that many customers were underserved by Moroccan financial institutions, and that Chari was uniquely positioned to fill the gap. Building on their access to a large amount of data on transactions in the stores, they decided to offer credit and Buy Now, Pay Later products for small business owners and their customers. They obtained a banking license and prepared to help their small business customers become hubs for digital consumer transactions in rural Morocco.[13]

These examples just scratch the surface of financial innovation outside of the United States and Europe. Though largely outside the scope of this book, it is clear that nations with underdeveloped banking systems have a great incentive to use technology to leapfrog into a world of digital products that use novel data to power small business lending solutions. The United States will most likely evolve differently due to its robust banking infrastructure, but lessons from innovators in the developing world are emerging and are well worth the attention of U.S. financial players.

The Dark Side of the Black Box

The potential uses of big data, predictive algorithms, and artificial intelligence are both exciting and scary. As with all advances, there are a lot of potential downsides in the future world we have imagined for small businesses and their lenders. One significant risk is the possibility of unintended consequences as a result of algorithm-driven decision making and unchecked artificial intelligence.

Imagine a car insurance company that sifted through its customer data and identified a single factor that consistently correlated with a 30% increase in car accidents. Now imagine that the factor was whether the driver of the car bought frozen pizza. This example may seem absurd, since there is no obvious causal link between frozen pizza-buying behavior and auto accidents, but it is based on a true story. The real insurance company in the example decided not to use the data to determine their insurance premiums for two reasons. First, if people found out that buying frozen pizza would hike their premiums, they would stop buying it without changing the other risk factors that actually caused accidents. Second, the company felt that its use of the information, if known, would likely provoke public backlash.

But what if the insurance company had made the opposite decision or a small business lender used similar data to determine loan approvals and pricing? What recourse would the small business owner have if they were suddenly refused credit? Would the business have the right to a transparent review of the data used to make the decision? Who controls the algorithm?

As machines learn to identify who is more likely to default on their loans, the risk of discrimination and exclusion becomes significant. Most worrisome is the idea that data would be analyzed in a "black box," that no one would know exactly what inputs the machine used to make recommendations or decisions. So while the insurance company in the previous example could deliberately decide not to include frozen pizza purchases in its algorithm, a machine could discover the same correlation and—barring explicit rules preventing it from doing so—include it as a pricing factor. By the same token, a machine might identify a risk factor that correlates strongly with race, gender, or the characteristics of other protected classes. Absent instructions on how to proceed, machines that lack awareness of bias and discrimination could create serious problems.

What about the need for transparency? Are black box models un-auditable or just so complex that they are incomprehensible? Is it possible to make them explainable and to monitor or control them? What can a small business who is refused credit understand about the reasons for the denial? Without any feedback it would be difficult for the small business to develop a plan to improve, so they could be successful when they apply in the future.

Both companies and regulators will need to develop new technological methods to untangle the inner workings of the algorithms of the future. Some argue that there is a trade-off between predictiveness and explainability. Perhaps automation can be developed that is capable of detecting discrimination and other bad outcomes. Even if it can, humans—in both companies and regulatory agencies—need to make judgments about what outcomes are desired and what protections are important for the greater community.

Economists have begun to explore the implications of artificial intelligence on innovation. They view artificial intelligence as a "general purpose technology," which, like the semiconductor in our innovation story, has the potential to create significant advances in multiple industries.[14] Artificial intelligence has the possibility of becoming a powerful enabler of innovation because it is actually an "invention of a new method of invention."[15] These economists also suggest that the winners are going to be those who have control over large amounts of unstructured data.

This raises another potential risk of artificial intelligence. If certain companies are allowed to have a monopoly over collections of data, this could adversely affect future innovation and the shared benefits it would bring. As we will discuss further in Chapter 14, future regulation needs to both oversee the algorithms in the "black box" and ensure long term open access to safe and secure data streams, as these are the building blocks of the beneficial small business products of the future.

* * *

The technology to create "Small Business Utopia" is not a far stretch from what is available today. Big data, APIs, and AI are all in use in products and services we interact with daily. But as we saw in many examples of the innovation cycle, truly adapting the technology available to solutions that customers want and need is the key to creating transformative products that gain wide adoption. The complexity of small business lending means that may take some time, and that there may be more than one solution. As we will discuss in the next two chapters, there are a large array of players, from traditional banks to new entrants highly engaged in the new technology-driven landscape. Next we explore who will be the winners and losers, and what are the paths to achieving the better small business outcomes that innovations have promised.

11

Who Will Be the Winners and Losers?

Given the potential for technology to fundamentally change small business lending, who in the marketplace will be the winners, and who will exit or be outcompeted? This turns out to be a difficult question. Brand new competitors have entered the market, existing players have responded with investments, and several important tech companies have not yet announced financial products but have shown interest or have relevant capabilities. The playing field is full in a way that has not been seen in a century, boding well for new innovations and productive change.

New entrants include challenger banks who contend that the old ways of banking are dead, and that future activity will be online only. A myriad of fintech companies are busy providing infrastructure and B2B software solutions including data aggregation and customer-friendly online portals for loan applications and processing. There is certainly no lack of interest and activity in the sector, with venture capital and other investors eagerly looking for companies to back.

Yet the current competitors who dominate small business lending, large banks, regional banks, community lenders, credit card companies, credit unions, and even community development financial institutions (CDFIs) show no sign of ceding the field quickly. Large banks are investing billions in technology; community banks are partnering with fintechs, particularly during the pandemic, to bolt on the technology that they need to compete. These institutions already have customers and have access to large amounts of capital from customer deposits. Change is difficult in an established institution, but can the existing players really be counted out so fast?

K. G. Mills, *Fintech, Small Business & The American Dream*,
https://doi.org/10.1007/978-3-031-55612-8_11

The Small Business Lending Landscape

In the time between the first publishing of this book and the writing of this second edition, I have traveled in the United States and to Europe, Asia, and North Africa, meeting with banks and the fintech community. In each meeting, I have had audiences vote on four different categories of competitors, asking the same question: who will be the winners and losers? There has been no consensus. In part, that experience led to the writing of this second edition. The future of the small business lending marketplace is a complicated question, dependent on who has customer trust, the availability and cost of investment capital, the predicative ability of new data-driven credit models, and the willingness of old institutions to change in response to new competitive pressures. This chapter attempts to unravel these factors and paint a picture of what it will take to become a dominant force in the next era of small business lending.

The Four Categories

To take on the question of winners and losers, we divide the current and potential competitors in the small business lending market into four categories: traditional lenders such as banks and credit card companies, Big Tech, challenger banks, and infrastructure players (Figure 11.1).

Figure 11.1   Four Categories of Stakeholders
Source: Author's analysis.

These categories are imperfect, and many companies don't fit exactly into one of these slots, but they provide a helpful general construct. The first category of traditional lenders represents the dominant forces historically in small business lending, including banks of all sizes and credit card companies. The main theme is that they have existing customers and historical business expertise in assessing risk and underwriting small businesses. Most operate under the bank regulatory oversight structure. Big Tech includes the giant platform companies such as Google, Apple, Amazon, and Meta (Facebook). These large players currently have little engagement in U.S. financial services compared to other global tech giants such as Ant Financial and WeChat in China, a model in which Big Tech dominates lending, payments, and other banking activity.

The third category, challenger banks describes newly chartered banks and non-bank entities who compete with a largely online presence and use technology as their competitive advantage. Most of the best-known banks such as Monzo and Revolut began outside the United States and have only a small presence here. Other small business lenders such as OnDeck and many of the early entrants mentioned in Chapter 7 have had a rocky path. Yet, there has been some success. Square, which began as a payments company, reached a high penetration in lending with Square Capital and eventually received a banking license. This category also includes Live Oak Bank, which operates from a national online central point, but in many ways resembles a traditional bank in its underwriting and lending activities.

The final category of fintech infrastructure is the broadest. This area reflects the many ways that technology is being integrated into lending, as well as into other small business activities such as e-commerce and payments. The category includes large companies such as Stripe and Shopify which have the ability to embed financial products in the workflows of their customers. Also included are the enabling companies for the new technology-driven lending processes. For instance, Plaid provides seamless access to bank account data, and Codat, Enigma, and many others aggregate and reconcile small business information that has been traditionally difficult to access. A large number of fintechs are also billing themselves as the infrastructure partners of smaller community banks or CDFIs, providing automated front-end applications and other capabilities.

Each of these groups comes to the small business lending market with unique advantages, a different heritage of assets and many hurdles to overcome if they are to be successful in the fast-evolving landscape. We will explore each in turn with the objective of parsing out the common themes that might drive ultimate success.

Traditional Banks and Credit Card Companies

As we saw in Chapters 3 and 4, the U.S. banking system gets much of its unique strength in small business lending from the over four thousand community banks that have a local presence in rural and urban communities across the country. The United States also has some of the most important large banks, such as J.P. Morgan and Bank of America which have a long history in small business lending. Is it possible that these entities are dinosaurs that cannot change?

The Case for Success

The case for success for the traditional players is not hard to make. Banks have existing customers with whom they have long relationships, and these customers avail themselves of multiple banking services. Particularly with community banks, there is often a personal relationship. The banker provides financial advice and counsel, and personal knowledge plays a role in loan underwriting. Through these relationships there has historically been a high level of trust. Over 40% of small business owners have never switched their primary bank, and another 31% last changed over six years ago.[1]

Most of these loyal customers keep their deposits with the bank, which is generally insured by the Federal Deposit Insurance Corporation (FDIC) up to certain limits. This leads to the second key advantage of existing banks—their access to low-cost deposits. With over two trillion in deposits (from both consumers and small businesses) at J.P. Morgan, they and other large banks have access to very cheap capital. This gives them a significant advantage over non-bank lenders who must raise money in more expensive parts of the capital markets. It is noteworthy that Goldman Sachs' 2016 entry into consumer lending, Marcus, raised deposits aggressively by paying above market rates on accounts. This successfully put them into the top 10 U.S. banks by deposit level by 2023 (Figure 11.2). However, cheap capital was not enough to ensure success. Despite a splashy start in consumer lending and some discussion of expansion into small business loans, by 2022, Goldman announced it was pulling back from retail operations.[2]

Challenges for Traditional Players

The largest challenge to the established banks is their long-standing history of operating success and the traditional concerns about change and adding risk

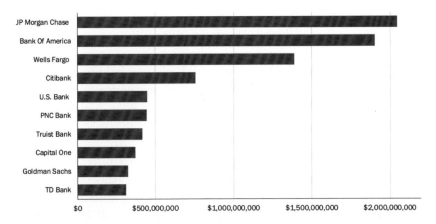

Figure 11.2   Largest U.S. Banks by Total Deposits as of Q1 2023
Source: Author's analysis of Federal Deposit Insurance Corporation (FDIC), BankFind Suite: Find Institution Financial & Regulatory Data, accessed August 2023.

in a highly regulated industry. As we will discuss in Chapter 12, incumbents often have trouble taking on the playbook of the disruptors, partly because they are less nimble and adventurous, but also because they have a large established businesses which have successfully generated profits. They are reluctant to jeopardize their operating models, particularly when the paths for success in the future marketplace have not been fully illuminated.

Even more worrisome is the trend for large banks to deemphasize small business lending, and their lack of focus on the transformation of their small business processes. One might look at J.P. Morgan, who even with over $11 billion annually in technology spending has not cracked the code on data enabled, automated small business lending. In fact, they have lost ground in the sector (perhaps by choice). Despite mentioning small business 55 times in their 2022 Annual Report, their position slipped from first or second in Small Business Administration (SBA) lending between 2010 and 2013 to 8th in number and 15th in dollars in 2023.[3] Part of the issue might be that in their organization the smallest businesses are served by the consumer lending division, making it more difficult to deliver the differentiated products and services that small businesses need.

Other large banks have also slipped competitively or deliberately changed their focus. Bank of America, who in 2018 had been driving for leadership in technology-driven small business lending, has focused on developing these products and services for its existing categories of customers. These tend to be larger, more established sectors, such as dental practices. Citibank has tightened its lending criteria and has not aggressively sought out additional small business lending volume. The relative lack of interest was also evident in the restrained participation of the large banks in PPP lending where they focused mainly on their own customers.[4]

For community banks, the focus on small businesses has remained strong, but there are other barriers to their ability to compete with new digital products. Community banks tend to have lower technology budgets and less expertise within their staff to take on transformational initiatives. The natural solution would be a partnership with a fintech infrastructure player who could provide a plug and play technology solution that interfaces with the bank's clients in a friendly efficient manner and uses the bank's own data and underwriting criteria to provide an automated lending solution. Although such fintech companies do exist, the implementation of these partnerships has proven to be more difficult than initially anticipated.

At the heart of the frictions is the fact that community banks rely on their core systems providers to handle any changes involving their data and systems. Three core systems providers dominate the U.S. community banking market: FIS, Jack Henry, and Fiserv, and given the risks and complexity of these systems, customers have been essentially captive to their provider. Historically, these large core systems companies were known for their lack of innovation, long lead times, and high costs for any requested changes.

That is beginning to change. Next-generation core banking systems have been developed that are more modular, allowing easier coupling with outside applications.[5] In addition, the traditional core system providers have recognized the necessity of making APIs available to allow new inputs into banks' decision models.[6] With these changes, community banks with their focus on small business lending and their interest in relationship lending are better positioned to be important players in the future landscape.

Credit Card Companies

Large credit card companies and processors have the ability to jump ahead of other competitors in the new era of technology and small business lending. Credit cards have long filled the gap in small-dollar lending to small businesses. Companies such as American Express, Visa, Mastercard and Capital One have large numbers of small business customers with whom they have trusted relationships. They have sophisticated technology budgets and staff and are focused on data-driven risk management. In addition, they tend to have good information on a company's transactions, either by their involvement in the payments streams that represent revenue to a retail operation, or the business expenses charged on the company credit card. All these factors are building blocks to small business lending products beyond cards and to the potential for success in the new landscape (see box for American Express's product suite and small business strategy).

American Express Business Blueprint™

In a move signaling a stronger focus on small business growth, American Express (Amex) unveiled American Express Business Blueprint™ in January 2023, with a suite of financial tools specifically designed for small business customers. The products were built on technology from their important 2020 acquisition of Kabbage. Central to the offerings were features that allowed small businesses to "check their financial vitals" and pay certain of their bills through a centralized cash flow management hub. Blueprint also included a business line of credit to streamline cash flow, tackle unexpected expenses, or capitalize on growth opportunities. Impressively, the digital loan application process meant that businesses could apply in minutes, and if approved, see loan funds post in their designated bank account in as little as 1 to 3 business days. "We want to provide an ecosystem that simplifies the lives of small business owners in an accessible, digital way," said Gina Taylor, Executive Vice President and General Manager of Small Business Products & Business Blueprint at American Express.[7] American Express Business Blueprint has been promoted by Amex as a testament to how even established financial giants can continually innovate.[8]

Neither Visa nor Mastercard has significantly evolved their existing relationships with small businesses into greater penetration of non-card lending. Capital One, on the other hand, reengineered its internal technology to better serve the small business customer. In 2016, the company started rebuilding 1300 internal applications to allow handling of big data in real time. This early commitment gave the company an edge in recruiting tech talent, and they employed over 10,000 developers by 2022.[9] Capital One has also partnered with data provider Enigma in its small business automated lending start up, Prime. This activity could give the company an edge in expanding its non-card small business lending.

Winners and Losers

Existing banks and credit card companies each have the potential to lead in the future of small business lending. They have large numbers of customers with whom they have a trusted and highly sticky relationship. Their deposit bases give them the lowest cost of money in the competitive landscape which means they can lend at almost 10 percentage points below the new challenger banks. Difficulties stemming from their antiquated systems seem likely to diminish over time as core providers evolve and fintech infrastructure players develop better workarounds. Already community banks leaders across the country, like Jill Castilla, CEO of Citizens Bank in Oklahoma, are innovating—even in the most unlikely small markets (see box).

Jill Castilla

In 2014, Jill Castilla stepped into the role of CEO for a community bank nestled in Edmond, Oklahoma. The former military officer with expertise in modern banking technologies recognized a glaring issue: small businesses, the backbone of communities like Edmond, grappled with limited access to efficient banking services, particularly loans. The core challenge was the outdated banking model that lacked the agility to meet modern demands. However, Castilla believed that technology could bridge this gap. Her first move was to overhaul traditional banking systems, integrating advanced digital solutions. In 2021, she launched a digital banking initiative, spotlighting a veteran-focused bank. In 2023, the bank partnered with fintech firm Narmi, rolling out a platform that enabled seamless account openings, directly synced with the central banking system managed by Jack Henry.[10] She paired these advances with community outreach. In collaboration with the Independent Shopkeepers Association, her bank provided physical storefront spaces for 50 local ventures.[11] Under Castilla's leadership, Citizens Bank not only champions digital banking innovation but sees itself as a beacon of support for the community's small businesses.

The story of Jill Castilla highlights a key differentiator in the future winners and losers among traditional players: the winners will be those with a real commitment to small business. Small businesses like their banks, but they are frustrated by the frictions they face in trying to operate seamlessly and get the attention and the capital they need. They are looking for providers who are responsive and knowledgeable about them and their businesses. And they want products and services that fit them and their business needs. Existing financial services companies have the capacity to create these compelling small business solutions and earn margins that can widen as the technologies become more tailored and easier to adopt. The key success variable is whether the current lenders decide to make small businesses a true priority and begin a journey of listening to their customers and developing new approaches that work for them.

Big Tech

When I ask audiences who might be the winner in small business lending of the future, Big Tech is a popular answer. The reasons are logical. Tech companies such as FAAMG (Meta formerly Facebook, Amazon, Apple, Microsoft, and Alphabet's Google) are well-known brands, trusted for their customer focus and ease of use. Each of them does business with a significant percentage of America's small businesses. Some, though not all, have dipped a toe into the water of small business lending or related financial services. They should be naturals to develop the products and services that small businesses crave.

Even more compelling is the fact that they have interactions on their platforms with millions of small businesses on a daily basis. This gives the large tech players two powerful advantages: first, they have masses of data points that can contain valuable signals on the well-being, growth, and profitability of each business. Second, the interactions with businesses on their platform give these tech companies a perfect place to embed new financial offers and gain trial, thus avoiding the costly marketing and customer acquisition costs most new fintechs face.

Given these clear strengths, it is surprising that there is little activity by Big Tech firms in financial services for small businesses. Why might this be the case? The most obvious issue is the highly regulated nature of banking and financial services. Given the vast array of growth sectors that these companies might choose to pursue, the baggage (and risk) of becoming a regulated bank or financial firm just to support the needs of a few small businesses makes lending a nonstarter.

That is not to say that Big Tech firms are doing nothing. In fact, the top tech firms made investments in about 20 fintech deals a year from 2018 to 2022, spending about $2 billion annually.[12] Google led the activity with 39 investments (largely through their Gradient Ventures fund), followed by Amazon who did 14 deals. These acquisitions were not generally in banking or small business financial services. Both Apple and Google have been active in developing digital wallets and digital IDs, as well as new payments methods, which sometimes include lending in the form of Buy Now, Pay Later.[13] The creation of these capabilities may not directly impact the ability of small business owners to access capital, but they could lead Big Tech companies into future forays in areas closer to banking.

Amazon

Amazon is the one Big Tech firm to offer small business lending. Starting in 2011 the firm began advancing small and medium businesses cash to build inventory. The small business which is selling on Amazon for the first time can expect a large bump in orders. Amazon decided to provide a suite of services for third-party sellers who are capital constrained. Using its visibility into the sellers' revenue through its platform, Amazon could encourage the business to build inventory to service the rising interest from customers—and provide a convenient and preapproved line of financing, based on these digital insights. Outstanding seller loans (called "seller receivables" in Amazon's financial reporting) rose steeply in the post-pandemic period, and totaled $1.3 billion in 2022, up 30% from 2021.[14] They also offered Amazon Business Credit Cards (provided by Amex) and a Buy Now Pay Later credit line called Pay By Invoice.[15,16]

This ecosystem was extremely convenient for small businesses that were enjoying a positive rise in business from their Amazon presence. The information from the platform allowed Amazon to make seamless credit decisions based on real-time insights, and incentives were aligned because when the small business sold more, Amazon also made money. However, many small businesses have had concerns about their relationship with Amazon and its lending products. Some have complained that when Amazon observes a fast-growing product with strong customer appeal, they source a similar competitive product and sell it under the Amazon brand for less. A small business may then see an impact on their sales, and many were concerned about having a financing relationship with a lender who was also then a competitor.

Meta

Meta has determined that it will be the digital wallet for the metaverse, in a move that is consistent with its rebranding. However, in the current world, its efforts have been focused on enabling e-commerce on its platform. This means building capacity around payments to make it easier for businesses to sell on Facebook and Instagram. In addition, outside the U.S. the ubiquitous use of WhatsApp has allowed them to experiment with financial services like money transfers. This buildup of expertise could be a back door into other financial products as the company sees a need to serve its users and the small business vendors using its platforms.[17]

Apple

The company that has shown the most interest in a broad suite of financial services is Apple. Through their partnership with Goldman Sachs, Apple launched a successful credit card which reached over 6 million users from August 2019 to May 2021. By 2023, however, the relationship soured as

Goldman pulled back from its consumer lending activities. As a result, Apple began to build its own in-house capacity for payments processing, credit risk assessment, fraud detection, and dispute resolution.[18] In March 2022, Apple acquired the U.K.-based Credit Kudos for approximately $150 million which uses open-banking data to make more informed credit assessments of loan applications.[19] Though their products are mostly consumer focused, this infrastructure could also work for small businesses. Overall, Apple's focus on expanding Apple Pay worldwide (and the related expansion into Buy Now, Pay Later) makes the company one of the more likely to find a path to success in digital lending and other relevant small business financial services.

Google

Google has been the most cautious about entering digital financial services but given their capabilities, they could be the wild card Big Tech player that makes the largest impact. Google has not been ignoring the sector. In 2021, they cancelled the launch of Google Plex, a mobile-first bank account that would have been integrated into Google Pay. Consumers liked the idea: nearly one in five said they would have opened a Google Plex account when it launched, and the product's waitlist had 400,000 sign-ups when it shut down.[20] The idea was not to replace banks but to partner with them. Over 11 major banks had already signed up to provide the savings and credit accounts that would be accessed through Google Pay.[21]

Instead of Plex, Google began focusing on its digital wallet and digital IDs in competition with similar Apple products. In addition, it is continuing to work on e-commerce through a partnership with Shopify. The Google/Shopify integration allows merchants to feature their products across Google on Search, Maps, Images, Lens, and YouTube. This has great appeal to small businesses looking to reach broad audiences and provides competition to Amazon. If Google is successful in its e-commerce strategy, there could be follow-on development of small businesses financial services to attract and support the vendor community.

Could Big Tech Win?

Although the major tech players are not currently engaged deeply in the small business lending and banking landscape, they should by no means be counted out. As my audiences suggested, there is tremendous power in the data and platforms Big Tech companies control that is relevant to success in small business lending. They have known and trusted brands whose equity transfers to the financial services sector. These companies create massive amounts of relevant data and have the internal expertise to use the information for credit insights. And they have a core capability of building integrated, customer-friendly interfaces, which have been a long-time pain point in banking. Finally, they are showing interest in some of the consumer segments of financial services, particularly as they relate to digital wallets and e-commerce.

Even if Big Tech successfully enters consumer financial services, the question remains whether they will pursue the small business products segment. As we have discussed, small business products tend to have smaller markets and be more difficult to execute. Given the high level of competing priorities, it seems likely that Big Tech players will only enter the small business markets under two conditions: first, if they view the success of the relevant small businesses as a key part of a larger strategy, for example as vendors. In that case, they would provide small business products (as Amazon does) as part of a broader ecosystem. In a second scenario, it is possible that a Big Tech player such as Apple (or even Elon Musk at X) would directly target segments of the banking system such as deposit taking and lending especially after gaining credit experience through products like Buy Now, Pay Later. In such a case, they could partner with banks (if they did not want the full regulatory burden) and build successful, ubiquitous financial services options. Even if these are first rolled out to consumers, they could migrate to small businesses. Under these scenarios, Big Tech could certainly become a powerful and transformative force in at least some segments of small business lending and banking services.

Challenger Banks

The third potential category of winners in the small business lending landscape is the new banks and non-bank lenders that depend on technology to service customers and assess loans. At their core, these new digital solutions are perhaps the most powerful force in the global fintech transformation. In countries from China to Kenya, banking is now dominated by digital first options. In particular, where traditional banking infrastructure is poor, new solutions are quickly embraced by a consumer and small business population that is starved for access to capital. In contrast, in the United States and other parts of the developed world, the established networks of banks and other financial institutions may not be the perfect service providers, but they have the advantage of being known and trusted, in part because of stiff government regulatory oversight. To win in the United States the new challengers must convince customers to switch, largely to fairly new financial services entities, which are not fully regulated.

The challenger bank category could also be called online lenders and is defined to include banks and other lenders who do not have physical branch networks but operate instead from a central digital hub. The assets these competitors bring to the lending market are the ability to give customers a much faster, customer-friendly, automated process eliminating the stacks of Xeroxed paperwork and the three week (or three month) wait for an answer. However, they also bring disadvantages such as higher costs and real or perceived lack of security and safety of the financial assets under their control.

U.K. Digital Banks

Challenger banks have reached surprisingly high penetration levels in the U.K. According to the British Business Bank, challenger banks and "specialist rivals" took 55% of the SME lending market in 2022, leaving "High Street" and traditional banks with less than half of the pie.[22] About 12% of U.K. consumers use a digital bank as their main bank, but a larger number (nearly 38%) have a digital only bank account alongside a traditional account. Penetration is much higher among the younger demographics, with only 19% of 18- to 34-year-olds preferring in-person banking. However, among individuals aged 45 to 54, the percentage was 30%, and 44% of those who were 55 years old and older wanted an in-person experience and wanted access to staff in branches.[23]

The success of U.K. challenger banks was a deliberate strategy of government regulators to increase competition and was facilitated by the adoption of Open Banking. Early on, regulations were enacted that made it clear that customers owned their banking data and that it could be safely ported to another financial institution. This has helped customers in the U.K. feel more confident about the safety and security of digital banking solutions than their U.S. counterparts. Some banks such as Starling were conceived from the start to give a new customer-focused banking experience, particularly to small businesses that were poorly served by existing options (see box).

Starling Bank

When Anne Boden founded Starling Bank in 2014, her vision was to revolutionize the banking world with "fast technology, fair service and honest values." Starling Bank became the U.K.'s first digital bank in 2017 and reached 2.7 million accounts, including 475,000 business accounts by the end of 2021.[24] In business banking, the bank focused on developing features to help owners efficiently track expenses, manage invoices, and gain insights into their financial health. One of the features introduced by Starling Bank, named "Saving Spaces," was conceptualized to assist small business owners in earmarking funds for distinct purposes within their accounts.[25] This enabled better budgeting and financial planning and ensured that funds were allocated appropriately for taxes, growth initiatives, or emergency funds. Its emphasis on innovative features that simplified financial management for small business owners made Starling a popular alternative to traditional lenders and earned it an award as Best Business Bank in the U.K. in 2019.

In the United States, due to the large number and long tradition of national and community banks, new challenger banks must meet a high bar. In a recent consumer survey, 53% said they were "satisfied enough with their current banking and financial service provider setup."[26] And 34% of respondents were worried about the "safety and security of [their] money and information and did not trust the reliability of digital banks."[27] For U.S. banking customers, digital solutions need to be easy to access, have superior customer interfaces and services, and perhaps even be cheaper than their traditional banking relationships.

As in the U.K., bank attitudes are different by age, with 56% of millennials saying they are at least "somewhat interested in switching to a digital bank." New solutions are also appealing to 54% of small business owners and 54% of freelancers, customers who are less well served by current banking options.[28] Thus, many believe that as the population ages and digital natives dominate, it is only a matter of time before the digital banks take over, even in the United States.

Non-Bank Lenders

Despite a promising start, non-bank lenders in the U.S. like LendingClub and OnDeck have struggled. The largest issues have been cost disadvantages in two key areas: cost of customer acquisition and cost of capital. Without a trusted brand, these new entrants have had to spend at high levels often in the range of 15% or more to attract customers. On top of those costs, non-banks lenders have to source the funds that they lend from expensive debt markets. Particularly in the period from 2011 to 2021, interest payments on bank deposits were very low, even close to zero, giving banks a large cost advantage over non-bank lenders. Loans from the digital non-bank lenders were often priced in the 18 to 35% range, higher even than credit card debt. This made them dangerously unaffordable for most small businesses.

In contrast to many other players, Square Capital had strong success in building its lending business. It benefited from the trusted brand that founder Jack Dorsey had built based on the small easy-to-use Square credit card processing device. The merchants using this device already had a relationship with Square. They went to the platform daily to access their credit card proceeds. These businesses were happy with the simple customer-friendly interface and were willing to try the new loan products despite their higher cost. Square Capital also benefited from the installed payments platform by using the data on card receipts to estimate the business's health and make credit assessments. They could also offer products such as merchant cash advances which allowed them to be paid back first out of the collateral of the card receipts, rather than waiting for a check for principal and interest payments. The lesson from Square's success is important: platforms that already are part of a small business's workflow have a huge advantage, both for gaining access to customer trust and for gathering critical data for credit or other decisions.

Live Oak Bank

In 2010, Chip Mahan came to the Small Business Administration with an unlikely proposal. His new bank, Live Oak was operating on a national basis—without a branch network—with all applications received digitally. His customers were all veterinarians, a group that needed capital for equipment and offices, but would often find it hard to get bank loans, particularly at the initial set up of the practices. Concentrating on one sector solved one of the key frictions in small business lending, the heterogeneity of the customer base. With a growing data set of similar loans, it would be easier for Live Oak's underwriters to differentiate a good veterinarian from a bad one. Over time Live Oak expanded its segments, first to dentists, then on to pharmacists, funeral homes, and finally to over 35 current small business sectors. By 2018, Live Oak was the largest SBA lender.[29]

Live Oak could be included in the first category of banks and credit card companies. We include it among the challenger banks because it is a relatively new lender, operating without branches from a single location with largely digital interfaces. It is, in fact, a great combination of traditional banking methods and new technology and holds many lessons for new entrants in small business lending. Live Oak did not start with brand recognition, so it built its reputation sector by sector using word of mouth to build trust and source new business. As a bank it had low-cost deposits to fund its loans (and sold the SBA-guaranteed portions of the loans in syndicated markets to keep its capital base liquid). The bank digitized as much of the process as possible to provide automated services that were accurate and low cost, and supplemented the digital activities with live, knowledgeable customer service agents. It even developed its own core operating system suited to the data-centric activities of the modern digital bank and spun it into a separate company, nCino, to sell the system to other banks.

Advantages and Constraints of Digital Banks

The learnings from the current digital landscape point to a clear but possibly controversial conclusion: the best way for a new digital lender to compete is to become a bank. Competing as a bank and taking deposits has great advantages in terms of lowering the cost of capital, and knowing there is strong oversight improves the level of trust from customers. Being regulated was once viewed as a disadvantage in fintech. The notion of "regulatory arbitrage" defined the advantage a digital non-bank lender had over a traditional bank, operating under the costs and constraints of the U.S. bank regulatory regime. It is true that bank regulation comes with some high costs and compliance burdens. But, particularly after the bank crisis of 2023, involving Silicon Valley Bank, many customers and lenders are seeing the benefits of oversight.

The successful digital lenders of the future will likely be banks or non-banks operating in a transparent, regulated environment. This is the model that has been successful in the U.K. and, thanks to the competency of their regulators and regulatory schemes, the oversight has encouraged rather than stifled innovation. Chapters 13 and 14 discuss the extensive work that must be done to attain a productive regulatory environment in the U.S. for digital banks and non-bank lenders. However, such an environment is worth developing so that digital banks can compete safely and deliver innovative products and services to the marketplace.

Infrastructure Players

Infrastructure players comprise the final category in the landscape and are an interesting group of diverse companies working on a wide range of lending-related issues. In general, infrastructure players are not lenders themselves. Instead, they use technology to provide the foundational elements that support new forms of fintech lending. We group these companies into three broad categories: (1) digital lending enablers, (2) data aggregators and providers of data analytics, and (3) non-lending platforms such as Intuit, Shopify, and Stripe who provide important environments in which lending can be embedded.

These groupings are not mutually exclusive, nor are they collectively exhaustive. There are lots of innovative ideas and new companies testing products that could be part of broader fintech solutions. But the three categories seem to capture much of the current activity in enabling infrastructure.

Digital Lending Enablers

We define digital lending enablers as those firms that are trying to provide digital lending infrastructure to banks, or those that are creating marketplaces to foster easier access for customers to a wide array of small business lending solutions.

A large number of new entrants over the last 5 to 10 years have developed pieces of the digital lending solution such as application processing, credit assessment, and underwriting. The hope was that smaller banks without the resources of a J.P. Morgan could find a plug and play solution through one of these third-party vendors, without each bank having to build their own from scratch. Two early examples of these digital lending facilitators were Numerated and Fundation. Numerated was created and incubated inside of Eastern Bank (see Chapter 12) and then was spun out to provide external services for any community or regional bank that wanted to set up automated lending for small-dollar loans. The company grew slowly until the arrival of the Covid-19 pandemic, when much of the early reluctance to change was swept away, and banks clamored for an easy to set up digital experience that could use their own underwriting criteria.

Despite these enabling companies, the conversion of smaller U.S. community banks to digital lending has proven slower and more laborious that originally anticipated. As mentioned earlier, a key factor has been the resistance and early lack of engagement from the major core systems providers on which most community banks rely. The big three, FiServe, FIS, and

Jack Henry, had little incentive to respond to digital innovation because their customer base was held captive. One banker described the challenge of changing core systems as doing open heart surgery while the patient is still walking around and talking. Until the core systems providers bought into the infrastructure changes required, small banks were unable to make progress.

Finally in 2023, Jack Henry began to implement an API-driven environment within their data walls, where a bank could bring in third-party data and more securely use it to augment their own information for credit or other decision making. FIS launched Code Connect, which enabled more customized data features and drastically cut the integration time. The pace at which the core systems facilitate engagement with third parties and/or develop their own infrastructure for data and analytics will dictate the ability of the community banking segment to compete and win.[30]

A final type of digital lending infrastructure is the creation of small business lending marketplaces. One of the great frictions in small business lending is the inability of small business borrowers to quickly get multiple lenders to offer a quote on their loan. A constraint in the past has been long paper applications that take weeks or months to process, making the loan application process often linear, meaning that an applicant applied to only one bank at a time and waited for an answer or rejection before trying a second bank. A part of the optimal environment that we call Small Business Utopia is to have multiple banks competing to provide each loan, with a seamless digital application process.

Marketplaces that create such a competitive environment would produce better pricing for the borrower. And borrowers could see a variety of offers that might include different loan sizes, duration, and terms as lenders have different products that they like to offer. It benefits both the borrower and the lender if the borrower is matched with a loan and a lender that is right for them, as the chance of a default is reduced. Early marketplaces such as Lendio are attractive examples, but even more options in this area would powerfully change the small business lending environment for the better.

Data Aggregators and Data Analytics Providers

The key to success in the new digital lending world lies in having the right data and being able to use analytics to gain actionable insights from the information at hand. This is no easy task. As we have discussed, one of the key barriers in small business lending is information opacity, the inability to see inside a business and know what is actually going on. What are their prospects? Are they growing and profitable? How do they perform versus their industry? Do they have the cash flow to repay the loan?

It helps that wildly innovative advances have been made in data analytics including the use of predictive algorithms, machine learning, and more and more complex and insightful forms of artificial intelligence. However, algorithms are only as good as the underlying data, so the providers and aggregators of data, particularly hard to access small business information, play an important role in the small business lending landscape. For example, Enigma, a data aggregator featured in Chapter 10, has been building its small business data assets for almost a decade from public and private sources. Using a unique identifier, Enigma can match data to the correct small business entity even if multiple businesses have the same name. This entity verification is an important breakthrough as more lenders draw in data from third-party sources, some of which don't include an EIN or other identifier. If they can correctly match new data to the business under consideration, they can create the rich picture of a company's activities and prospects that is key to understanding its creditworthiness.

It used to be that local banks claimed a better understanding of their business customers as they saw the daily transactions in the business's bank account. These cash flows turn out to be highly predictive of loan paydowns and defaults and form the basis of credit analysis by cash flow-oriented fintech lenders. (Surprisingly, large banks such as J.P. Morgan and Wells Fargo did not historically use bank account transactions in their underwriting and in many cases did not even have easy access to the information due to the siloed nature of the bank information systems.) In recent years, any lender can access any potential borrower's bank account data, even if they bank in a different place. With the customer's permission, infrastructure players like Plaid (and other similar systems) securely transmit bank transactions in a standardized format through APIs. In the EU and elsewhere Open Banking regulations oversee this data sharing, providing a critical way to prevent data monopolies and encourage innovative competition in the small business lending arena.

Bank transactions are not the only predictive data for small business credit assessments. Accounting records also turn out to be highly useful. But in many cases, it is difficult to read and analyze data from accounting software such as QuickBooks, as it may be full of quirky or inconsistent entries. Enter sophisticated companies such as Codat and competitors like 9Spokes. These companies use advanced data science techniques to clean and standardize accounting and other information making it easier for lenders to assess credit quality and for business owners to see their own financial position and needs (see box on Codat). In yet another example, Ocrolus (described at the beginning of Chapter 8) has the ability to digitize information from paper forms and put it into a reliable data format so it can become a useful input in automated loan decisions and other processes.

Codat—A Business Data API

In the heart of London's bustling fintech sector, Pete Lord, Alex Cardona and David Hoare identified a pressing small business need. Witnessing the burden that exchanging financial data created for both service providers and small and medium enterprises when accessing credit, they teamed up to form Codat to harness the power of APIs for financial data sharing. It turned out to be a non-trivial task and they have now been refining their methods for cleaning and standardizing business data for over 6 years. However, the efforts were successful. Codat now provides data from third-party systems including bank records, accounting software (e.g. QuickBooks, Sage, NetSuites, Xero), payments systems (e.g. Square, PayPal, Stripe, Shopify) in a single point of connection. This technology powers specialized products for loan decisioning, credit monitoring and accounting automation. By 2023, Codat was backed by leading organizations such as Paypal, American Express, J.P. Morgan, Plaid and Shopify, and expanded to the U.S. and Australia.

The rapid pace of technological advances has been matched by a surge of entrepreneurial companies each focused on a different piece of the data and analytics tool kit. These companies may not each have enough breadth to be large transformational players, but they will be critical lynchpins in enabling the new small business digital lending ecosystem. And they might also provide better operating intelligence to more small businesses, lowering the failure rates and helping more to succeed.

Non-Lending Platforms and Embedded Lending

For lenders to cost effectively make loans, they must find and communicate options to small businesses just at the moment when they are considering a loan. It is notoriously difficult to reach small businesses in general, because they are busy running their businesses. The heterogeneity of small businesses means that there is not one or even a few business verticals where they can be easily aggregated. It is highly valuable, therefore, to have access to a platform that knows which small businesses are potentially in need of capital, and to have a means of speaking to them in a timely and credible format. This is the appeal of embedding financial offers into platforms where small businesses are already engaged on a daily basis. The possibilities of embedded lending come into view when we examine the activities of two relatively new but large and important platforms: Shopify and Stripe.

Shopify provides a cloud-based commerce platform for small and medium-sized businesses to help create and manage their online businesses. The company delivers online businesses their website setup, product showcase, payment processing, and shipping. With Shopify, users can choose from various templates to design and customize their store to fit their brand and product goals. Shopify uses Stripe to provide its online payments infrastructure. Behind the scenes Stripe creates the linkages to the banks that allow e-commerce payments to flow smoothly and securely. Because Stripe and Shopify know the activity levels of the small businesses who use their platforms, they are well positioned to build underwriting models and establish a credit box that indicates who might be a good prospect for a loan.

Stripe is engaged with multiple banks for payments processing. Those banks or others can agree to be the originating banks for loans that might be analyzed by Stripe and offered to small businesses on the Shopify platform. The banks can then hold the loans or sell them to other investors. Each layer in this infrastructure performs a critical piece of the lending process in a new way. Shopify uses its relationship with the customer to offer credit in a trusted environment to businesses who have a real financing need. Stripe creates the underwriting analytics and the secure pipelines to the banks. The banks enjoy a new source of loan volume, at a low acquisition cost, which they can hold or sell.

Shopify is not the only customer-facing entity that is exploring credit as an additional product. Every horizontal platform, including Xero, Square and Intuit, and even Lyft, Instacart and DoorDash, is looking to deepen their relationship with their customers. Many are looking at ways to help the small businesses with whom they engage keep their money on the platform and transact seamlessly from one operating dashboard. For example, if a Door-Dash courier stores their money on the site, the Dasher is more likely to be locked in and engaged. Shopify Balance was developed to let small businesses create a business account to operate their financial transactions within the digital Shopify world. Offering credit is a logical extension of these efforts.

Every vertical software provider from Toast which serves restaurants to Squire, a platform for barber shops, sees the same opportunity. In addition to processing payments and creating operating insights, they can offer credit products that are seamlessly available on their platform. The data that they gather from their digital relationship with the small business informs the underwriting algorithms and allows the loans to be tailored to the business owner's needs. For the small business owner, these embedded offers are more convenient and timely than a traditional bank process. These products are also appealing to small businesses with bumpy cashflows because having access to liquidity at the right time can make the difference between growth, success, stagnation or failure.

The list of platform companies goes on. Intuit/Quickbooks provides the world's largest small business accounting product and has customers on the platform daily who think of the brand as a trusted partner. The accounting data allows Intuit to know which businesses are growing, which are using cash to build working capital, what the cash realization cycles might be, and therefore, which might be a good candidate for a working capital line or other product. The platform's access to customers, coupled with data that can be used to develop predictive insights, is a powerful format for winning in the new small business landscape.

Each platform requires a bank or other financial institution at the back end and perhaps a middle layer of connectivity like Stripe. This sandwich of infrastructure describes how embedded lending of the future will be constructed. Customer-facing platforms might originate the loan, holding a relationship with the small business owner that has unique insight into the right product and timing that fits their needs. A middle layer might hold the analytics and underwriting engine, benefiting from good information from other similar businesses in the sector, and trained risk models. Banks could then have the opportunity to provide "banking-as-a-service", benefiting from a new stream of revenues and profits. This formula delivers many winners, including small business owners who have greater access to the credit they need to grow and prosper.

The Recipe for Winners

Given that the four categories all have some strengths (and some disadvantages), how do we determine who will be the winners and losers in this transformational moment of small business lending? The early impulse to say that the old dinosaurs (i.e., traditional banks) would soon be overcome by the nimble new innovators (neo-banks) was quickly proven to be wrong. But the clear outline of the winners of the future has yet to fully become apparent. In fact, there are likely to be many formulas for winning, given the diversity of small businesses and the range of needs they have for capital.

We do see a few patterns, however, that could be predictors of success (and failure). First, cost of capital and cost of customer acquisition are such large components that getting them right as a lender is critical to a profitable business model. For cost of capital, it is very hard to compete with funding from low-cost deposits—so that leads to the conclusion that one way to success is to compete as a bank. To have a competitive customer acquisition cost, the business must either have a known and trusted brand name or access to a stream of embedded customers. This leads to the second conclusion—that platforms who have trusted access to small businesses, particularly through daily interactions, have an enormous advantage in launching new lending products and services.

The combination of these two conclusions has resulted in the powerful trend of embedded finance. Embedded finance in the business-to-business sector is projected to more than triple over the next several years from $1.9 billion in 2021 to $6.7 billion in 2026.[31] For embedded finance to work platforms need a partner who can deliver lending products. The nature of the partnership between the platform and the lender can vary greatly, depending on who takes control of creating the offer and who is making the credit decision. The financial arrangements would have to reflect who is taking the credit risk.

Venture investors have begun to target embedded finance in their software as a service (Saas) portfolios. According to Jeff Bussgang of Flybridge Capital, the traditional focus of starting with a vertical SaaS company and adding fintech (such as with Toast) should be flipped. He argues "Determining the sequence of products or services offered to your customers should be primarily guided by their specific needs, with a particular focus on addressing their greatest pain or "must-have" requirements. For instance, consider businesses that have a high demand for working capital. The optimal strategy to attract these customers might be to initially address their working capital challenges with a direct offering ('must-have') rather than proposing front or back-office software solutions to improve their business processes ('nice to have')." He suggests starting with fintech as the first product: Fintech + Vertical SaaS instead of Vertical SaaS + Fintech.[32] Such strategies should mean that venture funding focused on solutions to pain points in small business lending will increase, and the pace of innovation will grow.

* * *

In the end we will see diverse winning strategies that are successful in the small business lending market, not just one that dominates. This conclusion reflects the complexity of the market and the dynamism of the technology that is now available to address market gaps. Small businesses exist in every size and every industry. Owners vary greatly in their ambitions for their businesses and the degree they desire to take on risk. Each needs a different kind of loan product, one with a size, price, and duration that fits with the business. Lenders and other loan originators from banks to platform providers have different objectives for their lending activity. Some want to facilitate access to capital as part of a broader offering to small businesses. Others, like banks, are in the business of taking risk on their stock of capital to earn returns.

In this complex array of supply and demand for small business loans, one could worry that the market might never work smoothly. I have a more optimistic view based on observing the extraordinary potential of the technology that is now available and the innovative capacity of the new market players. Data aggregators described in this chapter produce streams of relevant small business data in standardized formats. Lenders are using machine learning and sophisticated algorithms to develop more insights on who is creditworthy. And artificial intelligence allows a bot to be more than a personal assistant, but in fact a co-pilot to the small business owner. Innovators in all corners of the market are using these layers of technology to experiment with more products and solutions. Acceptance in the marketplace will encourage the winners and close critical market gaps, allowing more small businesses to access the capital they need to grow and succeed.

12

A Playbook for Banks

It was a cold, winter day in January 2017 as Eastern Bank CEO Bob Rivers stared out the window overlooking downtown Boston, reflecting on Eastern's recent innovation adventures. Rivers had just become Eastern Bank's Chairman and CEO, starting his career as a bank teller 35 years earlier and working his way up through the ranks in several banks, before becoming Eastern's President in 2007. Rivers had seen the signs of disruption—technology seemed to be taking over the world and banking was no different. Now the bank was at the end of a three-year internal innovation project designed to bring new technology solutions to its customers. Eastern Labs had developed a hugely successful, fully automated small business lending product that was recognized as an industry leader and had strong adoption by Eastern customers.

Rivers was proud of what they had accomplished. Eastern Bank was by all accounts a traditional bank. Founded in Salem, Massachusetts, in 1818, Eastern was the oldest and largest mutual bank in the country. Being a mutual bank meant Eastern had no shareholders and was instead owned by its depositors—a model that restricted the bank's capital stock to retained earnings. Begun as an attempt by some wealthy New England merchants and ship owners to provide access to capital for those in the community to build homes, Eastern Bank originally opened once a week—on Wednesdays from 12 to 1 PM. It offered a 5% passbook account and a precursor to the modern home mortgage. In addition to repaying the principal and the interest on their loans, borrowers incurred one additional "fee." They had to volunteer at the bank in order to help expand the hours. This community focus and

© The Author(s), under exclusive license to Springer Nature
Switzerland AG 2024
K. G. Mills, *Fintech, Small Business & The American Dream*,
https://doi.org/10.1007/978-3-031-55612-8_12

the mutual ownership structure had been part of the fundamental identity of Eastern Bank for almost 200 years.

Through most of the 1980s and 1990s, Eastern operated as a traditional community bank, serving the New England region with a large branch network, specializing in small and middle-market business lending, consumer banking, and insurance brokerage. In 1997, Eastern began a massive expansion push, aiming to double the size of the bank within ten years. More than a decade later, as the nation emerged from the worst financial crisis since the Great Depression, Eastern found itself in a relatively fortunate position. With few risky loans on its books, it had escaped the crisis with minimal losses and without closing a single branch. As the crisis came to an end, Rivers realized that Eastern had the capacity to meet the needs of small businesses whose credit had been constrained during the crisis. As Rivers put it, his team felt they had "both an opportunity and a responsibility to step up." They decided to focus on Small Business Administration (SBA) guaranteed lending and, within six months of ramping up their small business operation, Eastern was the top SBA lender in Massachusetts and eventually became a top 10 SBA lender nationally.

But Rivers was still worried. Small business lending was a core part of their business, but fintech disruptors were providing a better customer experience and processing the loans faster than Eastern's manual process would ever allow. Determined to compete, Bob Rivers and Chief Information Officer Don Westermann decided to take a walk around Kendall Square, home to Massachusetts Institute of Technology (MIT), where many of these fintech entrepreneurs were incubating their companies. With few connections in this field, Rivers and Westermann cold called people and took meetings with whomever they could find. Rivers ultimately wanted to find someone to transform Eastern's technology, arguing, "We should worry about people putting us out of business, but we should also put ourselves out of business." One day, Rivers picked up the Boston Globe and noticed that PerkStreet Financial, an online bank headquartered in Boston, was struggling to make ends meet. Once thought to be the future of banking, PerkStreet was closing after just four years in business. But the talented innovator behind Perk-Street piqued Rivers' interest. He picked up the phone, called his network in Kendall Square, and asked if they could put him in touch with PerkStreet's CEO Dan O'Malley. By the time Rivers called, O'Malley had already been searching for a bank with whom to partner for about one month. He believed that his project at PerkStreet would have been more easily executed within a bank rather than through an independent entity. After three months of negotiating, O'Malley officially joined Eastern Bank as their Chief Digital Officer, responsible for the bank's product team, customer support, and "Eastern Labs"—the new innovation group located in the lobby of Eastern Bank's headquarters. With a $4 million annual investment from the Board, Eastern Labs began running a series of tests.

Initially, they simply set up a basic web page and used the customer support team to reach potential customers by phone and email. Once a customer applied, their information was processed manually within two hours, cutting turnaround time dramatically without having to build an automated system. As O'Malley said, "We decided to fake it until we made it."

But having an innovation team work inside of a traditional bank was not easy. The process of experimenting with new products was messy and involved risk. For example, in O'Malley's first test, he wanted to run what he called a "universe test," approving loans for anyone who applied just to see if there was a demand for the faster, online process. One team member's response was, "So you want me to open the window, take taxpayer-guaranteed money and just hand it out to anyone who shows up. That's the stupidest idea I've ever heard." Even those who did not work with Labs felt its influence—after all, they saw it in the lobby every day. Some felt that the money and attention going to Labs could be better spent supporting their day-to-day operations, or on other new projects.

Despite this tension, Labs developed a successful product. Over three years, $12 million, and multiple tests, a project that began with a basic web page ended with a product that fully automated Eastern's small business lending and improved customer acquisition through digital marketing, all while meeting the bank's regulatory and internal underwriting requirements. O'Malley saw an opportunity to sell the product to other community banks and believed this combination of automated loan processing and improved marketing gave the product unique appeal. As he put it, "Real-time loan origination reduces back-office costs but doesn't itself drive growth. Growth comes from automating sales in new [digital] channels." Eventually, O'Malley spun out the product into its own company called Numerated Growth Technologies, in which Eastern Bank had an equity stake.[1]

The State of U.S. Small Business Banking

The story of Eastern Bank illustrates the challenges facing U.S. community and regional banks, particularly the smaller ones. Already under pressure, these banks do not have the resources or often the inclination to invest in innovation. Few can mount an effort like Eastern Labs within their own walls. Industry groups have been disappointingly not inclined to help, preferring instead to devote most of their efforts to lobbying in Washington against fintech competition in any way possible.

Yet the future landscape of banking—including community banking—more and more clearly involves change. Customers are demanding the ease of digital options, even if some still appreciate in-person engagement and the local branch presence. New products informed by masses of relevant data have become the norm. Rather than trying to build their own solutions, small banks have access to an increasingly rich pool of third-party options, each of which operates in a different way. Thus, investing in innovation in the current environment involves selecting and then building partnerships with outside providers of technology, data, and solutions. The questions for banks today are first, do they want to serve small business customers, and if so, how can they pick the right products and partners?

Decision to Serve Small Businesses

Profits in the U.S. banking sector have been under pressure. Costs have increased from investments in technology and regulatory compliance, and margins have been squeezed in traditional lines of business. Many banks are increasingly reliant on extra fees that annoy customers and leave the bank vulnerable to competition. Large non-bank platforms are offering financial options that cut into banks' traditional service areas. Facing these pressures U.S. banks, large and small, have strategic decisions to make. The most critical decision is: who are the customers I want to serve in the future?

Several recent strategic reviews of the banking sector including work by all the major consulting firms have identified this as a moment of opportunity.[2] This is particularly true in small business banking. The International Finance Corporation (IFC) suggests that micro, small, and medium-sized enterprises globally have unmet financing needs of approximately $5.2 trillion a year, roughly 1.5 times the current lending market for this type of business.[3] For many smaller banks, small business deposits and small commercial and real estate loans have been a traditional core of their business proposition. Why not also increase their small business lending? This segment tends to have good margins and, importantly, less overt price competition than consumer business lines.

Banks who are considering a small business focus need to ask: what are the products and services that the small business customer wants? And does the bank want to make these areas a priority? Small business banking includes a suite of products from deposits, bill paying, small business credit cards, lines of credit, and advice and counsel. Some customers even use selected treasury services and fraud management. Banks have an advantage in offering small business loans to customers who already use them for other services. Surveys tell us that most small businesses (up to 70%) still want to borrow from their primary institution.[4]

This is a broad area of opportunity because fewer than 600 U.S. banks have more than 20% of their portfolio concentrated in small business lending.[5] But, success in this segment will require focus and investment. Small businesses value saving time and getting quick responses in addition to (or maybe even above) competitive rates. Borrowers also want integrated tools that make their payments and deposits seamless, reflecting the new standards that tech companies have set for this type of customer experience. Small businesses want the safety and security of the traditional relationships they have with their banks, but only if the service levels and product options are a good fit with their needs. The bar has been raised.

Big Banks

Large banks still play an important role in small business lending but they have chosen to compete in an increasing narrow part of the market. Over the past 15 years, two large banks, J.P. Morgan and Bank of America, have grown their assets by about 3.5 trillion and 1.5 trillion, respectively.[6, 7] Despite this growth, their shares of small business lending have not grown over time, reflecting the growing attraction of other business lines, and their narrow focus on a select segments of traditional small businesses. Yet large banks cannot be counted out of the market. For the segments they chose to serve, large banks are making aggressive strides, particularly by using data and intelligence to improve their interactions with existing and potential customers.

One part of their approach has been to take what has been working with consumers in terms of digitization and adapt those tools to the unique needs of small business owners. Bank of America has developed a small business dashboard similar to that envisioned in "Small Business Utopia" that can integrate with third-party applications such as QuickBooks and ADP. This information feeds a personalized experience with the bank where the business receives offers that are preapproved and relevant to their business and cash flow needs.

Large banks are also investing in mining the data they accumulate to create new business opportunities. In one example, if customer says "self-employed" on a personal mortgage application, the bank's software will then identify them as a small business owner, use third-party data from an integrated API to identify the industry and revenues of the business and designate that customer and their business as a marketing opportunity. If the business is in a target segment that the bank likes, such as doctors or dentists for Bank of America, a specialist can give that customer a call with a personalized offer for their business. These capabilities, also present at J.P. Morgan, make large banks strong competitors in their traditional small business niches where they choose to play.

Wells Fargo, a historically strong small business lender, has suffered from management and organizational weaknesses and has fallen behind, while Citibank has chosen to deemphasize small business lending in its strategic priorities. This has left the way clear for regional banks like Eastern and others such as PNC, Regions and Fifth-Third, and community banks with the inclination to invest in new approaches and the technology solutions that small businesses are seeking.

Community Banks

The segment of banks with the best chance to capture the untapped opportunity in the small business lending segment is community banks. But they also face the greatest challenges. The opportunity comes from their traditional focus on small businesses in their community and on their wrap-around approach to small business needs, including advice and counsel. Those banks who want to grow their small business revenues need to reassess their game plan for winning in the new technology-enabled banking environment. The first step is to fully define the incremental small business customers the banks is seeking to serve. Is there a segment of small businesses where the bank has expertise? The focus could be industry related, or it could be on businesses of a particular size or state of growth and development. Silicon Valley Bank, before its demise, built a large business focusing on early-stage growth companies that were seeking their first bank loan.

The bank then needs to identify the pain points of their target segments. For instance, are these businesses unsophisticated at preparing the documentation for a loan application? If so, how could the data accessible by the bank allow a more automated and informed loan decision process? Perhaps the small business needs help understanding what loan they really need. With the time they save by using an automated credit review and cash flow projection of the business' activity, the bank relationship personnel could be advising the business owner on the type of credit product that would best fit their borrowing needs.

To execute such a strategy to go after small business lending, most community banks need a fairly aggressive digital transformation. This path is more possible than in the past but is not without hardship. Of the three elements required, the one that represents the greatest challenge is the lack of innovation by the bank core processors FIS, Jack Henry, and FiServ. These systems have long been inflexible, making the integration of new technologies and features cumbersome. Thankfully over the past few years, the block the core providers had on adoption of innovation by their customers has begun to dissipate.[8] It is becoming more possible for community banks to access the first of three key components for a digital transformation: a more flexible core which can work with new internal or third-party data and processes.

There has also been progress on second and third elements: the ability to integrate high-quality point solutions such as Plaid and various data and decision support software providers, and the development of a customer-friendly digital front end. The entry of many competent and innovative infrastructure players made it easier for banks to see a path to acquiring digital capacity to add new information to their decision making and significantly improve their customers' experience. Forty percent of banks report investing in technologies to use APIs and almost a third are changing their front ends to do digital account opening.[9]

Using technology to reimagine small business banking can have a large impact on banks' performance. In one analysis, McKinsey calculated that using new data to create more targeted customer acquisition can create higher conversion rates and increase revenues by 10 to 15%. They add "embracing digital transformation and streamlining the customer journey can lead to operational-efficiency gains of 20 to 30%. Furthermore, with enhanced risk models and consistent decision-making, the peril of nonperforming loans can be curtailed by 10 to 25%."[10] These are significant incentives to embark on the journey of change to a more digitally savvy approach.

A Playbook for Small Business Banking

Besides overcoming the technology hurdles described above, what constitute the keys to success in the new small business lending environment? As we argued in Chapter 11, a key differentiator is that winners will have a deep commitment to small businesses and their success and a strong strategic understanding of which small business customers they want to serve. Live Oak is a great example of the benefits of a strategy that emphasizes specific industry verticals—as is Bank of America and its focus on doctor and dentists. Citizens is building a bank around military customers and veterans. Others are concentrating on automation to address the customer pain point of needing rapid responses and a flexible array of products that are convenient to access. Still other local banks are concentrating on relationships and being the trusted advisor in their local communities. Deciding which customers to serve, identifying their pain points and then using technology to develop fast, personalized customer-friendly solutions are the new playbook for the future.

The technology components of success are advancing at a more rapid pace, and legacy systems issues will be less of an impediment to future change. The most challenging aspect facing banks on this journey is then the organizational and leadership challenges of these transformations.

Innovating in a Traditional Bank—Why Is It so Difficult?

Any innovation inside of a traditional organization, such as a bank, is difficult. Banks tend to have risk-averse cultures, in part because they are heavily regulated and must protect customer deposits. What if the technology doesn't work? What if customers don't like it? What if internal personnel don't want to change? When the management of a traditional business feels threatened by an innovation, they may try to stymie it. The management's role is to protect the key profit engines that drive the bottom line. New technologies will more than likely be disruptive to critical parts of the bank's core business. After all, an innovation that is not at all threatening to an important business line is probably tangential to the bank and may not be worth taking up in the first place. So how should banks think about structuring whatever innovation activity they decide to pursue?

One prominent theory of organizational behavior suggests initially separating the innovative activity from the day-to-day operations of the business, creating an "ambidextrous" organization, in which each activity has a separate budget, personnel, processes, and metrics for success. This approach (such as we saw in Easter Labs) allows the traditional organization to continue to pursue the profit-generating activities that sustain the current success of the business and provides a protected environment for the innovators to take risks and explore new and disruptive paths.[11]

In addition to the need to create a separate structure, these efforts have little chance of success without the personal attention and active oversight of the top leadership—in particular, the CEO. Bob Rivers clearly showed his commitment, providing significant time, attention, and financial resources to Eastern Labs. Developing senior team buy-in is also critical and requires a narrative and logic about the identity of the company that is broad enough to encompass the innovation activity. In addition, incentives, culture, and metrics, particularly compensation and bonus plans, must be modified to support the new goals across the entire senior team.

The most challenging aspect of ambidexterity is that, after innovations have been incubated in a separate, protected environment, they need to be successfully integrated back into the organization. This is an easier process if the benefits of the innovation are a two-way street. Rather than something that is done "over there," there must be aspects of the innovation that create immediate value to the traditional organization. For example, in Eastern Bank, loan officers began to realize that the new automated loan process was creating a better experience for their customers. Both loan officers and small business owners could get an answer more quickly, and the underwriting was generally aligned with the bank's own standards, making the process more efficient for everyone.

The new process also allowed the team to outmaneuver competition, by making sure that every creditworthy borrower who walked in the door or logged onto their website had a good experience and received a loan from Eastern. Rather than being a threat to the employees in the core business, technology was an opportunity to enable their success. As a final benefit, the innovation activity changed the image of the bank, particularly externally. Even though they ended up losing the initial team of innovators in the spin out, the CFO of the bank noted that Eastern Labs increased their reputational capital within the entrepreneurial community, making it easier to recruit new talent. As he put it, "We certainly got a lot of publicity and cache out of it. When I'm recruiting prospective hires, I'm always surprised at how interested they are in Labs."[22]

Banking as a Service (BaaS)

There is a final strategic option for banks which is born from the evolution of embedded finance in non-bank platforms. Banking as a Service (BaaS) is a broad term describing the provision of banking services in non-bank environments. This is an exploding area as customer-focused platforms are embedding financial products into all kinds of activities, capturing the customer at the exact moment when they need the relevant service. The actual financial service is often outsourced to a bank who may take on risk or may just facilitate the activity. BaaS revenue has been estimated to grow from $1.7 billion in 2021 to over $17.2 billion in 2026.[12]

These estimates include the full array of fees available to all participants in the embedded finance product or value chain. For purposes of this section, we focus on the possibilities for banks as partners with the fintechs or other platforms who are engaged with the customer directly.[13] Dozens of banks have already made a decision to perform this role including Cross River, Green Dot, and Emigrant. Is this an advantageous path for other banks to follow? Clearly, many different arrangements are possible including ones that bring tremendous risk to the banking partner. But with the right abilities and the right partnerships, BaaS can bring future opportunity and growth. For example, bank partners who develop a strong ability to assess lending risk using new and existing data sources will be in demand by platforms who are engaging with small businesses and trying to develop credit products that meet their needs. Banks know how to operate as regulated entities and have the benefits of deposit guarantees. These advantages should be able to be monetized in partnerships of the future.

* * *

Many banks and banking organizations view the up-and-coming fintech revolution as an existential threat, and have organized, particularly in Washington, to thwart the new competition however possible. This attitude has some validity. Technology has changed customer expectations for speed and ease of use. New platforms like Toast, Shopify, and Square are integrated into the work streams of small businesses as trusted partners, and by using the available data and intelligence, they can offer loan products in a seamless way at exactly the moment the small business has needs. How will banks, large and small, compete in this new landscape?

In the face of these challenges, it is important to remember the strengths that the incumbent banking institutions hold. Banks have exclusive access to low-cost capital from deposits. They have loyal customers who already use other banking services and prefer to get their loans from their primary banking institution. They operate in a regulatory framework that despite its constraints allows them access to profitable Banking-as-a-Service market segments. With the increase in infrastructure products, banks have more access to plug and play technology options. If a bank leans into innovation and change, there is every reason to believe it can win against the new competitors. In particular, one can imagine community banking being revitalized as technology frees up the time of bankers from gathering paper documents and filling out excel spread sheets for the underwriting process, allowing a return of relationship banking and the advice and counsel about possible loans that business owners value so highly.

Part IV

The Role of Regulation

13

Regulatory Obstacles: Confusion, Omission, and Overlap

In the mid-1960s, banks began to realize that a relatively recent innovation—credit cards—could become the next big contributor to their bottom lines. The first card that was usable at multiple merchants, Diners Club, was issued in 1950. This spurred financial firms to work out how to make offering them profitable and attractive enough to be adopted *en masse* by consumers and merchants. Among other improvements, they developed cards that could be used at any merchant—not just restaurants—anywhere in the country and experimented with how to sign up more customers.[1]

By 1966, a group of Chicago banks thought they were ready to jump into the market with both feet. Just before that year's holiday season, these banks began to mail millions of unsolicited credit cards to Chicago residents, especially targeting affluent suburbanites. The effort turned out to be a disaster. The banks' mailing lists were full of errors. Cards were sent to children, pets, and dead people. And since the banks publicized their effort, criminals were enticed to steal the cards, which did not require customers to activate them, from mailboxes and post offices. Some merchants even conspired with thieves to put banks on the hook to pay for fraudulent charges. In all, the Chicago Debacle led to an estimated $6 million to $12 million in losses.[2]

The scandal also produced scrutiny from legislators and reformers who realized that the financial regulatory system had not been adapted to handle the new cards. Some called for credit cards to be banned, but lawmakers took a more measured approach. During the late 1960s and 1970s, Congress passed several major consumer protection laws that banned a variety of abusive and predatory practices, and empowered consumers to dispute billing errors. In 1978, a Supreme Court ruling allowed banks to set credit card

© The Author(s), under exclusive license to Springer Nature Switzerland AG 2024
K. G. Mills, *Fintech, Small Business & The American Dream*,
https://doi.org/10.1007/978-3-031-55612-8_13

interest rates based on the home state of the bank, rather than having to abide by different interest rate caps in each state, which made broad credit card issuance more attractive to banks. Updated banking rules and regulations better protected consumers while creating more regulatory certainty for banks. As a result, the groundwork was laid for credit cards to become nearly ubiquitous in America.

* * *

Financial innovation has brought new lenders and loan products to the small business market that are dramatically changing the small business lending landscape. However, fintech entrepreneurs and non-banks are operating under a legal and regulatory system that never anticipated their presence. New lending products are proliferating, often from entrants who are not overseen by the existing bank regulatory structure. Complex third-party arrangements are powering embedded finance which involve customer-facing applications layered on top of banks. Regulation has not yet caught up to the creative solutions that technology has begun to power in the marketplace.

Some argue that a hands-off approach to regulating the new products and services may result in more innovation. That view has merit, but it is also true that innovations are not inherently good; some players might maximize their own profits at the expense of borrowers or the financial system. Algorithms with unexpected biases and arrangements with inadequate data security and privacy can have dangerous unintended consequences. At the same time, heavy-handed regulation may provide more protections at the cost of a well-functioning market and the widespread development of affordable small business financial services.

The solution we need involves a balanced regulatory system that encourages innovation and helps small businesses find better financing options, while simultaneously identifying and stopping bad actors and unsafe arrangements. Unfortunately, the current financial regulatory system is flawed in ways that prevent the market from reaching this optimal state. New innovation is thriving, despite the burden of overlapping rules and requirements, but the complexity of the current system and the vagueness of how the rules apply to the new activities are likely to result in suboptimal products and risky processes. This chapter and the next take on the question of what work is needed to make the regulatory environment ready for the technology driven future of small business lending.

Fintech Oversight Falls Through the Cracks of the Fragmented Regulatory System

No one would design the current U.S. financial regulatory system if they were to start from scratch. The existing structure was cobbled together piecemeal over more than 150 years, with Congress often responding to financial crises by creating at least one new federal financial regulatory agency. For example, in 1863, Congress created the Office of the Comptroller of the Currency (OCC) to help finance the Civil War and address inconsistencies in banking regulations among the states. The legislation that created the Federal Reserve (Fed) grew from the Panic of 1907, while the Great Depression led Congress to establish the Federal Deposit Insurance Corporation (FDIC) to prevent runs on bank deposits and the Securities and Exchange Commission (SEC) to provide oversight of securities markets. The creation of the Office of Thrift Supervision (OTS) was a response to the savings and loan crisis of the 1980s.

Following the 2008 financial crisis, Congress eliminated the OTS, which had failed to adequately supervise several large financial firms that were at the heart of the crisis, including American International Group, Inc. (AIG), Countrywide, and Washington Mutual. However, through the Dodd-Frank Act of 2010, Congress also created three new entities: the Consumer Financial Protection Bureau (CFPB), the Office of Financial Research (OFR), and the Financial Stability Oversight Council (FSOC). The result is not a model of efficiency or effectiveness. The U.S. financial regulatory system is fragmented, featuring multiple agencies—both state and federal—with overlapping jurisdictions engaged at times in duplicative, and even conflicting, activities.

Banks, thrifts (also known as savings and loans), and credit unions can all take customer deposits, but they are governed by different rules, and each can be chartered at the state or federal level. Each state has different rules for the depository institutions that it charters, while four different agencies—the Fed, the FDIC, the OCC, and the National Credit Union Administration (NCUA)—oversee federally chartered depositories and also have some authority to oversee state-chartered depositories. Collectively, these agencies are sometimes called "prudential" regulators because their primary mission is to ensure the safety and soundness of the individual financial firms they oversee. Other financial regulatory agencies focus on oversight of certain activities rather than on individual firms. For example, the CFPB writes and enforces rules aimed at protecting consumers from predatory financial products. The SEC regulates securities activities with rules for trading, broker licensing, and transparency.

Few disagree that the financial regulatory structure is problematic. According to a recent report by the Government Accountability Office (GAO), the current regulatory structure, despite some strengths, "has created challenges to effective oversight. Fragmentation and overlap have created inefficiencies in regulatory processes, inconsistencies in how regulators oversee similar types of institutions, and differences in the levels of protection afforded to consumers. GAO has long reported on these effects in multiple areas of the regulatory system."[3] Figure 13.1 depicts the current U.S. regulatory structure which resembles a "spaghetti soup"—a tangle of interconnected entities, relationships, and rules.

The problems of fragmentation, overlap, and duplication never seem to get solved, but not for lack of ideas. Researchers from the Volcker Alliance catalogued no fewer than 45 legislative and official proposals to restructure the financial regulatory system between 1915 and 2013.[4] This does not include many of the proposals made by think tanks and other policymakers during the same period.

There are several reasons for the lack of reform. Opponents of reform have, over the years, argued that competition among regulatory agencies improves the overall quality of regulation and avoids overregulation, that reform will create uncertainty, or that the system works fine as it is. Regulators themselves

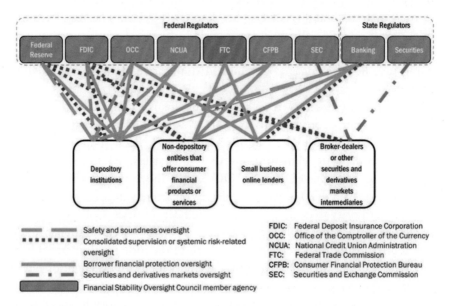

Figure 13.1 Small Business Online Lending Falls Through the Regulatory Cracks
Source: Adapted from GAO-16-175, "Financial Regulation: Complex and Fragmented Structure Could Be Streamlined to Improve Effectiveness," February 2016.

may lobby to protect their jurisdictional "turf," and so too might members of congressional committees who would lose oversight authority over an agency within their jurisdiction if it were merged into another. Financial firms may also resist change because reform could mean extra costs of adjusting to a new supervisor and new rules.

Recent innovations in financial services, particularly in lending, have challenged regulators because new fintech firms are different entities than banks and other traditional financial institutions. Fintechs are subject to some of the same rules as other financial firms, to the extent that their activities are similar. But some of the regulatory regimes either apply differently to fintechs or do not apply to them at all. In fact, in its current state, small business lending has, in several important ways, fallen through the cracks of the current regulatory system. We will look at several of these issues: first, there is no clear path for a non-bank to obtain a federal charter leaving many of the new entrants largely unsupervised. Second, due to the complexity of "third party rules," governance of multi-layered lending arrangements in embedded lending can be murky. Finally, and of even more concern, under the current regulatory structures, many of the protections consumers enjoy do not apply to small business borrowers.

Insufficient Federal Oversight of Non-bank Lenders

There are at least seven federal agencies—not to mention states, each of which conducts its own banking and securities oversight—that have some regulatory authority over the banks and credit unions that lend to small businesses. But despite some attempts, there is no comprehensive federal oversight of non-bank lenders.

The Federal Reserve (Fed). The Fed oversees state-chartered banks and thrifts that are members of the Federal Reserve System, foreign bank organizations operating in the United States, and all holding companies that include banks or thrifts. The Fed has additional duties, including promoting the stability of the financial system, promoting consumer protection, and fostering a safe and efficient payment and settlement system.[5] The Fed also has a mandate to understand and monitor market conditions, including the small business lending market.

The Federal Deposit Insurance Corporation (FDIC). The FDIC provides deposit insurance and is the primary federal regulator for state-chartered banks that are not members of the Federal Reserve System.[6]

The Office of the Comptroller of the Currency (OCC). As an independent bureau of the U.S. Department of the Treasury, the OCC oversees all national banks, federal thrifts, and federal branches and agencies of foreign banks.[7]

National Credit Union Administration (NCUA). The NCUA regulates and supervises federal credit unions and insures the deposits of all federal and most state credit unions.

The Federal Trade Commission (FTC). The FTC was created in 1913 to prevent unfair competition and business practices that affect commerce generally, including lending to consumers and small businesses. The FTC has enforcement authority over the Fair Credit Reporting Act (FCRA), which oversees consumer credit report disclosures.[8]

The Consumer Financial Protection Bureau (CFPB). In 2010 the Dodd-Frank Act, Congress created the CFPB and gave it the mission to monitor consumer financial markets, including activities such as student loans, retail mortgages, and consumer credit cards. The CFPB has jurisdiction over a wide range of financial products and activities to ensure that the marketplace works for both lenders and borrowers, but only it only governs consumer borrowers.[9]

The Securities and Exchange Commission (SEC). The SEC protects investors in public markets, including publicly traded small business loan securities. The agency also supervises securitization markets and new securities, such as funds that invest in small business loans.

Despite some of the gaps in direct authority, several federal agencies keep an eye on some fintech activities. Regional Federal Reserve banks include fintech questions in their coordinated credit surveys on small business lending. The SEC monitors the activities of online lenders that raise capital in securities markets, paying special attention to protecting investors in those markets and ensuring that appropriate disclosures are made. State-level regulators grant charters and licenses to fintechs in their states. Yet, to date, the federal regulatory system does not have a central mechanism to oversee non-bank small business lending.

Benefits of a Federal Charter Overseeing Non-bank Lenders

Many fintech small business lenders are governed by a patchwork of state-by-state oversight that makes compliance expensive, complicated, and time-consuming. Non-bank lenders essentially have two options: (1) lending directly to borrowers by acquiring licenses and being supervised in each state in which they operated, or (2) originating loans through a partnership with a national or state bank. Some entrants specifically designed their products so they did not qualify as loans, to avoid regulation and regulatory uncertainties. The tangle of multi-state oversight has raised compliance costs, especially for new and small firms, which might cause entrepreneurs eying the sector to wait until regulation becomes more certain, thus stifling innovation.[10]

State Banking Supervision

To their credit, state regulators recognized these issues, and the Conference of State Bank Supervisors (CSBS) began efforts to coordinate and align regulation across states. In 2018, they issued an ambitious plan to adopt an "integrated, 50-state licensing and supervisory system, leveraging technology and smart regulatory policy" by 2020.[11] Impressively, in 2020, the State Examination System (SES) was launched. By 2023, over 3,800 company examinations were performed, and 53 state agencies had implemented SES.[12] Further coordination of bank oversight like this at the state level would certainly be helpful.

OCC Charters

In 2016, the OCC announced that it would allow non-banks to apply for a special purpose federal bank charter. Under the category of "no good deed goes unpunished," this proposal was met with objections from multiple parties, including existing fintechs that had already gone through the pain of registering in every state and did not want to see new competitors find an easier path. Banks thought the charter would be "banking light" and disadvantage them. The state bank supervisors went so far as to file a complaint against the OCC proposal in U.S. District Court. In July 2018, the OCC went forward with a charter that would allow non-bank lenders to become special purpose national banks saying, "Companies that provide banking services in innovative ways deserve the opportunity to pursue that business on a national scale as a federally chartered, regulated bank."[13] Sadly, further progress has been halted in part by the banking lobby, and no institution has applied for or been approved under the OCC special purpose charter, so we remain without a mechanism for consistent federal oversight of non-bank competitors.[14]

Third-Party Regulation and Entity Coordination

There are also regulatory frictions facing banks that want to partner with fintechs to bring innovative lending options to their small business customers and some uncertainty about the rules governing multi-party arrangements in embedded lending. These partnerships fall under the category of "third-party arrangements" and historically have been subject to oversight from a number of entities.

In a sign of great progress, in 2023 the FDIC, the OCC, and the Department of Treasury jointly issued guidance for banks on how to manage risks that may arise from their relationships with third parties, such as fintechs, brokers, payments processors, and IT vendors.[15] This document replaced the previous regime of separate and sometimes contradictory guidelines issued by each of the three agencies.[16,17,18] The new guidance set out an eight-phase process for managing risk with third parties, including due diligence, contract negotiation, ongoing monitoring, documentation and reporting, and independent reviews.[19] These rules, and the ongoing work on Dodd-Frank Section 1033, have direct bearing on one of the most innovative parts of the evolving financial services space, the ability to share data between financial institutions to provide better products and services to customers, including small business customers seeing loans.

In the United States, Section 1033 is the home of activities that could provide the interconnectivity known in the United Kingdom and other countries as Open Banking. Section 1033 has not yet been finalized but the rules as drafted contain many critical elements, including the requirements for banks to share consumer data and a more specific delineation of the obligations of the third parties. There is only one glaring omission: Section 1033 refers only to consumer data and does not explicitly cover small businesses.

Given the amount of frictions and barriers we have described around information opacity for small businesses in the credit process, having access to the streams of data relevant to a business's prospects—including bank records, payment streams, and accounting records—all in one place seamlessly is critical to the important new lending products and services we have imagined. Small Business Utopia (described in Chapter 10) depends on this convergence of data in a safe and secure way. Without clear regulatory guidance it is hard to know whose responsibility it is if critical data is compromised. The small business could be greatly harmed if their financial information is stolen or misused. Clearly, the answer is to create a strong regulatory framework with explicit standards for secure data sharing and accountability for breaches. Without an expansion of Section 1033 to cover small businesses, the entire ecosystem will be without clear guidelines for information sharing and transfer, stifling the benefits from innovation and competition that we have described in this book.

The Current Regulatory System Is Not Well Designed to Identify and Thwart Bad Actors

Section 1033 is not the only place in the current regulatory system small business have been left out. Sadly, several other consumer protections put into place after the 2008 financial crisis are restricted to consumers, largely because small business owners have historically been viewed as sophisticated enough to fend for themselves in lending markets. This means that many rules, including those related to providing borrowers with standardized and understandable information about the terms of their loans (such as annual percentage rate—APR—and repayment terms), are not required for small business or other commercial loans.

Consumer Lending Protections Don't Apply to Small Businesses

In 2015, the Fed interviewed a group of "mom & pop" small businesses about lending options. The 44 participating businesses had between 2 and 20 employees and less than $2 million in annual revenues, representing a variety of industries and regions of the United States.[20] The owners were asked to compare several sample loan products, as shown in Figure 13.2.

They were then asked to answer the following question: "what is your 'best guess' of the interest rate on product A?" (Figure 13.3). The participants'

Figure 2	Product A	Product B	Product C
Amount borrowed	$40,000	$40,000	$40,000
Information you provide	Your sales history and bank account information, tax returns, etc. You send the information directly to the lender through mail or email.	You give permission to have your records pulled electronically for your sales history, bank accounts, inventory, and online reviews of your business.	Your bank account information, tax returns, and three years of financial statements. You send the information directly to the lender through mail or email. You pledge collateral to secure the loan.
Credit score	You need at least a 500 FICO	You need at least a 650 FICO	You need at least a 700 FICO
Waiting period for decision	3 to 5 days	2 hours	7 days
How soon funds arrive in your account	3 to 5 business days after you are approved	The same day you are approved	4 weeks
Repayment information provided	You owe $52,000. The company takes 10 percent of your debit/credit card sales receipts each day until it is paid off.	You owe the original $40,000 plus 28 cents for every dollar you borrow. The loan is paid off in one year.	You owe monthly payments of $3,440. Your effective APR is 6.0%. The loan is paid off in one year.

Figure 13.2   Loan Options Presented to Small Business Owners—2015
Cleveland Fed Focus Groups and borrower interviews
Source: Barbara J. Lipman and Ann Marie Wiersch, "Alternative Lending through the Eyes of 'Mom & Pop' Small-Business Owners: Findings from Online Focus Groups," Federal Reserve Bank of Cleveland, August 25, 2015.

answers were all over the map, ranging from 5% to over 50%. In reality, it is a trick question. The interest rate on Option A cannot be calculated with the information provided because the effective rate would vary depending on how long it took for the borrower to pay back the loan. But many small business owners in the focus groups had answers they perceived to be correct.

From 2015 to 2017, we presented this same exercise to several groups of students and alumni at Harvard Business School and got a similar range of answers. The truth is, even with a financially sophisticated audience, the costs related to a relatively simple small business loan can be difficult to understand and compare. The Fed conducted another set of focus groups in 2017, presenting small business owners with financing and loan descriptions similar to those on online lending sites. Again, they saw that small business owners found the descriptions of the loans confusing.[21]

Nearly all of the small business owners in the 2017 Fed focus groups said they wanted clear, easy-to-understand disclosures about all costs, payment policies, and potential penalties to help them make informed decisions and compare credit offerings. And why shouldn't they? Such disclosures are helpful in making decisions and are required for consumer, mortgage, and student loans, so why should the standard be different for small business loans?

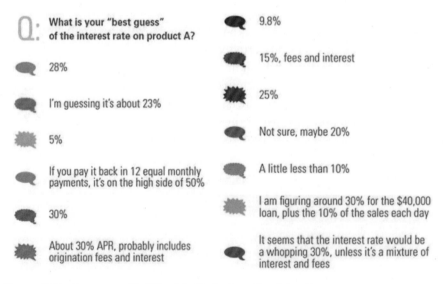

Figure 13.3 Borrowers Had Trouble Understanding Loan Terms
Small business owners' guesses of APR on product A
Source: Barbara J. Lipman and Ann Marie Wiersch, "Alternative Lending through the Eyes of 'Mom & Pop' Small-Business Owners: Findings from Online Focus Groups," Federal Reserve Bank of Cleveland, August 25, 2015.

Issues in Small Business Lending

Small businesses should be empowered not only to make better credit decisions, but also to protect themselves from predatory and otherwise unscrupulous lenders. Several problems emerged in the early online lending market, causing great concern among regulators, policymakers, consumer protection advocates, and responsible lenders. The most worrisome ongoing issues relate to high loan costs and terms that may not be fully disclosed and can make the loan difficult to sustain and repay. The APRs of some non-bank financing products can run well above 50% and can reach more than 100%.[22,23] Although lenders often argue that disclosing APRs does not paint the full picture—and for short-term credit they can be correct—some of these prices are high enough that one wonders how a small business can sustain the loan.

Borrowers may not even know they are paying high prices because such disclosures are not required. While some responsible lenders have chosen to provide extensive and transparent disclosures, others might include the information differently, or not at all. The result is that borrowers don't have access to clear metrics they can use to shop and compare loans across products and lenders, as they do with consumer loans or auto insurance.

Small business owners who borrow short-term credit that they fail to repay are often forced to roll over their debt into another loan, which piles additional fees onto the underlying loan. Rollovers can easily turn into a debt trap which ends up becoming difficult to escape.[24] One practice that creates this trap for the small business owner is known as "double dipping," in which a lender charges a borrower additional fee when their loan is renewed, before the term of the original outstanding loan is complete.

Policymakers Lack Data on Small Business Lending

One overarching issue facing regulators and small business advocates is that it is not clear how pervasive predatory activities and high costs are in the small business lending market. This is because there is no comprehensive data on real-time loan originations and pricing for small business lending. The sources now available—FDIC call report data on commercial and industrial (C&I) lending, Fed surveys, and private sources—are all rough proxies for small business lending. There is no systematic data collection on a host of important areas, such as loan applications and approvals, and the ability of different demographic groups to acquire credit. And there is no information on the costs of the loans. All of this makes it difficult to adequately assess, particularly in real time, the dynamics of the small business lending market, identify gaps and to develop sound policy to address worrisome issues.

Imagine being a member of Congress during the next recession, pandemic, or other crisis wondering how you should act on reports of small businesses shuttering their doors around the country and in your home state due to tight credit markets. It would be hard to respond effectively without good data. And yet, that is the position in which U.S. policymakers have long placed themselves.

A partial solution to this data collection issue was included in Section 1071 of the Dodd-Frank Act, which was passed in 2010. The provision requires the CFPB to gather and review certain data on small business lending. This includes collecting data on loan originations and on fair lending practices, with a particular goal of ensuring that women and minority-owned small businesses receive equitable access to credit. An initial statement from the CFPB indicated that it would act "expeditiously to develop such rules," but the Bureau focused first on its consumer regulations and fell behind.[25] It was not until 2017 that an official request for information was released to help formulate the rules, and then little additional progress was made for an additional five years.[26] Finally, in March 2023, thirteen years after the Dodd-Frank became law, the CFPB issued the rules regarding the detailed suite of small business lending data that needed to be reported and announced plans to begin collection. If people generally agree on the utility of this data, why was the regulation stalled for so long?

Section 1071 encountered strong resistance from many banks and others concerned about the increased cost burden of collecting the required data. They were also concerned that the information would be used after the fact to show bias in lending patterns that was unknown or unintended. In fact, in 2023 after the rule was made final, the Senate passed a bill to reverse it arguing that the costs and risks of compliance would cause lenders to turn away from small business lending and reduce availability of credit. The concerns about unintended consequences are understandable, but the repeal of Section 1071 would be a grave mistake. The answer cannot be to simply do nothing and allow policymakers and regulators to "fly blind" when it comes to small business lending. Compliance costs and oversight risks can be managed, and more granular information will undoubtedly improve the ability of both regulators and the market to meet the needs of small business borrowers.

* * *

There is something to be said for light-touch regulation, which can stimulate innovation and benefit borrowers as well as lenders. Early digital lenders, operating outside traditional banking regulations, experimented with more creative, automated underwriting techniques that allow them to make faster lending decisions. They extended credit to a broader range of borrowers than traditional lenders and made the credit application experience faster and accessible. These innovations spread though the marketplace and an entire landscape of competitors are experimenting with even more innovative lending arrangements. Yet, this activity is in many ways falling through the cracks of the current bank regulatory framework.

As the Chicago Debacle of 1966 illustrates, limited regulatory oversight has drawbacks. Responsible regulation needs to protect borrowers and investors, and mitigate systemic risk, while at the same time promoting innovation. It can be a tricky balance to strike, but it is a balance that is necessary to improve the state of small business lending. In Chapter 14, we suggest some principles for financial services reform that should guide the small business lending regulatory system of the future.

14

The Regulatory System of the Future

Fintech innovations will alter the financial system. In the small business lending segment, there will be new lenders and new products and services, many of which will use data in ways that have never before been contemplated. The ownership, security, and use—or misuse—of data and the governance of the related artificial intelligence systems will be defining issues in this coming era. Regulatory challenges will accelerate as technology becomes integral to more aspects of banking and payments. We cannot predict the future exactly, but we can be proactive and reform our financial regulatory system to better prepare for the kinds of changes that are coming.

We propose three core principles for how to approach reform and shape future governance. The first principle is to promote innovation by creating an environment that encourages new approaches and does not allow risk aversion to stifle the potential for exciting and valuable small business products and services to emerge from this fintech revolution. At the same time, there must be guiderails and protections, both for the borrowers and for the financial system as a whole. So the second principle is to protect small businesses, both from "bad actors" and also from risks stemming from the use of data and artificial intelligence. Third, the U.S. regulatory system needs to simplify and coordinate its efforts, so it can function more effectively and provide oversight to both new actors and to activities currently outside its scope and expertise. This reform is necessary to create an environment where U.S. financial service firms can continue to be world leaders.

© The Author(s), under exclusive license to Springer Nature
Switzerland AG 2024
K. G. Mills, *Fintech, Small Business & The American Dream*,
https://doi.org/10.1007/978-3-031-55612-8_14

Industry Efforts to Self-Regulate

As hundreds of new fintech players entered the market, many of the first movers in the industry were aware of problems emerging in online small business lending and took steps to self-regulate. The objective was to weed out the predatory lenders and avoid a "race to the bottom" characterized by low transparency and high pricing that could result in responsible players being shut out of the market. The industry also hoped to avoid more stringent government regulation through effective self-regulation.

One of these efforts, the Small Business Borrowers' Bill of Rights, was developed in 2015 and updated in 2017 by online lenders such as LendingClub and Fundera, and by non-industry stakeholders such as the Small Business Majority, and the Aspen Institute.[1] The Small Business Borrowers' Bill of Rights proposed six "fundamental financing rights" to which the signatories believed small business borrowers were entitled, including the right to transparent pricing and terms, non-abusive products, responsible underwriting, fair treatment from brokers, inclusive credit access, and fair collection practices.[2]

Despite widespread advances in the fintech landscape and the impact of a global pandemic, the Small Business Borrowers' Bill of Rights remains a worthy template. However, it is only a set of guidelines, not a detailed map for implementing regulation. Self-policing and voluntary disclosures alone will unfortunately be not enough since innovation requires clear rules, and principles, and best practices do not have the force of law. Another complicating factor is that the scope of issues that require oversight has grown as data science and artificial intelligence have become more sophisticated and integrated into novel lending solutions. Thus, there is a pressing challenge to policymakers to create a legal structure that works for industry, for small businesses, and for the integrity of the financial system.

Lessons from Other Countries

America is not the only nation facing these questions. Since fintech innovation is a global phenomenon, there are already lessons—good and bad—that U.S. policymakers can learn from the experiences of foreign regulators.

Positive Lessons from the United Kingdom

During the 2008-9 financial crisis, former U.K. Chancellor of the Exchequer, George Osborne, recalled being flooded with calls to help small businesses get access to credit.[3] The crisis and recession hit the United Kingdom's small and medium-sized enterprises (SMEs) hard. Osborne and then Prime Minister David Cameron soon realized that the government had few tools available to address SME lending and thereby help stabilize the economy. Unlike the United States, which had a network of more than 5,000 community banks, over 80% of U.K. SME lending was done by four large banks, and all four were in trouble.

The crisis triggered aggressive steps by the U.K. government to help SME lending recover. There are several lessons from that effort, which the United States could do well to learn. These fall into five categories: (1) the benefits of creating a central oversight agency with a mandate to protect the financial system and encourage competition; (2) the need to create mechanisms in the regulatory environment that encourage and support innovation; (3) the adoption of a systematic review of new rules that regulate new entities in order to make sure they are working properly; (4) the value of collecting data that allows policymakers to monitor the levels of and gaps in small business lending; and (5) the conclusion that markets will be more innovative and more secure if consumers and small businesses control their own data.

The Financial Conduct Authority

In 2013, the British government created a new agency, the Financial Conduct Authority (FCA), to supervise the business conduct of about 45,000 financial services firms to make sure that financial markets were "honest, competitive, and fair." It also became the prudential regulator for about 17,000 firms, charged with ensuring their safety and soundness.[4]

But unlike most regulators, the FCA was given a third strategic objective: to promote "effective competition in the interest of consumers." This competition mandate allowed the FCA to take on a proactive agenda around fintech and innovation, in a way few regulators had ever envisioned. The approach led to the creation of Project Innovate, a much-discussed program for innovative fintech firms to try out some of their business ideas before taking them to the broader market. Perhaps the most interesting aspect of this initiative was the Regulatory Sandbox, a place for businesses to "test innovative products, services, business models, and delivery mechanisms in a live environment without immediately incurring all the normal regulatory consequences of engaging in the activity in question."[5]

For example, say a start-up had a new algorithm that might better predict the creditworthiness of potential borrowers. Once the firm was in the sandbox, they received individualized regulatory guidance from the FCA staff, became eligible to receive waivers or modifications of existing FCA rules, and could apply for "no enforcement action" letters that limited disciplinary action if the firm dealt openly with the FCA.[6,7] All of these activities were designed to help start-ups test new ideas while simultaneously allowing the FCA to monitor industry developments. In the first year the sandbox was in operation, the FCA received 146 applications for its first two six-month cohorts and accepted 50 of those into the program.[8]

Since its inception, the FCA sandbox has overseen 170 new firms and in August 2021, the Regulatory Sandbox moved to an always open model, allowing firms to submit their applications throughout the year.[9] This initiative also spurred other nations to launch similar concepts: in September 2020, Australia developed the enhanced regulatory sandbox (ERS) exemption for fintech businesses testing innovative financial services. Canada, India, and Singapore also launched similar concepts.

By 2023, the FCA was an established regulator with oversight over the large and growing fintech lending entities and a leading role in U.K. Open Banking products and services. Along with a sister agency, the Prudential Regulation Authority (PRA) which was the prudential regulator of large lenders, the FCA took on the dual responsibilities of making sure that the financial services providers had solid capital structures and safe practices, while also keeping an eye on the competitiveness of the market and the availability of credit. For example, in March of 2023, when Silicon Valley Bank (SVB) failed, the FCA played a key role in arranging and approving the sale of its U.K. subsidiary to HSBC, a large U.K. lender over a critical weekend, creating a stable solution for SBV customers to access their deposits on Monday morning.

Routine Reviews of Regulatory Effectiveness

In 2010, in response to the financial crisis, Her Majesty's (HM) Treasury implemented a series of regulations that provided an oversight structure for fintechs involved in the U.K. peer-to-peer lending markets, which were growing rapidly. The regulations were enacted quickly, in less than nine months. Because the markets were new, HM Treasury officials built in an additional provision—the entire set of rules would be reviewed in one to two years to be sure they were working. This idea of quickly implementing, then reviewing and adapting legislation, is absent from U.S. lawmaking and may be hard to effect, but the concept would be useful as fintech regulation needs to evolve in response to new innovations as they reach the marketplace.

Mandated Industry Data Collection

The United Kingdom also took aggressive actions post the 2008-9 crisis on the data collection front. The newly created British Business Bank (BBB) became responsible for gathering quarterly data from banks and online lenders on loan originations and loan stocks, including metrics on costs and defaults, to better track the availability of credit and the progress of market reforms. The BBB focused particularly on the SME lending market and on the fintech marketplace in general. Further, banks were required to share commercial loan data in confidential formats with regulators and policy-makers and make this information available to competitors via credit agencies to improve credit assessments and oversight of potential discrimination. The result of this effort was that U.K. policymakers had accurate measures of small business lending which they were able to use during the Covid-19 pandemic to assess the needs of the small business segment and impact policymaking.

Data Ownership—PSD2 and Open Banking

In 2018, a landmark set of regulations governing financial data took effect in Europe. The Revised Payments Services Directive (PSD2) upended the status quo in the financial system by giving customers explicit ownership of their financial data and requiring banks to share this data with third-party service providers through APIs at a customer's request.[10] PSD2 leveled the playing field between banks and fintechs since incumbent firms were not allowed to monopolize customer data. The United Kingdom implemented its own version of PSD2, called Open Banking, which, in addition to requiring that banks share data with third-party providers, required banks to provide that data in a standardized format.[11]

Over the next five years, the U.K. took an independent path in developing its own standards for Open Banking. Under the oversight of the FCA, data exchange rules and safeguards were developed so that customers could permission the sharing of their data. Banks resisted many of these efforts due to concerns that they would lose customers who would switch to new providers. Interestingly, that has not proven to be the case. Bank relationships are surprisingly sticky. Of the 76 million current accounts in the U.K. less than 12% have switched since the launch of these options in 2013, though many have opened second accounts.[12]

The largest impact to date of Open Banking infrastructure has been in the area of payments—not lending. Currently, the Open Banking connections allow a customer to connect their accounts seamlessly. This means payments can be made directly to trusted third parties in seconds without the delays and costs of wire transfers or exchanges. Though not transformative for lending, this ease of rapid payment reduces frictions and expenses in financial services and has massive customer appeal. In addition, Open Finance is very much on the horizon with discussion of extending the networks to public utilities, investment managers, and pension providers.

Although the long-term shape of Open Banking in the U.K. has yet to fully be determined, its progress is a helpful guide for U.S. policymakers. Having small businesses own their financial data and be the decision makers about who gets access to it, changes the competitive dynamics of the market. Under an Open Banking framework, providers have an equal opportunity to gain access to critical customer information and create novel small business products and applications, particularly in lending. Getting this regulation right will make markets more innovative in ways that substantially benefit customers like small business owners.

Cautionary Tales from China

The regulation of alternative lending in China started out with a light-touch approach, with the benefits and consequences one might expect. In China, peer-to-peer lending had a long history, with people lending directly to friends and relatives, and indirectly through rotating credit and savings associations.[13] Online lenders built on this tradition and flourished, with rapid growth in the number of platforms. The Chinese government encouraged innovation in the sector starting in 2013.[14] By 2015, peer-to-peer trading volume in China was four times what it was in the United States.[15] Online lending proved particularly appealing to Chinese small businesses, which had long found it difficult to secure financing from traditional banks that were often at least partially controlled by the state. In 2015, an average of three new lending platforms came online each day, and the volume of loans grew by hundreds of percent annually.

Despite the fact that the Chinese financial regulatory system had been known to be heavy-handed and conservative in general, oversight of peer-to-peer lending was almost nonexistent until 2016. With no formal disclosure guidelines from national regulators, problems arose. As the number of online platforms mushroomed, so did the share that had been investigated by the police and those where the owners had walked away with investor funds or where loan repayments had ceased (Figure 14.1). The 2016 Blue Book of Internet Finance backed up this assessment, finding that more than one-third of Chinese platforms either had cases of fraud, or had gone or were going out of business.[16]

In December 2015, authorities shut down Ezubao, an online peer-to-peer broker that was found to be a giant Ponzi scheme that collapsed after taking in about $9 billion from more than 900,000 investors.[17] Ezubao had promised some investors returns of nearly 15% per year, much higher than banks were offering. But one senior manager at the firm later said that "95 percent of investment projects on Ezubao were fake." Near the end, police had to resort to digging up 80 travel bags full of financial documents buried 20 feet underground by company officials.[18] Ezubao helped spark a government crackdown on numerous problems in China's peer-to-peer lending market.

In 2016, the Chinese government announced a series of new guidelines and rules. They defined online lending, banned platforms from engaging in certain activities such as pooling lender funds, required that platforms use a qualified bank as a fund custodian, and set 65 mandatory and 31 encouraged disclosures.[19]

However, by 2019 it became impossible to oversee the widely dispersed peer-to-peer lending activity, and regulators essentially shut down the sector

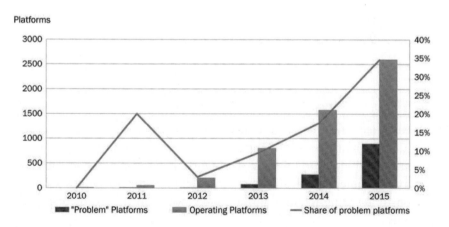

Figure 14.1 Number of Online Chinese Peer-to-Peer Platforms and Share of "Problem" Platforms
Source: Martin Chorzempa, "P2P Series Part 1: Peering Into China's Growing Peer-to-Peer Lending Market," Peterson Institute for International Economics, June 27, 2016.

(to the dismay of investors).[20] The market shifted to a small number of large platform companies that had entered the small business lending space. In 2018, Ant Group, the parent company for Alipay and an affiliate of e-commerce giant Alibaba, cemented itself as the largest fintech firm in the world by establishing a $150 billion valuation.[21] Ant and Alipay became "the modern gateway to an ecosystem of financial services," not only dominating the mobile wallet and payments space, but also providing wealth management, insurance, credit scores, and consumer lending services.[22]

This growth did not go unnoticed by the Chinese authorities, who took steps to limit Ant Group's ambitions, such as curtailing its effort to create a national credit scoring system. In 2021, Ant Group was about to complete the world's largest initial public offering (IPO), but the operation was stopped at the last minute by the Chinese authorities, and in 2023, Ant Group's dynamic founder Jack Ma shared that he would remove himself completely from the company.[23]

The rise of dominant players in China's fintech market proved to be a positive development for small businesses, giving them access to state-of-the-art digital banking options. The new credit models used transaction data to give loans quickly and effectively, a process which state-owned banks had been unable to develop.[24] Yet, their success posed a new problem for China's regulators who were concerned about large platforms using their market power to the detriment of borrowers (and as important national actors). Interestingly, U.S. regulators share some similar concerns about platform companies such as the Big Tech players and their monopoly power, though these companies are still far from becoming a powerful force in financial markets in the United States.

* * *

U.S. regulators can learn from the experiences of both China and the United Kingdom as they develop financial regulatory systems that include the new fintech innovators. China's initial experience showed the dangers of too little oversight, though the open competition did spur vibrant technical innovation and high early market acceptance. Later regulatory activity shows a government intent on creating a safer marketplace for consumers and a high aversion to anything resembling monopoly power in the hands of Big Tech companies.[25,26]

The U.K. model provides useful guideposts, as the government and regulatory activities have been robust yet measured, straightforward yet comprehensive, and have produced real successes. The U.K. example demonstrates an effective balance of encouraging innovation and risk-taking with oversight and data collection. Even with the rigidity and polarization of American politics around regulatory reform, the U.S. regulators can draw useful lessons from the U.K. work on encouraging innovation while maintaining a safe and sound system, and from their ongoing work on Open Banking and Open Finance.

Principles for U.S. Financial Reform

For the good of America's small businesses, we must move on from the polarized view that any new financial regulation is bad for the banking industry and its consumers, as well as the opposing view that financial firms are untrustworthy, and must have ever-more rules piled upon them. In their 2003 book, *Saving Capitalism from the Capitalists*, Raghuram Rajan, and Luigi Zingales make the argument that protecting free markets requires government intervention.[27] But that too much government regulation of finance can benefit incumbents and insiders rather than encourage dynamic markets and benefit consumers and investors. The question is not "should there be more or less regulation", but "what kind of regulation does the current ecosystem require"?

Innovation has made its way into financial services, and the changes technology will bring to products and markets will continue. The more pervasive use of data and artificial intelligence is already impacting lending markets dramatically. The Basel Committee on Banking Supervision summarized the moment: "fintech has the potential to lower barriers of entry to the financial services market and elevate the role of data as a key commodity and drive the emergence of new business models. As a result, the scope and nature of banks' risks and activities are rapidly changing and rules governing them may need to evolve as well. These developments may indeed prove to be more disruptive than previous changes in the banking industry."[28] Change is coming, and our regulatory system is not yet prepared to meet these challenges.

Remaking the U.S. financial regulatory system will be difficult, but we need an active agenda to meet the new challenges, and create a new set of balanced, sensible rules that operate in a transparent environment. For small business lending, three broad principles must guide the effort for financial regulatory reform: (1) supporting innovation; (2) enhancing protections for small business borrowers while ensuring the safety of the financial system; and (3) streamlining the regulatory environment so it can take on oversight of the new and complex technologies and partnership arrangements that will be part of the financial system of the future.

Principle 1: Promote Innovation

Allowing small businesses to have a wider variety of financing choices will benefit lenders, small businesses, and the entire economy. There are several ways that the regulatory system can help to achieve this goal.

Engage with Innovators

An important lesson from the U.K.'s fintech innovation journey is the productive engagement of government with business and fintech innovators in a series of policymaking councils. In 2020, the U.K. government commissioned a wide review of the fintech environment, led by a respected private sector actor, Ron Kalifa. Formerly an entrepreneur who built Worldpay, a global payments company, Kalifa brought a pragmatic view to the fintech regulatory landscape, developing a roadmap for regulation and policy. The government backed, but private sector led, Center for Finance, Innovation, and Technology was formed at the recommendation of the Kalifa Report and now sits at the center of policy formation and discussion for Open Banking and fintech regulation.[29] Such a respected entity does not exist in the U.S. regulatory landscape. As a result, the banking lobby and fintech entrepreneurs vie for attention of Congress, leading to policy inputs that are less rigorous and fact-based than would be optimal.

Data Ownership, Privacy, and Transparency

Data is a key ingredient of many of the new innovations that will transform small business lending. This leads to a series of challenging questions for financial services regulators since data security and privacy issues are especially acute when it comes to sensitive financial data. The lending solutions of the future involve multiple parties such as customer-facing platforms, middleware analytics companies, and banks, with data flowing in real time between the parties. Clear rules around data ownership and responsibility are critical foundations for these new arrangements to flourish.

U.S. regulators watched European experience closely, as they crafted the proposed rules for Dodd-Frank Section 1033. As we mentioned in Chapter 13, the rule gives ownership of financial data to consumers and allows them to permission the transfer of that data to authorized third-party entities through secure channels. This guidance and the unified principles governing third-party relationships and risk management (also discussed in

Chapter 13) are major steps forward in creating a clear regulatory structure for the U.S. banking and fintech community. One critical issue remains: explicitly expanding the rules of Section 1033 to include small businesses.

Principle 2: Look Out for Small Businesses

The absence of small business in Section 1033 is a vivid example of the way small business is overlooked in the current regulatory environment. Several regulations need to be adjusted to make sure that small businesses have greater protections, particularly as new innovative products and services emerge in the market.

Require Appropriate Disclosures in Small Business Lending

If a person applies for a loan to buy a pickup truck for themselves, they are protected by numerous consumer laws and regulations, including standardized price and term disclosures. But if that same person applies for a loan to buy a pickup truck to expand their small lawn care business, many of those same protections do not apply. Given that small business borrowers are often hard to distinguish from consumer borrowers, this dichotomy makes little sense. And, at a more fundamental level, all borrowers should be able to easily understand and compare their credit options.

A 2007 Federal Trade Commission (FTC) study found that disclosures that enabled cross-comparisons dramatically increased borrowers' ability to understand mortgage options.[30] Loan disclosures already exist for consumers in formats that work, so lenders can begin by using these as examples in their small business documentation.[31] As we have seen, small business owners want to be aware of the cost, fees, and terms of loans in order to make good credit decisions. Simply extending the Truth in Lending Act (TILA) provisions to small businesses might be the easiest solution.[32] However, given that consumer and small business loan products may have increasingly different characteristics, a more tailored set of protections may be required.

Collect Small Business Lending Data

A critical gap for policymakers has been the absence of high-quality data available on small business lending. Fortunately, this data is being collected under Dodd-Frank Section 1071 first for the largest banks and then, over several years, for smaller banks. Of key interest is the basic data on loan originations which can be used to identify market gaps and the impact of policy on closing those gaps. The Small Business Administration data has for some time reflected the fact that more good loans to women and minority-owned businesses can be made than the market is currently supporting. Getting additional capital into the hands of creditworthy small business owners that are currently underserved will create more opportunity and more economic growth.

Regulating complex financial markets is a demanding job. A lack of good data about the transactions in those markets has historically made it difficult to identify and stop bad actors, and design good small business protections. Information on small business loan originations from Section 1071 will illuminate pricing and risk in lending markets, which will be particularly important as new digital lending options proliferate.

Protect Small Businesses from Discrimination

With the influx of large amounts of data in the underwriting process comes new responsibilities. As lenders increasingly rely on personal information and transaction data as part of their underwriting algorithms, it will be imperative to design oversight to avoid adverse discriminatory effects. Our story in Chapter 10 about predicting a driver's accidents based on whether or not they buy frozen pizza may have seemed like an innocuous example. But, it foreshadows real dangers about how artificial intelligence will be used and its potential to marginalize certain populations. These are not imaginary concerns—troubling examples of bias in applied artificial intelligence have already emerged and financial services will not be far behind.

The federal government has recognized the need to regulate algorithmic bias. In October 2023 the White House issued an executive order on AI oversight that put the United States in a leadership position on global AI regulation.[33] The order calls for work ranging from identifying deep fakes to disclosure of training data for highly sensitive algorithms, particularly those with national security implications.[34] This follows a joint statement in April 2023 by four federal agencies (The Civil Rights Division of the United States Department of Justice, the Consumer Financial Protection Bureau, the Federal Trade Commission, and the U.S. Equal Employment Opportunity Commission) highlighting the risk of algorithmic bias in lending, as algorithms trained on historical data can reproduce past discrimination.[35] These are positive efforts, but just reflect early steps and fall short of the congressional legislation and full rulemaking that will be required.

Building a smart oversight environment in a financial services world driven by big data will be complicated. Financial firms that use artificial intelligence (AI) or other algorithms to guide how they lend to customers will likely need to share some information about the inner workings of their models with regulatory agencies. Regulators will need the expertise to assess these complex activities and gather data to see if discriminatory outcomes are occurring. A priority for financial regulators should be to develop transparent and secure communication with lenders about the algorithms and machine learning tools they are using, and the outcomes from those algorithms on protected classes.

A final challenge is developing ways to communicate the output of these complicated models to customers. Regulations under both the Equal Credit Opportunity Act (ECOA) and the Fair Credit Reporting Act (FCRA) require that lenders need to be able to explain their decisions to borrowers in a useful way. (Note that only ECOA covers small businesses while FCRA is restricted to consumers.) Recent guidance from the CFPB suggests that if the underwriting rule cannot cite an actual understandable rule, the lender should not use that tool. Given advances in machine learning, and the complexity of models, this may prove challenging, causing lenders to have to trade-off predictiveness for explainability.

However, it could be that AI itself could help. One creative solution might be to ask AI to analyze the underwriting model and provide the explanation to the customer for any denial. The customer could then ask the AI for suggestions about how to improve their chances for getting an approval the next time. Another idea is to use adversarial AI to check for algorithmic bias. For example, one model could be programmed to optimize for risk and another to assure that there is no bias, and have them compare the results.[36] The possibilities are wide-ranging, but the overall objective is to protect small businesses with appropriate disclosure and transparency.

Principle 3: Streamline the Financial Regulatory System

The often-conflicting authorities of individual regulatory agencies make compliance needlessly difficult for industry participants. Even before fintechs came into the picture, many small banks expressed frustration and anxiety about conflicting directives received from different agencies about the same loan. In addition, each agency has its own examination process, which results in duplicative requests for information, and other inefficiencies.

Numerous proposals have been made over the years to reduce the fragmentation and overlap in the U.S. financial regulatory system. A 2014 Bipartisan

Policy Center report recommended creating a consolidated task force made up of examiners from the OCC, the Fed, and the FDIC, who would jointly conduct their bank examinations. The relevant state bank regulatory agency would also have the option of joining the task force. The task force would submit a single set of questions to the entity being examined and publish a joint examination report that would be immediately available to each of the agencies involved.[37]

Coordination would make U.S. financial regulation both more effective and more efficient. Fintech and the dramatic changes in technology provide an opportunity, and in fact, an imperative, to streamline the system. The new technologies and complex partnership arrangements cannot be overseen effectively in a piecemeal fashion.

A 2022 Treasury Report to the White House Competition Council focused on the opportunities and challenges of a world where both fintechs and banks participate and partner. After making the case for the benefits of new digital financial products, they presented recommendations for improving the regulatory environment, many of which have been covered in this chapter.[38] Rules regarding data sharing and the interagency coordination of third-party guidance all get a mention. And there is a commendable discussion of improving the availability of small-dollar loans. However, the report has one great flaw; it focuses exclusively on consumer financial products and does not cover the particular needs of small businesses or even mention the small business lending market.[39] Small business deserve a regulatory framework that is built to meet their unique challenges and provide them and their marketplaces appropriate protections.

Develop Broad Principles Instead of Restrictive Rules

No matter how well developed a policy or law is, the world does not stand still. Good policymakers recognize the need to consistently adapt to changing circumstances with new approaches and regulations. This is especially important when technology is changing as quickly as it is today.

One good way to ensure adaptability is, when possible, to rely on broad principles of conduct, rather than restrictive rules, for regulation. One such principle would be to supervise like activity in like ways. This would mean that an entity making a small business loan would fall under the same guidelines for disclosure or conduct of its business, whether it is a bank or a non-bank lender. Basic tenets like those embodied in the Small Business Borrowers' Bill of Rights could be important foundational principles for more specific legislative or regulatory actions.[40] Another overarching principle might be around transparency, including promoting clear product disclosure in ways that customers can understand and compare, and allowing customers to see inside opaque decisioning tools like algorithms as much as possible. A principles-based approach would also provide more consistency—and avoid conflicting or confusing guidance as different agencies make their own rules around data ownership and privacy.

Use Innovation to Improve Regulation

Innovation is also important in regulatory compliance, where the use of regulatory technology, or "regtech," is growing. Regtech applications help in several ways. Firms can increasingly use technology to ensure that they are complying with rules and other requirements. For example, algorithms can be trained to look for bias and disparate impact. Regulators can use innovation to find more effective and less costly ways to audit compliance, find anomalies, and identify potential bad actors for further review. Some countries, including the United States, have even used regulatory sandboxes, and "sprints" and "hackathons," to solve specific compliance problems. In general, more data, more transparency, and more streamlining of activities are good watchwords in order for both regulators and policymakers to make continuous improvement in regulatory processes and outcomes.

* * *

Getting regulation right is difficult, as it requires balancing appropriate oversight with promoting innovation. Too little oversight could lead to the emergence of bad actors or another financial crisis, while too much regulation could stifle new products and innovations that would make life easier for small businesses.

Unfortunately, while other countries proactively sought out solutions to this dilemma, the United States fell behind and is still working to make up lost ground. But it is not too late for regulators to step up to the task. Indeed, how regulators respond to the challenges before them will determine how well the United States takes advantage of the enormous opportunity to lead in financial technology and innovation—and to help the nation's small businesses.

Part V

Conclusion

15

The Future of Fintech and the American Dream

Small businesses have been around since the time of early civilizations, and lending to small businesses is almost that old. In researching this book, we set out to find the earliest known small business loan. We found that the roots of traditional lending can be traced back to 3,000-year-old written loan contracts from Mesopotamia, which show the development of a credit system and include the concept of interest.

These ancient records include a loan to one Dumuzi-gamil, a bread distributor in the Mesopotamian city of Ur. He and his partner borrowed 500 grams of silver from the businessman Shumi-abum, who appeared to be acting as a banker. Dumuzi-gamil became a prominent bread distributor within the region by operating institutional bakeries that supplied the temple. In fact, one tablet describes him as the "grain supplier to the King." This early businessman paid an annual rate of 3.78%. Some of his colleagues were not as lucky. Other loans of silver to fisherman and farmers were documented at rates as high as 20% interest for a single month.[1]

Even 3,000 years ago, the structure of commercial activities required capital that the merchant could use to fund the business, and the owner of the capital required a return for the use of those resources. Remarkably, this initial contractual relationship still forms the foundation for the arrangements between small businesses and their lenders.

Small business lending has been so consistent over time because the basic math of small business operations has remained constant. A business sells a good or service for some margin over the cost of providing the product. Even in a high-margin business, the profits from each transaction are a small percentage of the sale. This makes it hard to accumulate the large amounts of

K. G. Mills, *Fintech, Small Business & The American Dream*,
https://doi.org/10.1007/978-3-031-55612-8_15

capital that investments in land, buildings, equipment, or even animals can require.

Enter the small business lender, and the resulting arrangements of loan contracts, interest, and repayment over time. Over the centuries, many facets of these arrangements have evolved, with the establishment of money, banks, and traditional loan products such as term loans and lines of credit. But at their core, the needs of small businesses for capital have not changed.

The modern market for small business capital has operated adequately, though not optimally. Large and small banks in the United States provided various loan products and relationship activities designed to address the needs of small businesses for working capital and expansion investments. For most of the twentieth century, small business lending saw little innovation and only incrementally used technology to automate existing processes. The customer experience was slow and paper-intensive, but the market felt little pressure to change.

That is no longer true. The financial crisis of 2008–2009 and the entrance of new fintech competitors galvanized a new cycle of innovation in small business lending. Frozen credit markets highlighted the importance of small business lending to the economy and the slow recovery exacerbated credit gaps that the market was not inclined to fill. Entrepreneurs demonstrated that technology could fill those gaps by eliminating the built-in frictions in the traditional processes, and a new era of innovation was born.

In 2020, the Covid-19 Pandemic and the resulting lockdownsreiterated the importance of small businesses to our economy and to the fabric of our daily lives. The bias of banks as they distributed the first round of the government aid, the Paycheck Protection Program (PPP), mainly to their customers and larger businesses revealed the barriers that smaller and underserved business owners faced from traditional lenders. When fintechs were authorized to participate, they quickly created automated applications that allowed the smallest businesses and many minority-owned businesses to access the next rounds of funding. This was a transformative moment as it became clear that even the smallest businesses would embrace technology if it delivered the capital they needed in a customer-friendly manner.

Reflecting on the new era of technology-driven solutions, we ask a final set of questions: What will the small business lending environment of the future look like? Will credit be more widely available? Will the new environment allow more small businesses to succeed? Given the fundamentals of small business needs and the changes in the lending markets we have explored, what exactly will be different in the future—and what will stay the same?

Truths of Small Business Lending

Change is flourishing in small business lending because the innovators are finding new ways to address some of the fundamental barriers in the marketplace. Many of these obstacles have been there for a long time and have been hard to ameliorate. They have been so constant that we call them the "truths" of small business lending.

The first truth is that not all businesses succeed. In fact, small businesses fail at an alarming rate. Over 45% of businesses started in the United States failed before they reached the fifth year.[2] Providing a loan to most of these businesses would not have been a good idea because they failed for some reason other than lack of credit. Often, their product or idea was something that customers did not want, or something that they could not deliver profitably.

Even in robust economic times, when credit is relatively easy to obtain, an estimated 40% of loan applications don't get all the funding they request.[3] If an unqualified business were to get a loan and fail, that loan would turn into an additional burden the owner would be desperately trying to pay off. Thus, the goal is not to get loans to every small business, but only to those who are creditworthy, meaning that they will be able to effectively use the capital to help themselves succeed. A related objective is to pair each creditworthy owner with a loan that fits their business: one that is the right amount, duration, and cost, with terms that the borrower can successfully handle and repay.

The second truth is that it is difficult to know who is creditworthy. Many small business owners do not understand their cash flows well and, as a result, can suffer unexpected cash shortages. Businesses sometimes need cash to bridge a slow period, and sometimes they need funds because they are doing better than expected. One of the least understood realities is that growth usually requires cash to fund increases in working capital or fixed assets. Thus, a fast-growing business can run out of cash, and even fail, if it does not plan ahead for a way to access the credit it will need.

Lenders have a hard time determining whether a small business owner is creditworthy for two reasons that we have discussed earlier. The first is their information opacity. It is hard to know if a small business is profitable, especially given that they often don't know themselves. The second issue is their heterogeneity, the fact that all small businesses are different. Because of this heterogeneity, it is hard to generate that "truth file"—the formula that can automatically give a credit approval to a loan applicant. In traditional small business lending, a banker might spend weeks with a small business, understanding their operations, only to ask at the end for a personal guarantee. A corollary to the second truth is that bankers seek collateral whenever possible, especially when the prospects of a business are opaque.

These two truths are the foundations for the story we have told in this book. Despite the importance of small business to the economy, lending to small businesses hasn't changed much because this lending is risky, and the information issues, along with the complexity of the world of small business, make the loan process costly and difficult to automate. Bankers have compensated by viewing the business as an extension of the business owner and making personal guarantees the standard for anyone but the most creditworthy.

These long-standing frictions in the small business lending market have been the most difficult for newer or smaller businesses, because these businesses are the hardest to understand, have the least collateral, and are the most likely to fail. But most of the 33 million U.S. small businesses are indeed small and, if they seek capital, are likely to want small loans. Many do not have banking relationships and are underserved by traditional lenders. The result is gaps and inefficiencies in the marketplace, and creditworthy borrowers who are either rejected or discouraged from getting the capital they need.

The Future of Small Business Lending

Technology that is available today has the power to create information and intelligence to which small business owners and their lenders have never before had access. This will improve the small business lending market in fundamental ways.

What Will Change in the Future?

Let's imagine a future state in which lenders and borrowers have much better and more transparent information, and there is an active and fluid market matching supply and demand for loans. What would be the benefits of a more perfect market for small business lending?

Reduced Gaps

In a market with perfect information, there would be no gap in access to credit for any borrower who met the credit criteria. The result: more creditworthy businesses would be funded, particularly those seeking small-dollar loans. When Square Capital reached a broad market with an average loan size of $6,000, many business owners could finally buy the piece of equipment they needed to operate. The lower costs of automated risk assessment and transactions allowed even very small loans to be made profitably.

In the United States, no one knows the size of the gap in access to credit or what the improvement would look like if technology made markets work optimally. However, one estimate based on the size of Small Business Administration (SBA) lending is that the gap of creditworthy borrowers who do not get funded is approximately 5% of those seeking capital. If that gap were closed by innovations contemplated in this book, prospects could be transformed for over 500,000 small businesses .[4]

Lower Search Costs

The perfect small business lending market will clearly offer a better customer experience. Applications exist today that are short and easy to fill out or even filled out already by automation that has access to the relevant data. Small businesses that used to spend 25 hours on an application can now have a digital experience and a near immediate response. Sometimes there is no application at all. A business owner might receive an embedded offer that is preapproved, before they even decide to seek capital. Small businesses that have been deterred by the time commitment and length of the process will find lending of the future to be more open, transparent, and usable. This should bring more borrowers into the process and improve their ability to get matched with a loan if they meet the lending criteria.

Transparency and Choice

Comparison shopping with full transparency and choice needs to be part of the future small business loan market, and the technology exists to make it so. In the optimum marketplace, borrowers will be able to understand the costs, benefits, and risks of loan options, and be able to compare those options on an apples-to-apples basis. We have already seen this story play out in the personal credit card space. In the 1990s, almost all credit card offers came to consumers in the mail or could be found at bank branches. Then, in the early 2000s, banks began offering products online, which allowed consumers to shop and compare from the comfort of their own homes. Now, shopping sites like NerdWallet and LendingTree are providing aggregation services that enable consumers to compare prices and other offerings online. Consumers have complete information written in plain English about all available products, pricing, and approval odds in a central location.

Although small business loan products are more complicated, comparison marketplaces such as Lendio already exist, and one can imagine an improved environment where a potential borrower could get lenders to bid on particular loan they are looking to take on. The question facing credit providers in this new environment will be, as one investor puts it, "Would a rational consumer armed with perfect information choose your product?".[5]

Risk-Based Pricing

In a perfectly functioning market, every small business that wanted a loan could get one—if three conditions were true:

1. Business owners were sophisticated and well-informed enough to understand the full costs of the loan, both the monetary costs and the "life" costs. That would mean borrowers were able to rationally assess the consequences of failure, as well as success for themselves and their families.
2. Lenders were incentivized both economically and by regulation to create full disclosure about all loan fees and costs.[6]
3. Lenders were able to perfectly match the price of credit with the risk of the credit offered.

If these three principles were operating, then theoretically, the market would match the risk of each loan with a price. If the borrower was willing to pay that price, the loan would be made. It would be the personal choice and responsibility of each small business owner to decide if the cost was too high.

But risk-based pricing and a free market solution for small business lending come with several concerns. Behavioral economists have demonstrated that humans are wired to downplay long-term negative consequences and overemphasize short-term wins. Entrepreneurs and small business owners are even more likely than most to have an optimistic view of the potential future outcomes. If small business owners were not generally optimistic, far fewer would take the risk of starting a business in the first place. Will these entrepreneurs be able to rationally assess the future risks of loan defaults, or will they just take the money and believe it will all work out well?

The high costs of some loans in the fintech market raise another question: What level of pricing are we willing to tolerate in the market? Should there be caps, or should we allow the levels to be set by the market and let borrowers use their own judgment in taking on loans? Although there are sharp disagreements on these questions, logic says that at some point, the costs will simply be too much for the small business owner to ever repay.

The risk of debt traps has long been recognized by usury laws and more recent efforts to regulate payday lenders. Yet, some argue that a fast short-term cash option can be a necessary lifeline for a business, even if it is costly. My view is that leaning on the side of a cap on rates, and living with the market inefficiencies, is perhaps a better solution than allowing too many small businesses to fall prey to overly optimistic forecasts and end up losing their businesses and maybe more. An interest rate cap or limit is particularly appropriate in an environment without full transparency of loan terms and small business borrower protections.

Small Business Utopia

The future of small business lending is enabled by the transformative technologies of big data, APIs, and artificial intelligence coming together in a way that is relevant to small business owners. We have called this future state, "Small Business Utopia." In the first edition of this book, it felt like Small Business Utopia might be right around the corner. The technology to build a cash forecasting dashboard already existed, and the assumption was that small business owners and lenders would immediately seek out the information, find it valuable, and put it to use. However, the idea of a "one size fits all" information portal proved too simplistic.

The perfect information platform of the future has proven more difficult to develop because it is really a stack of three layers of intelligence, and each layer needs to be able to interact with a variety of different users who have different needs (Figure 15.1).

At the bottom significant innovation was required to build a "universal API," one place that was a reliable source of data about each small business. Technology existed early on to gather data from multiple sources, for example accounting software, payment streams, bank accounts. The difficulty lay in standardization and the creation of high-quality intelligence that could reliably create a picture of the health of a business and even predict future cash flows. Instead of a big information mess, software is now available

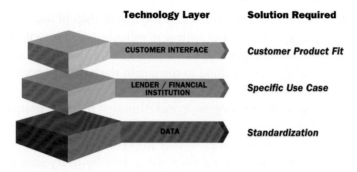

Figure 15.1   The Small Business Lending Product Stack
Source: Author's analysis.

that delivers clean data, aggregated by entity in a highly automated software solution available for purchase by any lending entity.

The second layer involves lenders, each of whom has their own use case for the newly available data streams. Many traditional lenders have no way to include this much information in their underwriting process. What was traditionally done on a spreadsheet or in a committee meeting with paper files, now requires a digital process. In addition, each lender needs to decide how to use the available data to predict the ability of a borrower to repay the loan. Complicated algorithms and data science are new skill sets for many risk management organizations. Even if the algorithms are available from a third party, the lender needs to determine the specific customers and loan products they want to provide.

The final layer is the customer-facing digital interface. A customer needs a clear line of sight to a product that solves their pain point. In Small Business Utopia a customer wants to see a seamless digital picture of their financial world including past and projected cash flows. They want to know what loans might be available to them that would fit their needs: options with the right amount, cost, and duration. If they take on a loan with a good customer-product fit, they have a better chance to successfully repay the obligation.

Customer-facing software solutions are complicated because small business owners vary greatly in their business objectives and their technical sophistication. Today, the user of the software has to actively navigate to an answer that works for them. But what if they had an intelligent automated advisor who would help them through the journey? What if the business owner could ask the bot, "Tell me what my future cash flows look like and what different options I might consider for financing my business," and receive appropriate and valuable advice powered by new modes of artificial intelligence? With such a tool, it is likely that fewer businesses would fail, at least from unexpected cash surprises and more could find their way to credit options that meet the needs of their individual business.

The Dark Side of the Black Box

The use of big data, algorithms, and generative AI will bring new products and services, but also bring some new concerns. For example, it is not yet clear what impact the changes we anticipate from technology will have on access to capital for traditionally underserved markets. In the past, women and minorities have struggled to find willing lenders. The hope is that with more efficient markets and new data sources, more creditworthy borrowers from underserved segments of the market will get loans. However, "black box" algorithms, where the formulas are not open to review, could lead to an outcome of more discrimination, not less.

More innovation can take place if there is a way to track potential poor market outcomes. Collecting this information and using it to identify and correct market gaps is a critical foundational element of a highly functioning small business credit market, as artificial intelligence becomes an integral part of lending decisions.

The Voice of Small Business

Small businesses don't go unnoticed, but sometimes they do go unheard. As we noted at the beginning of Chapter 2, small businesses have a special place in the hearts of Americans and are one of the few areas where there is bipartisan agreement. But the voice of small business is sometimes missing at the table, particularly in Washington. Small business owners are an independent, diverse group, and are busy running their companies, so they rarely convene and express their priorities. And aside from oversight by the head of the U.S. Small Business Administration, there is no policy mechanism to continuously check in on how government policy decisions will impact the small businesses that employ 46% of our country's workforce. And the economists whose job it is to track the well-being of the economy and its citizens have few metrics to track the health and contribution of the small business segment.

Interestingly, at the height of the pandemic, when it looked like the shutdown might severely impact small businesses' survival, the country came together and made small businesses aid a top priority of relief efforts. Let's keep that spirit, even as memories of the Covid-19 pandemic thankfully fade. This book is written to provide a fact-based guide to the importance of small business in our economy, and the frictions and gaps that prevent our small business sector from reaching its full potential. It is a playbook for regulatory solutions that will help be sure we optimize the opportunities that technology will bring in the critical area of access to capital. Those "smarter" regulations will need champions in Washington, beyond small business owners themselves, if they are to get and keep the attention of Congress and regulators and become law.

Predictions for the Future of Fintech and Small Business Lending

What is going to happen next? Of course, we don't know for sure. But based on the narrative described in the preceding chapters, it is possible to make some predictions:

Prediction #1: The Winners Will Be Small Business Friendly Platforms and Their Banking Partners

The narrative of this book begins with the fact that small businesses are important, but often get less attention than they deserve. The winners of the future will flip that script. Platforms already exist that have made themselves part of the daily activity of the small business owner. Shopify, Stripe, Square, QuickBooks, Toast, and more have each found a way to identify frictions in the operations of a group of small businesses and deliver better solutions. Several successful platforms have turned their eyes to providing credit options, embedded in the services they already provide.

In the past, technology platforms have been reluctant to provide capital because of the highly regulated nature of banking activities. But advances now allow a third-party bank to provide the lending as a service, seamlessly integrated into the customer's workflow, and informed by the customer's own data. Banks and platforms will make a variety of arrangements about sharing of revenues and apportionment of risk. Some like American Express will look to add small business services to their already robust banking, card, and lending activities. Other banks may stay in the background providing risk assessment and underwriting, and perhaps loan servicing, but grateful not to worry about the customer acquisition. In this environment, there is an opportunity for banks to win, if they build the capacity to engage digitally, choose the right partners, and set appropriate rules under which they are comfortable participating.

The key to success in these partnerships will be a focus on seamlessly serving the small business owner. Both the platform and the bank benefit when the business gets the right loan, at the right time with the right cost and terms, and can pay it back successfully. Innovators in these partnerships will likely develop a high functioning bot that provides helpful small business advice and counsel, but there may also be a return to human relationship banking which could be delivered more cost effectively when data analysis is automated. All these creative solutions are likely to benefit small business owners who will have an array of avenues to get the help they need to grow and succeed.

Prediction #2: Small Businesses Will Lean in to Tech

Small businesses have traditionally not been early adopters of technology. That is changing. The tech of today is more intuitive and does not require big systems installations and lots of capital. It lives in the cloud and can be accessed through a cell phone. Go to a farmers market and every vendor can take contactless payments with a device taped to their stall. Once it is clear that a solution works well in a particular sector, word of mouth will spread the information inside that vertical, making customer acquisition cheaper and faster.

We saw a sharp increase in new business applications after the Covid-19 pandemic that appeared to be sustained. One hypothesis is that this represents younger entrepreneurs making the choice to pursue a more independent path to their dreams. The younger generation requires easy to use, effective technology solutions as part of their basic operating life. Banking and lending will need to keep up to win their business. And again, when there is a solution that beats the competition, they will spread the word quickly through social media.

The message to traditional banks and financial services providers is clear. Make products that understand the pain points that small business owners face and provide solutions that are intuitive and easy to adopt. This means that banks, fintechs and others who want to serve the small business market must immerse themselves in the activities and issues of the sector they want to serve.

If they do this successfully there is one more benefit. Small business owners are willing and able to pay more for solutions that actually work for them and meet their needs. As technology becomes more a part of the world of financial services, margins will compress. We have already seen this in many consumer products, including mortgages. Small business products are more complex and less likely to become commoditized, providing a much longer runway of good profits for those who make the effort to invest and effectively serve the market.

Prediction #3: Regulation Will Fail to Keep Up

While it would be ideal for policymakers to be proactive, history shows that human nature is more often prone to reaction. Congress in particular is a reactive body, if only because voters reward elected officials for responding to problems, rather than preventing them from happening. U.S. financial regulatory agencies have the advantage of greater independence from Congress and the executive branch, including independent funding in some cases. This gives them greater latitude to be proactive, and sometimes they are. But addressing the risks technology will bring without stifling innovation is a difficult challenge, even for a high functioning regulatory system. The United States, with its overlapping and duplicative jurisdictions, will find it difficult to develop well-coordinated, forward-thinking policy, and in the current environment, it will be hard to develop the bipartisan commitment required to pass such a regulatory package.

Therefore, we expect that regulation will struggle to keep up, to the detriment of the market, allowing bad actors to prey on unsuspecting small businesses and fueling a confusing and costly regulatory environment. Unintended consequences in a world of increased data usage, such as issues around privacy, data security, and discrimination due to algorithmic bias will also result if policymaking does not become more proactive.

Fintech, Small Business, & the American Dream

The view of this book is largely optimistic. Additional data and efforts to innovate in small business lending markets are generally good trends, which we predict will have a positive impact on small business outcomes. The entry of fintech entrepreneurs has awakened the competitive instincts of banks and traditional lenders, who have realized that they don't want to cede the small business market to the new disruptors. Large technology companies have shown indications that they might view small business lending as a place to play. This heightened competition is good for small businesses, who too often have been an afterthought for lenders, in the shadow of consumers and large businesses.

Of course, the full picture of the future is not entirely rosy. The U.S. regulatory system in its present state is ill-equipped to protect small business owners and deal with the change that technology will bring, and political realities seem likely to prevent adoption of "smarter" rules. Nonetheless, we could be on the brink of one of the most positive transformations in small business lending in at least a century. As new entrepreneurs enter, and older players innovate, the attention will be on understanding what small businesses want and delivering new options that will make it easier for small businesses to succeed.

There is a long debate within economics about the degree to which finance causes economic growth, as opposed to just following economic activity. In a seminal 1997 article, Ross Levine outlined several key functions performed by the financial sector that drive economic growth, including allocating capital.[7] Levine saw the development of financial markets as a critical influence on growth, and not as an inconsequential or passive "side show." Thus, innovations that reduce frictions in critical functions like lending and make financial markets work better are a positive force that should drive more prosperity. From the evidence we see today, fintech may be just such a force for small business lending and the small businesses that depend on America's financial markets for their growth and success.

* * *

Fifteen years ago, Ron Siegel decided to start a bakery, and wondered what he would call his new business. "It was difficult and scary to break out of my daily work routine to pursue a dream that had an unknown outcome," Ron said. "The name 'When Pigs Fly' means 'I doubt it's possible' and that's why it was the perfect name for my bakery."[8] Today, Ron tells his story on the packages of millions of loaves of his bread. And following in the footsteps of Dumuzi-gamil, our bread distributor from Mesopotamia, "When Pigs Fly" sells its bread all over New England from its operating plant in York, Maine.

The American spirit of entrepreneurship has been a defining element since the founding of our nation. Today, innovators have brought new ideas and technology to the small business lending market and, as we have described in this book, a consequential transformation has begun. The outlook for small businesses is getting brighter, as these changes create more opportunities for people like Ron to do what often seems impossible—open and operate a small business and successfully pursue the American Dream.

Notes

Chapter 1

1. "United States Small Business Profile, 2022," U.S. Small Business Administration Office of Advocacy, 2022, https://advocacy.sba.gov/wp-content/uploads/2022/08/State_Profiles_2022.pdf.
2. R.W. Fairlie, Z. Kroff, J. Miranda, and N. Zolas, *The Promise and Peril of Entrepreneurship: Job Creation and Survival Among US Startups* (MIT Press, 2023).
3. "Comprehensive New Data Reassesses the MSME Finance Gap in Developing Countries," *International Finance Corporation*, November 2017, https://pressroom.ifc.org/all/pages/PressDetail.aspx?ID=18268.
4. Karen G. Mills, and Annie Dang. "Building Small Business Utopia: How Artificial Intelligence and Big Data Can Increase Small Business Success." In *Big Data in Small Business*, edited by Carsten Lund Pedersen, Adam Lindgreen, Thomas Ritter, and Torsten Ringberg (Edward Elgar Publishing, 2021).
5. Interview with Frank Rotman of QED Investors, April 13, 2018.
6. Note: The Dodd-Frank Wall Street Reform and Consumer Protection Act was the U.S. Congress' main legislative action that changed regulations after the financial crisis of 2008.

Chapter 2

1. Lydia Saad, "Historically Low Faith in U.S. Institutions Continues," *Gallup*, July 6, 2023, https://news.gallup.com/poll/508169/historically-low-faith-institutions-continues.aspx.
2. https://www.youtube.com/watch?v=00wQYmvfhn4.
3. Paul M. Romer, "Implementing a National Technology Strategy with Self Organizing Industry Investment Boards," *Brookings Papers on Economic Activity: Microeconomics*, no. 2 (1993): 345, https://www.brookings.edu/wp-content/uploads/1993/01/1993b_bpeamicro_romer.pdf.
4. Robert Atkinson and Howard Wial, "Boosting Productivity, Innovation, and Growth Through a National Innovation Foundation," *Brookings Institution and Information Technology and Innovation Foundation*, April 2008, https://www.brookings.edu/wp-content/uploads/2016/06/NIF-Report.pdf.
5. J.A. Schumpeter, *The Theory of Economic Development* (Cambridge, MA: Cambridge University Press, 1934).
6. Erik Hurst and Benjamin Wild Pugsley, "What Do Small Businesses Do?" *Brookings Papers on Economic Activity, 2011*, no. 2 (2011), https://www.brookings.edu/wp-content/uploads/2011/09/2011b_bpea_hurst.pdf.
7. J. John Wu and Robert D. Atkinson, "How Technology-Based Startups Support U.S. Economic Growth," *Information Technology and Innovation Foundation*, November 2017, https://itif.org/publications/2017/11/28/how-technology-based-start-ups-support-us-economic-growth.
8. "Consumers Now More Willing to Go Out of Their Way to Support Small Businesses," *UPS Store*, May 12, 2014, https://www.theupsstore.com/about/pressroom/consumers-support-small-businesses.
9. "Big Expectations, Small Businesses: What Customers Want," *Dimensional Research*, September 2019, https://d26a57ydsghvgx.cloudfront.net/content/Zendesk%20SMB%20Survey%20Report%20-%20US%20-%20Jul2.pdf.
10. "American Express Teams Up with Shaquille O'Neal and Friends to Drive Card Members to Shop Small and Earn Big Rewards," *American Express*, November 10, 2016.
11. "Robert Solow Talks About the Work of the Future" *MIT Work of the Future, Homepage*, accessed October 30, 2023, https://www.youtube.com/watch?v=Fv177H0xiMk.

12. "United States Small Business Profile, 2022," *U.S. Small Business Administration Office of Advocacy*, 2022, https://advocacy.sba.gov/wp-content/uploads/2022/08/State_Profiles_2022.pdf.

13. "Frequently Asked Questions About Small Business," *U.S. Small Business Administration Office of Advocacy*, March 2023, https://advocacy.sba.gov/wp-content/uploads/2023/03/Frequently-Asked-Questions-About-Small-Business-March-2023-508c.pdf.

14. "Business Employment Dynamics—Table E. Quarterly Net Change by Firm Size Class, Seasonally Adjusted," *Bureau of Labor Statistics*, accessed July, 2018, https://www.bls.gov/bdm/bdmfirmsize.htm.

15. David Madland, "Growth and the Middle Class," *Democracy Journal*, no. 20 (Spring 2011), https://democracyjournal.org/magazine/20/growth-and-the-middle-class/.

16. William Easterly, "The Middle Class Consensus and Economic Development," *Journal of Economic Growth 6*, no. 4 (July 2001): 317–335, https://williameasterly.files.wordpress.com/2010/08/34_easterly_middle classconsensus_prp.pdf.

17. Ben Hubbard and Kate Kelly, "Saudi Arabia's Grand Plan to Move Beyond Oil: Big Goals, Bigger Hurdles," *New York Times*, October 25, 2017, https://www.nytimes.com/2017/10/25/world/middleeast/saudi-arabias-grand-plan-to-move-beyond-oil-big-goals-bigger-hurdles.html.

18. Daron Acemoglu, Ufuk Akcigit, Harun Alp, Nicholas Bloom, and William Kerr, "Innovation, Reallocation and Growth," *Becker Friedman Institute for Research in Economics Working Paper*, no. 21, December 1, 2017, https://papers.ssrn.com/sol3/papers.cfm?abstract_id=3079898.

19. Edward L. Glaeser, Sari Pekkala Kerr, and William R. Kerr, "Entrepreneurship and Urban Growth: An Empirical Assessment with Historical Mines," *Review of Economics and Statistics 97*, no. 2 (May 2015), https://www.mitpressjournals.org/doi/abs/10.1162/REST_a_00456?journalCode=rest.

20. Tyler Richards, "Small Business Facts: Small Business Innovation Measured by Patenting Activity," *SBA Advocacy*, September 2022, https://advocacy.sba.gov/wp-content/uploads/2022/09/Fact-Sheet_Small-Business-Innovation-Measured-by-Patenting-Activity-1.pdf.

21. Mirjam Van Praag and Peter H. Versloot, "What Is the Value of Entrepreneurship? A Review of Recent Research," *Small Business Economics*, no. 29 (2007): 351–382, https://link.springer.com/content/pdf/10.1007%2Fs11187-007-9074-x.pdf.

22. William R. Kerr, Ramana Nanda, and Matthew Rhodes-Kropf, "Entrepreneurship as Experimentation," *Journal of Economic Perspectives 28*, no. 3 (Summer 2014): 25–48, https://pubs.aeaweb.org/doi/pdfplus/10.1257/jep.28.3.25.

23. Elizabeth Brown and Austin Nichols, "Self-Employment, Family-Business Ownership, and Economic Mobility," *Urban Institute*, May 2014, https://www.urban.org/sites/default/files/publication/33841/413134-self-employment-family-business-ownership-and-economic-mobility.pdf.

24. Ben R. Craig, William E. Jackson, and James B. Thomson, "Small Firm Finance, Credit Rationing, and the Impact of SBA-Guaranteed Lending on Local Economic Growth," *Journal of Small Business Management 45*, no. 1 (2007): 116–132, https://www.econstor.eu/bitstream/10419/100955/1/wp2005-28.pdf.

25. William R. Kerr, *The Gift of Global Talent: How Migration Shapes Business, Economy & Society* (Palo Alto, CA: Stanford University Press, 2018); Azoulay, Pierre, Benjamin F. Jones, J. Daniel Kim, and Javier Miranda, "Immigration and Entrepreneurship in the United States," *American Economic Review: Insights 4*, no. 1 (2022): 71–88. https://doi.org/10.1257/aeri.20200588.

26. "The 2017 Kauffman Index of Startup Activity: NationalTrends," *Kauffman Foundation*, May 2017, https://www.kauffman.org/kauffman-index/reporting/startup-activity.

27. Adam Bluestein, "The Most Entrepreneurial Group in America Wasn't Born in America," *Inc.*, February 2015, https://www.inc.com/magazine/201502/adam-bluestein/the-most-entrepreneurial-group-in-america-wasnt-born-in-america.html.

28. "United States Small Business Profile, 2022," *U.S. Small Business Administration Office of Advocacy*, 2022, https://advocacy.sba.gov/wp-content/uploads/2022/08/State_Profiles_2022.pdf.

29. Note: In 2022, 15.6 million people were reported as self-employed. Some of them operated firms that had employees. However, given that there were only 6 million employer firms in 2022, most of the self-employed were likely also non-employer firms. As an estimate, 12 million or just under half of the 27 million non-employer firms were full-time jobs for their owners, while the others were side businesses. Data for "Nonemployer businesses" is taken from the Nonemployer Statistics at the U.S. Census Bureau (https://www.census.gov/programs-surveys/nonemployer-statistics/data/tables.All.html); Data for Unincorporated Nonemployer Businesses is taken from the Bureau of Labor

Statistics table on Self-employed workers, unincorporated (not seasonally adjusted), (https://www.bls.gov/webapps/legacy/cpsatab9.htm).

30. Ian Hathaway and Mark Muro, "Tracking the Gig Economy: New Numbers," *Brookings*, October 2016, https://www.brookings.edu/res earch/tracking-the-gig-economy-new-numbers/.

31. Note: For example, from 2018 to 2019, the number of non-employer businesses grew by 618,000, while the number of self-employed grew by 233,000.

32. Mercedes Delgado and Karen G. Mills, "The Supply Chain Economy: A New Industry Categorization for Understanding Innovation in Services," *Research Policy 49*, no. 8 (October 2020), https://www.sciencedirect. com/science/article/pii/S0048733320301177. Note: This paper esti- mates a new industry categorization that separates supply chain (SC) industries (i.e. those that sell primarily to businesses or government) from business-to-consumer (B2C) industries (i.e. those that sell primarily to consumers). To our knowledge, this is the first systematic quantification of the supply chain economy. The supply chain includes both manufac- turers, and importantly, service providers. It is a large and distinct sector with higher wages and a higher degree of innovative capacity than B2C industries. See also: Mercedes Delgado and Karen Mills, "The supply chain economy: New policies to drive innovation and jobs." Economía Industrial, Volume 421, 2021.

33. Mercedes Delgado and Michael E. Porter, "Clusters and the 2008–9 Recession," June 8, 2017, https://papers.ssrn.com/sol3/papers.cfm?abs tract_id=3819293.

34. Aaron Chatterji, Edward L. Glaeser, and William R. Kerr, "Clusters of Entrepreneurship and Innovation," *NBER Working Paper*, no. 19013, May 2013, https://www.nber.org/papers/w19013.

35. Jorge Guzman and Scott Stern, "Nowcasting and Placecasting Entrepreneurial Quality and Performance," *NBER Working Paper*, no. 20952, February 2015, http://www.nber.org/papers/w20954.

36. Ramana Nanda, "Financing High-Potential Entrepreneurship," *IZA World of Labor*, 2016, https://wol.iza.org/articles/financing-high-potent ial-entrepreneurship.

37. Ryan Decker, John Haltiwanger, Ron S. Jarmin, and Javier Miranda, "The Secular Decline in Business Dynamism in the U.S," *University of Maryland Working Paper*, June 2014, http://econweb.umd.edu/~hal tiwan/DHJM_6_2_2014.pdf.

38. John Haltiwanger, Ron S. Jarmin, and Javier Miranda, "Who Creates Jobs? Small Versus Large Versus Young," *The Review of Economics and Statistics* 95, no. 2 (2013), https://www.mitpressjournals.org/doi/10.1162/REST_a_00288.

39. Jason Wiens and Chris Jackson, "The Importance of Young Firms for Economic Growth," *Ewing Marion Kauffman Foundation Entrepreneurship Policy Digest*, September 2015, https://www.kauffman.org/resources/entrepreneurship-policy-digest/the-importance-of-young-firms-for-economic-growth/

40. Ryan Decker, John Haltiwanger, Ron Jarmin, and Javier Miranda, "The Role of Entrepreneurship in US Job Creation and Economic Dynamism," *The Journal of Economic Perspectives 28*, no. 3 (2014): 3–24, https://pubs.aeaweb.org/doi/pdfplus/10.1257/jep.28.3.3.

41. Faith Karahan, Benjamin Pugsley, and Aysegül Sahin, "Understanding the 30-Year Decline in the Startup Rate: A General Equilibrium Approach," May 2015, http://conference.iza.org/conference_files/EntreRes2015/pugsley_b22364.pdf.

42. Jan W. Rivkin, Karen G. Mills, and Michael E. Porter, "The Challenge of Shared Prosperity: Findings of Harvard Business School's 2015 Survey on American Competitiveness," *Harvard Business School*, September 2015, http://www.hbs.edu/competitiveness/Documents/challenge-of-shared-prosperity.pdf.

43. Karthik Krishnan and Pinshuo Wang, "The Cost of Financing Education: Can Student Debt Hinder Entrepreneurship?" *forthcoming, Management Science,* November 2017, https://papers.ssrn.com/sol3/papers.cfm?abstract_id=2586378; Brent Ambrose, Larry Cordell, and Shuwei Ma, "The Impact of Student Loan Debt on Small Business Formation," *Federal Reserve Board of Philadelphia Working Paper*, no. 15–26, July 2015, https://papers.ssrn.com/sol3/papers.cfm?abstract_id=2633951.

44. John C. Haltiwanger, "Entrepreneurship During the COVID-19 Pandemic: Evidence from the Business Formation Statistics," *National Bureau of Economic Research*, April 2021; "Business Formation Statistics Monthly Release", United States Census Bureau.

45. John Haltiwanger, "Entrepreneurship During the COVID-19 Pandemic: Evidence from the Business Formation Statistics," *National Bureau of Economic Research*, 2021.

46. Ibid.

47. Ibid.

48. Catherine E. Fazio, Jorge Guzman, Yupeng Liu and Scott Stern, "How Is Covid Changing the Geography of Entrepreneurship? Evidence from the Startup Cartography Project," *NBER Working Paper*, no. 28787, May 2021, https://www.nber.org/system/files/working_papers/w28787/w28787.pdf.

Chapter 3

1. Interview with Pilar Guzman Zavala, August 31, 2017.
2. Nancy Dahlberg, "Passion, Perseverance Powered Empanada Maker Through Tough Start," *Miami Herald*, July 10, 2016, http://www.miami-herald.com/news/business/biz-monday/article88785767.html.
3. Author's analysis of data from the Business Dynamics Statistics, *U.S. Census Bureau*, last modified September 23, 2015, https://www.census.gov/ces/dataproducts/bds/data_firm.html.
4. Mark Gertler and Simon Gilchrist, "Monetary Policy, Business Cycles, and the Behavior of Small Manufacturing Firms," *The Quarterly Journal of Economics 109*, no. 2 (May 1994), http://www.uh.edu/~bsorense/Gertler&Gilchrist.MP%20business%20cycles%20and%20behavior%20of%20small%20manufactoring%20firms.pdf; Randall S. Kroszner, Luc Laeven, and Daniela Klingebiel, "Banking Crises, Financial Dependence and Growth," *Journal of Financial Economics 84*, no. 1 (2007), http://www.sciencedirect.com/science/article/pii/S0304405X0600208X; Gert Wehinger, "SMEs and the Credit Crunch: Current Financing Difficulties, Policy Measures, and a Review of Literature," *OECD Journal: Financial Market Trends*, no. 2 (2013), https://www.oecd.org/finance/SMEs-Credit-Crunch-Financing-Difficulties.pdf.
5. Diana Farrell and Chris Wheat, "Cash Is King: Flows, Balances, and Buffer Days: Evidence from 600,000 Small Businesses," *JPMorgan Chase and Co. Institute*, September 2016, https://papers.ssrn.com/sol3/papers.cfm?abstract_id=2966127.
6. "2022 Small Business Credit Survey: Report on Employer Firms," *Federal Reserve Banks*, March 2023, p. 13, https://www.fedsmallbusiness.org/survey/2023/report-on-employer-firms.
7. Brian S. Chen, Samuel G. Hanson, and Jeremy C. Stein, "The Decline of Big-Bank Lending to Small Business: Dynamic Impacts on Local Credit and Labor Markets," *NBER Working Paper*, no. 23843, September 2017, http://www.nber.org/papers/w23843.

8. Roisin McCord, Edward Simpson Prescott, and Tim Sablik, "Explaining the Decline in the Number of Banks Since the 2008–9 Recession," EB15-03 (March 2015), https://www.richmondfed.org/~/media/richmondfedorg/publications/research/economic_brief/2015/pdf/eb_15-03.pdf.

9. "FDIC Community Banking Study," *Community Banking Initiative*, December 2012, https://www.fdic.gov/regulations/resources/cbi/study.html.

10. Mark Gertler and Simon Gilchrist, "Monetary Policy, Business Cycles, and the Behavior of Small Manufacturing Firms," *The Quarterly Journal of Economics 109*, no. 2 (May 1994), http://www.uh.edu/~bsorense/Gertler&Gilchrist.MP%20business%20cycles%20and%20behavior%20of%20small%20manufactoring%20firms.pdf.

11. Randall S. Kroszner, Luc Laeven, and Daniela Klingebiel, "Banking Crises, Financial Dependence and Growth," *Journal of Financial Economics 84*, no. 1 (2007), http://www.sciencedirect.com/science/article/pii/S0304405X0600208X.

12. Burcu Duygan-Bump, Alexey Levkov, and Judit Montoriol-Garriga, "Financing Constraints and Unemployment: Evidence from the 2008–9 recession," *Federal Reserve Bank of Boston Working Paper*, no. QAU10-6 (December 2011), https://www.bostonfed.org/publications/risk-and-policy-analysis/2010/financing-constraints-and-unemployment-evidence-from-the-great-recession.aspx.

13. Gabriel Chodorow-Reich, "The Employment Effects of Credit Market Disruptions: Firm-Level Evidence from the 2008–9 Financial Crisis," *Quarterly Journal of Economics 129*, no. 1 (2014): 1–59, https://scholar.harvard.edu/chodorow-reich/publications/employment-effects-credit-market-disruptions-firm-level-evidence-2008-09.

14. Note: The Federal Insurance Deposit Commission (FDIC) requires banks to file quarterly call reports which include total assets on bank balance sheets by loan size, but do not include loan origination data. Thus, they describe the stock of loans but not the flows.

15. Interview with George Osborne, September 2016.

16. Author's analysis of data from "Loans to Small Businesses and Small Farms," *Federal Deposit Insurance Corporation Quarterly Banking Profile*, accessed August 23, 2018, https://www.fdic.gov/bank/analytical/qbp/.

17. Note: The Small Business Administration Loan Guaranty Program allows banks to make small business loans with the promise that if the borrower defaults, the federal government will bear a designated portion of the loss.

18. Robert Jay Dilger, "Small Business Administration 7(a) Loan Guaranty Program," *Congressional Research Service*, November 7, 2018, https://fas.org/sgp/crs/misc/R41146.pdf.

19. Karen Gordon Mills and Brayden McCarthy, "The State of Small Business Lending: Innovation and Technology and the Implications for Regulation," *Harvard Business School Working Paper*, no. 17-042 (2016): 121, http://www.hbs.edu/faculty/Publication%20Files/17-042_30393d52-3c61-41cb-a78a-ebbe3e040e55.pdf.

20. "Small Business Lending Fund," *U.S. Department of the Treasury*, accessed January 19, 2018, https://www.treasury.gov/resource-center/sb-programs/Pages/Small-Business-Lending-Fund.aspx.

21. Kevin T. Jacques, Richard Moylan, and Peter J. Nigro, "Commercial Bank Small Business Lending Pre and Post Crisis," *The Journal of Entrepreneurial Finance 18*, no. 1 (Spring 2016): 22–48, https://digitalcommons.pepperdine.edu/cgi/viewcontent.cgi?referer=&httpsredir=1&article=1275&context=jef.

22. Jeff Zients, "Getting Money to Small Businesses Faster," *The White House Blog*, September 14, 2011, https://www.whitehouse.gov/blog/2011/09/14/getting-money-small-businesses-faster.

23. Jean-Noel Barrot and Ramana Nanda, "The Employment Effects of Faster Payment: Evidence from the Federal Quickpay Reform," *Harvard Business School Working Paper*, no. 17-004, July 2016 (Revised July 2018), https://papers.ssrn.com/sol3/papers.cfm?abstract_id=2808666.

24. Federal News Radio Staff, "Necole Parker, Founder and CEO of the ELOCEN Group LLC," *Federal News Radio*, July 31, 2014, https://federalnewsradio.com/federal-drive/2014/07/necole-parker-founder-and-ceo-of-the-elocen-group-llc/.

25. "Helping Small Business Overcome Barriers to Growth," United States House of Representatives Committee on Small Business, Testimony of Steven H. Strongin, February 14, 2018, https://smallbusiness.house.gov/uploadedfiles/2-14-18_strongin_testimony.pdf.

26. Paul Davidson, "U.S. Economy Regains All Jobs Lost in Recession," *USA Today*, June 6, 2014, https://www.usatoday.com/story/money/business/2014/06/06/may-jobs-report/10037173/.

27. Collin Eaton, "Jamie Dimon Dishes on Small Business Lending, Regulatory Issues," *Houston Business Journal*, February 27, 2013, https://www.bizjournals.com/houston/blog/money-makers/2013/02/dimon-dishes-on-small-business.html.

28. William C. Dunkelberg and Holly Wade, "NFIB Small Business Economic Trends," *National Federation of Independent Business*, June 2012.

29. Small Business Survey Topline—3rd Qtr 2017," *Wells Fargo and Gallup*, July 19, 2017, pp. 8–9, https://assets.ctfassets.net/ewhhtaabqlyo/2yt UTLKjMcM4y4yEMYSMIs/4283c944c34c9345ea9b16bb028f226f/ Wells_Fargo_Small_Business_Survey_Q3_2017_FINAL7-19-2017.pdf.

30. Manuel Adelino, Antoinette Schoar, and Felipe Severino, "House Prices, Collateral and Self-Employment," *Journal of Financial Economics 117*, no. 2 (2015): 288–306, https://doi.org/10.1016/j.jfineco.2015.03.005.

31. Karen Gordon Mills and Brayden McCarthy, "The State of Small Business Lending: Credit Access During the Recovery and How Technology May Change the Game," *Harvard Business School Working Paper*, no. 15-004 (2014): 30, http://www.hbs.edu/faculty/Publication%20Files/15-004_09b1bf8b-eb2a-4e63-9c4e-0374f770856f.pdf.

32. "Small Business, Credit Access, and a Lingering Recession," *National Federation of Independent Business*, January 2012.

33. Michael D. Bordo and John V. Duca, "The Impact of the Dodd-Frank Act on Small Business," *NBER Working Paper*, no. 24501, April 2018, www.nber.org/papers/w24501.

34. Martin N. Baily, Justin Schardin, and Phillip L. Swagel, "Did Policymakers Get Post-Crisis Financial Regulation Right?" *Bipartisan Policy Center*, September 2016, https://cdn.bipartisanpolicy.org/wp-content/ uploads/2016/09/BPC-FRRI-Post-Crisis-Financial-Regulation.pdf.

35. Steve Strongin, Sandra Lawson, Amanda Hindlian, Katherine Maxwell, Koby Sadan, and Sonya Banerjee, "Who Pays for Bank Regulation?" *Goldman Sachs Global Markets Institute*, June 2014, https://www.goldma nsachs.com/intelligence/public-policy/regulatory-reform/who-pays-for-bank-regulation.html.

36. Thomas Hogan, "Costs of Compliance with the Dodd-Frank Act," *Rice University Baker Institute for Public Policy*, Center for Public Finance Issue Brief, September 6, 2019; Sam Batkins and Dan Goldbeck, "Six Years After Dodd-Frank: Higher Costs, Uncertain Benefits," *American Action Forum*, July 20, 2016, https://www.americanactionforum.org/ins ight/six-years-dodd-frank-higher-costs-uncertain-benefits/.

37. Llewellyn Hinkes-Jones, "How Much Did Dodd-Frank Cost? Don't Ask Banks," *Bloomberg BNA*, February 2, 2017, https://www.bloomb erg.com/news/audio/2017-02-02/how-much-did-dodd-frank-cost-don-t-ask-banks.

38. Ron Feldman, Ken Heinecke, and Jason Schmidt, "Quantifying the Costs of Additional Regulation on Community Banks," *Federal Reserve Bank of Minneapolis*, May 30, 2013, https://www.minneapolisfed.org/article/2013/quantifying-the-costs-of-additional-regulation-on-community-banks.

39. Drew Dahl, Andrew Meyer, and Michelle Neely, "Bank Size, Compliance Costs and Compliance Performance in Community Banking," *Federal Reserve Bank of St. Louis*, May 2016, https://www.communitybanking.org/~/media/files/communitybanking/2016/session2_paper2_neely.pdf.

40. "2017 Small Business Credit Survey: Report on Employer Firms," *Federal Reserve Banks*, May 2018, p. 7, https://www.fedsmallbusiness.org/medialibrary/fedsmallbusiness/files/2018/sbcs-employer-firms-report.pdf.

Chapter 4

1. Ruth Simon, "What Happened When a Town Lost Its Only Bank Branch," *The Wall Street Journal*, December 25, 2017, https://www.wsj.com/articles/what-happened-when-a-town-lost-its-only-bank-branch-1514219228.

2. Ann Marie Wiersch and Scott Shane, "Why Small Business Lending Isn't What It Used to Be," *Federal Reserve Bank of Cleveland*, August 14, 2013, https://www.clevelandfed.org/newsroom-and-events/publications/eco-nomic-commentary/2013-economic-commentaries/ec-201310-why-small-business-lending-isnt-what-it-used-to-be.aspx.

3. "Availability of Credit to Small Businesses," *Federal Reserve Banks Publications*, October 2022. https://www.federalreserve.gov/publications/2022-october-availability-of-credit-to-small-businesses.htm.

4. Ibid.

5. Allen Berger and Gregory Udell, "Relationship Lending and Lines of Credit in Small Firm Finance," *Journal of Business 68*, no. 3 (1995): 351–381, https://scholarcommons.sc.edu/cgi/viewcontent.cgi?article=1009&context=fin_facpub.

6. Jonathan Scott and William Dunkelberg, "Bank Consolidation and Small Business Lending: A Small Firm Perspective," *Proceedings* (1991): 328–361.

7. Brian Uzzi and James Gillespie, "Corporate Social Capital and the Cost of Financial Capital: An Embeddedness Approach," In *Corporate Social Capital and Liability*, edited by R.T.A.J. Leenders and S.M. Gabbay (Boston, MA: Springer, 1999), 446–459.

8. Robert DeYoung, Dennis Glennon, and Peter Nigro, "Borrower-Lender Distance, Credit Scoring, and Loan Performance: Evidence from Informational-Opaque Small Business Borrowers," *Journal of Financial Intermediation 17*, no. 1 (2008): 113–143, https://doi.org/10.1016/j.jfi.2007.07.002.

9. "2015 Small Business Credit Survey: Report on Employer Firms," *Federal Reserve Banks*, March 2016, p. 9, https://www.newyorkfed.org/mediali-brary/media/smallbusiness/2015/Report-SBCS-2015.pdf.

10. Ryan N. Banerjee, Leonardo Gambacorta, and Enrico Sette, "The Real Effects of Relationship Lending," *Bank for International Settlements Working Papers*, no. 662, September 2017, https://www.bis.org/publ/work662.pdf.

11. John R. Walter, "Depression-Era Bank Failures: The Great Contagion or the Great Shakeout?" *Federal Reserve Bank of Richmond Economic Quarterly 91*, no. 1 (2005), https://www.richmondfed.org/-/media/richmondfedorg/publications/research/economic_quarterly/2005/winter/pdf/walter.pdf.

12. "Commercial Banks in the U.S.," *FRED Economic Data (Federal Reserve Bank of St. Louis)*, last modified August 16, 2018, https://fred.stlouisfed.org/series/USNUM; "Number of Insured Banks," *Federal Deposit Insurance Corporation*, accessed September 2023, https://www.fdic.gov/.

13. "Commercial Banks—Historical Statistics on Banking," *Federal Deposit Insurance Corporation*, accessed September 14, 2018, https://www5.fdic.gov/hsob/SelectRpt.asp?EntryTyp=10&Header=1.

14. "FDIC Community Banking Study," *Federal Deposit Insurance Corporation*, December 2012, pp. 2–4, https://www.fdic.gov/regulations/resources/cbi/report/cbi-full.pdf.

15. "FDIC Community Banking Study," *Federal Deposit Insurance Corporation*, December 2020, p. 28, https://www.fdic.gov/resources/community-banking/report/2020/2020-cbi-study-full.pdf.

16. Note: A thrift, also known as a savings and loan, specializes in taking deposits for savings, and making loans, especially mortgage loans. Thrifts came into vogue in the United States starting in the 1930s after the passage of the Federal Home Loan Bank Act as a way to allow a greater percentage of Americans to own their homes. Thrifts have become increasingly similar to banks over time.

17. Kevin J. Stiroh and Jennifer P. Poole, "Explaining the Rising Concentration of Banking Assets in the 1990s," *Current Issues in Economics and Finance 6*, no. 9, (August 2000), https://pdfs.semanticscholar.org/5b0b/6879f388106468e74380414b60a9a565a4f4.pdf.

18. "FDIC Community Banking Study," *Federal Deposit Insurance Corporation*, December 2012, pp. I–II, https://www.fdic.gov/regulations/resources/cbi/report/cbi-full.pdf.

19. *Supervisory Insights 13*, no. 1 (Summer 2016): 3, https://www.fdic.gov/regulations/examinations/supervisory/insights/sisum16/sisum16.pdf.

20. Andrew Martin, "In Hard Times, One New Bank (Double-Wide)," *New York Times*, August 2010, http://www.nytimes.com/2010/08/29/business/29bank.html.

21. "Statistics at a Glance, Historical Trends", *FDIC Quarterly Banking Profile*, June 30, 2023, https://www.fdic.gov/analysis/quarterly-banking-profile/statistics-at-a-glance/2023jun/fdic.pdf.

22. Yan Lee and Chiwon Yom, "The Entry, Performance, and Risk Profile of De Novo Banks," *FDIC-CFR Working Paper*, no. 2016-03 (April 2016), https://www.fdic.gov/bank/analytical/cfr/2016/wp2016/2016-03.pdf.

23. Ruth Simon and Coulter Jones, "Goodbye, George Bailey: Decline of Rural Lending Crimps Small-Town Business," *The Wall Street Journal*, December 25, 2017, https://www.wsj.com/articles/goodbye-george-bailey-decline-of-rural-lending-crimps-small-town-business-1514219515.

24. Hoai-Luu Q. Nguyen, "Do Bank Branches Still Matter? The Effect of Closings on Local Economic Outcomes," *MIT Economics*, Working Paper, December 2014.

25. Ibid.

26. "Bank Mergers, Acquirer Choice and Small Business Lending: Implications for Community Investment." B.A. Minton, A.G. Taboada, and R. Williamson, National Bureau of Economic Research, 2021.

27. Oliver E. Williamson, "Hierarchical Control and Optimum Firm Size," *Journal of Political Economy 75*, no. 2 (April 1967): 123–138, https://www.journals.uchicago.edu/doi/10.1086/259258.

28. Rebel A. Cole, Lawrence G. Goldberg, and Lawrence J. White, "Cookie Cutter vs. Character: The Micro Structure of Small Business Lending by Large and Small Banks," *Journal of Financial and Quantitative Analysis 39*, no. 2 (June 2004): 227–251, https://condor.depaul.edu/rcole/Research/Cole.Goldberg.White.JFQA.2004.pdf.

29. "Small Business Lending Survey," *FDIC*, November 1, 2017, https://www.fdic.gov/communitybanking/2017/2017-11-01-sbls.pdf.

30. Governor Frederic S. Mishkin "Availability of Credit to Small Businesses," November 7, 2007, https://www.federalreserve.gov/Newsevents/Testimony/Mishkin20071107a.Htm.

31. John H. Cushman, Jr., "Credit Markets; Secondary Market Is Sought," *New York Times*, March 29, 1993, http://www.nytimes.com/1993/03/29/business/credit-markets-secondary-market-is-sought.html?mcubz=3.

32. Kenneth Temkin and Roger C. Kormendi, "An Exploration of a Secondary Market for Small Business Loans," *Small Business Administration Office of Advocacy*, April 2003, 12–13, http://citeseerx.ist.psu.edu/viewdoc/download?doi=10.1.1.186.8863&rep=rep1&type=pdf.

33. "Fall 2013 Small Business Credit Survey," *Federal Reserve Bank of New York*, September 2013, https://www.newyorkfed.org/medialibrary/interactives/fall2013/fall2013/files/full-report.pdf.

Chapter 5

1. Karen Gordon Mills and Brayden McCarthy, "The State of Small Business Lending: Credit Access During the Recovery and How Technology May Change the Game," *Harvard Business School Working Paper*, no. 15-004 (2014), http://www.hbs.edu/faculty/Publication%20Files/15-004_09b1bf8b-eb2a-4e63-9c4e-0374f770856f.pdf.

2. "2021 Small Business Credit Survey: Report on Employer Firms," *Federal Reserve Banks*, May 2022, pp. 8–14, https://www.fedsmallbusiness.org/survey/2022/report-on-employer-firms.

3. "2016 Small Business Credit Survey: Report on Employer Firms," *Federal Reserve Banks*, April 2017, p. 11, https://www.newyorkfed.org/medialibrary/media/smallbusiness/2016/SBCS-Report-EmployerFirms-2016.pdf.

4. "Joint Small Business Credit Survey Report 2014," *Federal Reserve Banks of New York, Atlanta, Cleveland and Philadelphia*, 2014, p. 11. https://www.newyorkfed.org/medialibrary/media/smallbusiness/SBCS-2014-Report.pdf.

5. "2016 Small Business Credit Survey: Report on Startup Firms," *Federal Reserve Banks*, August 2017, https://www.newyorkfed.org/medialibrary/media/smallbusiness/2016/SBCS-Report-StartupFirms-2016.pdf.

6. Ibid.

7. Ruth Simon and Paul Overberg, "Funding Sources Shift for Startups," *Wall Street Journal*, September 28, 2016, http://www.wsj.com/articles/funding-sources-shift-for-startups-1475095802?tesla=y.

8. Interview with Linda Pagan, August 2, 2018.

9. Note: The SBA has a portfolio of nearly $100 billion of guarantees, with a loss rate of less than 5%, indicating that there is a significant set of creditworthy small businesses in the market that might not otherwise qualify for loans. Since the cost of the losses is generally covered by SBA fees, the federal budget impact of this significant program is close to zero. The program is a great example of a public–private partnership that takes advantage of bank expertise to provide more access and opportunity for small businesses at little government expense. This is a useful model to consider for other market gaps or social purposes, and the program has been copied by other nations in order to better support their small business sectors.

Chapter 6

1. Michael Riordan and Lillian Hoddeson, *Crystal Fire: The Invention of the Transistor* (W. W. Norton, 1997), 254.
2. Joseph Alois Schumpeter, *Business Cycles* (New York: McGraw-Hill, 1939).
3. Joseph Schumpeter, *Capitalism, Socialism and Democracy* (New York: Routledge, 2010), 83.
4. Joseph Alois Schumpeter, *The Theory of Economic Development: An Inquiry into Profits, Capital, Credit, Interest, and the Business Cycle* (New Brunswick, NJ: Transaction Books, 1911), 66.
5. Rebecca Henderson, *Developing and Managing a Successful Technology & Product Strategy: The Industry Life Cycle as an S Curve* (Cambridge, MA: The Co-Evolution of Technologies and Markets, 2005), www.mit.edu/people/rhenders/Teaching/day1_jan05.ppt.
6. Priya Ganapati, "June 4, 1977: VHS Comes to America," *Wired*, June 4, 2010, https://www.wired.com/2010/06/0604vhs-ces/.
7. "Frequently Asked Questions About Check 21," *Board of Governors of the Federal Reserve System*, last modified August 6, 2013, https://www.federalreserve.gov/paymentsystems/regcc-faq-check21.htm#:~:text=The%20Check%20Clearing%20for%20the,legal%20impediments%20to%20check%20truncation.
8. "Availability of Credit to Small Businesses," *Federal Reserve Banks Publications*, October 2022. https://www.federalreserve.gov/publications/2022-october-availability-of-credit-to-small-businesses.htm.

9. Brian Riley, "Small Business Credit Cards; Growth Opportunities in a Post-COVID World," *Javelin Strategy & Research*, December 30, 2021, https://javelinstrategy.com/research/small-business-credit-cards-growth-opportunities-post-covid-world.

10. "FDIC Quarterly Banking Profile," *Federal Deposit Insurance Corporation 14*, no. 1, https://www.fdic.gov/analysis/quarterly-banking-profile/fdic-quarterly/2020-vol14-1/fdic-v14n1-4q2019.pdf.

11. "Total Consumer Credit Owned and Securitized, Outstanding," *FRED Economic Data*, accessed September 28, 2023, https://fred.stlouisfed.org/graph/?id=TOTALSL.

12. "Real Estate Loans: Residential Real Estate Loans, All Commercial Banks," *FRED Economic Data*, September 28, 2023. https://fred.stlouisfed.org/graph/?id=RREACBW027SBOG.

13. "Annual Report 2019," JPMorgan Chase & Co., 2020, p. 44, https://www.jpmorganchase.com/content/dam/jpmc/jpmorgan-chase-and-co/investor-relations/documents/annualreport-2019.pdf.

14. *CAN Capital*, accessed December 2023, https://www.cancapital.com/WhoWeAre/.

15. Rip Empson, "Smart Lending: On Deck Gives Your Startup a Credit Score So You Can Secure a Loan," *TechCrunch*, May 19, 2011, https://techcrunch.com/2011/05/19/smart-lending-on-deck-gives-your-startup-a-credit-score-so-you-can-secure-a-loan/.

16. Karen Gordon Mills and Brayden McCarthy, "The State of Small Business Lending: Innovation and Technology and the Implications for Regulation," *Harvard Business School Working Paper*, no. 17-042, 2016, http://www.hbs.edu/faculty/Publication%20Files/17-042_30393d52-3c61-41cb-a78a-ebbe3e040e55.pdf.

17. Michael Erman and Joy Wiltermuth, "LendingClub CEO Resigns After Internal Probe, Shares Plummet," *Reuters*, May 9, 2016, https://www.reuters.com/article/us-lendingclub-results-idUSKCN0Y01BK.

18. Leena Rao, "Once-Hot Online Lending Companies Go Cold in Face of Skepticism," *Fortune*, July 1, 2015, http://fortune.com/2015/06/30/lending-club-ondeck-shares/.

19. Sabrina T. Howell, Theresa Kuchler, David Snitkof, Johannes Stroebel and Jun Wong "Lender Automation and Racial Disparities in Credit Access," *The Journal of Finance*, 2023; Robert W. Fairlie and Frank M. Fossen, "The 2021 Paycheck Protection Program Reboot: Loan Disbursement to Employer and Nonemployer Businesses in Minority Communities," *AEA Papers and Proceedings*, vol. 112 (May 2022), https://www.aeaweb.org/articles?id=10.1257/pandp.20221028.

20. Kristine McKenna, "Lots of Aura, No Air Play," *Los Angeles Times*, May 23, 1982, L6.

Chapter 7

1. LendIt Archives, Courtesy of Peter Renton, accessed March 13, 2018.
2. "LendIt 2013 Official Conference Report," *LendIt Blog*, August 24, 2013.
3. Peter Renton, "Wrap-Up of the 2014 LendIt Conference," *Lend Academy*, May 9, 2014, https://www.fintechnexus.com/wrap-up-of-the-2014-lendit-conference/.
4. "The LendIt Story," *Lendit Conference*, 2018, http://www.lendit.com/about.
5. "LendIt USA 2015: Agenda at a Glance," *Lendit USA*, 2015.
6. Travis Skelly, "Larry Summers' Full-Throated Endorsement of Online Lending," *FinTech Collective*, April 16, 2015, https://news.fintech.io/post/102ceyr/larry-summers-full-throated-endorsement-of-online-lending.
7. Interview with Frank Rotman, April 13, 2018.
8. Rolin Zumeran, "The History of APIs and How They Impact Your Future," *OpenLegacy Blog*, June 7, 2017, https://www.openlegacy.com/.
9. "Open Banking's Next Wave: Perspectives from Three Fintech CEOs," *Business a.m.*, September 10, 2018, https://www.businessamlive.com/open-bankings-next-wave-perspectives-from-three-fintech-ceos/.
10. Parris Sanz, "CAN Capital Celebrates 20 Years," *CAN Capital*, March 21, 2018, https://www.cancapital.com/.
11. Note: APR refers to an Annual Percentage Rate, or what most think of as an "interest rate." This number represents the percent interest paid on a loan over the course of a year. Because MCAs are repaid using a percentage of a business's sales receipts, they could be repaid in a shorter time frame than a year. However, since the repayment amount is fixed, the calculation of APR can be quite high if the loan is repaid in a short time frame. As a result, some argue that APRs unfairly represent the true cost of MCA loans. Nonetheless, APRs remain the standard for interest rate disclosures and comparisons.
12. Jackson Mueller, "U.S. Online, Non-Bank Finance Landscape," *Milken Institute Center for Financial Markets*, Curated through May 2016, http://www.milkeninstitute.org/assets/PDF/Online-Non-Bank-Finance-Landscape.pdf.

13. "LendingClub Launches Business Loans," LendingClub, accessed March 27, 2018, https://www.lendingclub.com/.

14. Julapa Jagtiani and Catharine Lemieux, "Small Business Lending: Challenges and Opportunities for Community Banks," *Philadelphia Fed Working Paper*, no. 16-08 (March 2016), https://www.philadelphiafed.org/the-economy/banking-and-financial-markets/small-business-lending.

15. Kabbage, accessed September 17, 2018, https://www.kabbage.com/.

16. Interview with Kathryn Petralia, March 19, 2018.

17. Miranda Eifler, "The OnDeck Score: Making Targeted Small Business Lending Decisions in Real Time," accessed March 27, 2018, https://www.ondeck.com/resources/ondeckscore.

18. Jackson Mueller, "U.S. Online, Non-Bank Finance Landscape," *Milken Institute Center for Financial Markets*, Curated through May 2016.

19. OnDeck, accessed April 18, 2018, https://www.ondeck.com/company.

20. Interview with Peter Renton, March 28, 2018.

21. Peter Renton, "Funding Circle Raises $37 Million and Launches in the U.S.," *Lend Academy*, October 23, 2013, https://www.fintechnexus.com/funding-circle-raises-37-million-and-launches-in-the-u-s/.

22. Allen Taylor, "Will Amazon Lending Disrupt, Displace, or Prop Up Banks?" *Lending Times*, January 4, 2018.

23. Jeffrey Dastin, "Amazon Lent $1 Billion to Merchants to Boost Sales on Its Marketplace," *Reuters*, June 8, 2017, https://www.reuters.com/article/us-amazon-com-loans-idUSKBN18Z0DY.

24. Amy Feldman, "PayPal's Small-Business Lending Tops $3B as Company Launches New Tools for Small-Business Owners," *Forbes*, May 1, 2017, https://www.forbes.com/sites/amyfeldman/2017/05/01/paypals-small-business-lending-tops-3b-as-company-launches-new-tools-for-small-business-owners/#7a8014b34018.

25. Leena Rao, "Square Capital Has Loaned Over $1 Billion to Small Businesses," *Fortune,* November 7, 2016, http://fortune.com/2016/11/07/square-capital-1-billion/.

26. "Q2 2018 Shareholder Letter," *Square*, p. 7, https://s21.q4cdn.com/114365585/files/doc_financials/2018/2018-Q2-Shareholder-Letter-%E2%80%94-Square.pdf.

27. Note: As described in Chapter 2, small supply chain firms account for almost 1 million small businesses and about 10 million jobs, with high average wages and significant amounts of innovation.

28. Note: In April 2018, Orchard was acquired by Kabbage, helping Kabbage gain access to Orchard's data science technology, https://www.kabbage.com/pdfs/pressreleases/Kabbage_Acquire_Orchard.pdf.

29. Author's analysis and data from "Breaking New Ground: The Americas Alternative Finance Benchmarking Report," *Cambridge Centre for Alternative Finance*, 2016, https://www.jbs.cam.ac.uk/fileadmin/user_u pload/research/centres/alternative-finance/downloads/2016-americas-alt ernative-finance-benchmarking-report.pdf.

30. "Karen Gordon Mills and Brayden McCarthy, "The State of Small Business Lending: Innovation and Technology and the Implications for Regulation," *Harvard Business School Working Paper*, no. 17-042 (2016): 121, http://www.hbs.edu/faculty/Publication%20Files/17-042_ 30393d52-3c61-41cb-a78a-ebbe3e040e55.pdf.

31. "MoneyTree™ Report Q4 2018," *PwC/CB Insights*, 2019, https://www.pwc.com/us/en/moneytree-report/moneytree-report-q4-2018.pdf.

32. Geoffrey A. Moore, *Crossing the Chasm: Marketing and Selling Disruptive Products to Mainstream Customers* (HarperBusiness Essentials, 2002), 9, http://soloway.pbworks.com/w/file/fetch/46715502/Crossing-The-Chasm.pdf

33. Geoffrey A. Moore, *Inside the Tornado: Strategies for Developing, Leveraging, and Surviving Hypergrowth Markets* (HarperCollins Publishers, 2009), 26.

34. Securities and Exchange Commission, Form 10-K: OnDeck Capital Inc., 2015, http://d1lge852tjjqow.cloudfront.net/CIK-0001420811/ 2e36150d-a925-4b94-ad17-1d111b90ba94.pdf; "LendingClub Reports Fourth Quarter and Full Year 2015 Results and Announces $150 Million Share Buyback," *PRNewswire*, February 11, 2016, http://www.prnewswire.com/news-releases/lending-club-reports-fourth-quarter-and-full-year-2015-results-and-announces-150-million-share-buyback-300 218747.html.

35. Chris Myers, "For Alternative Lenders to Be Successful, Differentiation Is Key," *Forbes*, October 2015, http://www.forbes.com/sites/chrismyers/ 2015/10/15/for-alternative-lenders-to-be-successful-differentiation-is-key/#722f3110207e.

36. Karen Gordon Mills, Dennis Campbell, and Aaron Mukerjee, *Eastern Bank: Innovating Through Eastern Labs*, HBS No. 9-318-068 (Boston: Harvard Business School Publishing, 2017), https://www.hbs.edu/fac ulty/Pages/item.aspx?num=53399.

37. Peter Renton, "LendIt USA Returns to San Francisco in 2018," *Fintech Nexus*, October 30, 2017, https://www.fintechnexus.com/lendit-usa-ret urns-san-francisco-2018/.

Chapter 8

1. Interview with David Snitkof, July 17, 2023.
2. Ibid.
3. "CDC Museum COVID-19 Timeline," March 2023, https://www.cdc. gov/museum/timeline/covid19.html.
4. Ibid.
5. Note: All but Arkansas, Iowa, Nebraska and North Dakota.
6. "The U.S. Economy and the Global Pandemic", *Economic Report of the President*, 2022, chapt. 3, https://www.whitehouse.gov/wp-content/upl oads/2022/04/Chapter-3-new.pdf.
7. "United States Small Business Profile, 2022," *U.S. Small Business Administration Office of Advocacy*, 2022, https://cdn.advocacy.sba.gov/wp-con tent/uploads/2022/08/30121338/Small-Business-Economic-Profile-US. pdf.
8. "2023 Small Business Trends," *Guidant*, accessed June 2023, https:// www.guidantfinancial.com/small-business-trends/.
9. Robert W. Fairlie, "The Impact of COVID-19 on Small Business Owners," *NBER Working Paper*, no. 27462 July 2020, https://www.nber. org/system/files/working_papers/w27462/w27462.pdf.
10. Chuck Castro, "Coronavirus Impact on Small Business—Nearly One Month In," *Alignable Blg*, April 2020.
11. Robert W. Fairlie, "The Impact of COVID-19 on Small Business Owners," *NBER Working Paper*, no. 27462 July 2020, https://www.nber. org/system/files/working_papers/w27462/w27462.pdf.
12. Diana Farrell and Chris Wheat, *Cash Is King: Flows, Balances, and Buffer Days: Evidence from 600,000 Small Businesses* (JPMorgan Chase and Co. Institute, September 2016), https://papers.ssrn.com/sol3/papers.cfm?abs tract_id=2966127.
13. "CDC Confirms Possible First Instance of COVID-19 Community Transmission in California," *California Department of Public Health Office of Public Affairs*, February 26, 2020, https://www.cdph.ca.gov/Pro grams/OPA/Pages/NR20-006.aspx.

14. Meg Anderson, "President Trump Confirms 1st U.S. Coronavirus Death; U.S. Heightens Travel Warnings," *NPR*, February 29, 2020, https://www.npr.org/2020/02/29/810722517/seattle-area-patient-with-coronavirus-dies.

15. "Virus Cases in State Top 30000," *The New York Times*, March 27, 2020, https://www.nytimes.com/2020/03/26/nyregion/coronavirus-nyc.html.

16. Cecelia Smith-Schoenwalder, "U.S. Coronavirus Cases Top 143,000 as New York Passes 1,000 Deaths," *U.S. News*, March 30, 2020https://www.usnews.com/news/health-news/articles/2020-03-30/us-corona virus-cases-top-143-000-as-new-york-passes-1-000-deaths.

17. "COVID-19 Pandemic EIDL and PPP Loan Fraud Landscape," *Small Business Administration Report*, June 27, 2023, https://www.sba.gov/doc ument/report-23-09-covid-19-pandemic-eidl-ppp-loan-fraud-landscape.

18. "President Bush Discusses Gulf Coast Recovery," *The White House Archives*, August 28, 2006, https://georgewbush-whitehouse.archives. gov/news/releases/2006/08/20060828-5.html.

19. Devin Dwyer and Janet Weinstein, "As Loans Run Out, Small Businesses Face Reckoning Amid COVID-19 Surge," *ABC News*, July 11, 2020, https://abcnews.go.com/Politics/loans-run-small-businesses-face-reckoning-amid-covid/story?id=71678006.

20. "United States Small Business Profile, 2020," *U.S. Small Business Administration Office of Advocacy*, 2020, https://advocacy.sba.gov/wp-content/uploads/2020/06/2020-Small-Business-Economic-Profile-US.pdf.

21. Note: Of the 11.4 million loans, 2.9 million were second draw loans, meaning that some businesses which already got a loan in previous rounds were able to get a second loan. Second draws were added by the SBA in the third round of PPP reflecting the length of the pandemic and the continuing needs of small businesses.

22. Robert W. Fairlie and Frank M. Fossen, "The 2021 Paycheck Protection Program Reboot: Loan Disbursement to Employer and Nonemployer Businesses in Minority Communities." *AEA Papers and Proceedings*, vol. 112, May 2022, https://www.aeaweb.org/articles?id=10.1257/pandp.20221028; Sabrina T. Howell, Theresa Kuchler, David Snitkof, Johannes Stroebel and Jun Wong "Lender Automation and Racial Disparities in Credit Access," *The Journal of Finance*, 2023.

23. Michael W Faulkender, Robert Jackman, and Stephen Mira, "The Job Preservation Effects of Paycheck Protection Program Loans," *Social Science Research Network Electronic Journal*, February 15, 2023, https://ssrn.com/abstract=3767509; "Paycheck Protection Program, Borrower

Application Form Revised March 18, 2021," *Small Business Administration*, accessed August 2023, https://www.sba.gov/sites/default/files/2021-03/BorrowerApplication2483ARPrevisions%20%28final%203-18-21%29-508.pdf.

24. "Paycheck Protection Program," *Small Business Administration*, accessed November 4, 2023, https://www.sba.gov/funding-programs/loans/covid-19-relief-options/paycheck-protection-program.

25. Tetyana Balyuk, Nagpurnanand Prabhala, and Manju Puri, "Small Bank Financing and Funding Hesitancy in a Crisis: Evidence from the Paycheck Protection Program," *FDIC Working Paper Series*, September 2021, https://www.fdic.gov/analysis/cfr/working-papers/2021/cfr-wp2021-01.pdf.

26. Note: Definition of small and large banks based on Jessica Battisto, Nathan Godin, Claire Kramer Mills, and Asani Sarkar, "Who Received PPP Loans by Fintech Lenders?" *Federal Reserve Bank of New York Liberty Street Economics Blog*, May 27, 2021, https://libertystreeteconomics.newyorkfed.org/2021/05/who-received-ppp-loans-by-fintech-lenders/.

27. "Federal Reserve Actions to Support the Flow of Credit to Households and Businesses," *Federal Reserve Press Release*, March 15, 2020, https://www.federalreserve.gov/newsevents/pressreleases/monetary20200315b.htm.

28. Steven Kelly, "United States: Paycheck Protection Program Liquidity Facility," *Social Science Research Network 4*, no. 2 (July 2022), https://elischolar.library.yale.edu/journal-of-financial-crises/vol4/iss2/88.

29. Alexander Bartik, Zoe Cullen, Edward L. Glaeser, Michael Luca, Christopher Stanton and Aditya Sunderam, "The Targeting and Impact of Paycheck Protection Program Loans to Small Businesses," *NBER Working Paper*, no. 27623, July 2020. https://www.nber.org/system/files/working_papers/w27623/revisions/w27623.rev1.pdf.

30. Based on tabulations by Sabrina T. Howell of the NYU Stern School of Business.

31. Ibid.

32. Author's calculations based on: Robert W. Fairlie and Frank M. Fossen, "The 2021 Paycheck Protection Program Reboot: Loan Disbursement to Employer and Nonemployer Businesses in Minority Communities." *AEA Papers and Proceedings*, vol. 112, May 2022, https://www.aeaweb.org/articles?id=10.1257/pandp.20221028.

33. "First COVID-19 Survey of Black and Latino Small-Business Owners Reveals Dire Economic Future, Inaccessible and Insufficient Government Relief Funds," *Color of Change/Unidos US*, May 18, 2020.

34. Note: The average loan size of $33,289 only included first draw loans. The third round also allowed small businesses to access a second draw.

35. Robert W. Fairlie and Frank M. Fossen, "The 2021 Paycheck Protection Program Reboot: Loan Disbursement to Employer and Nonemployer Businesses in Minority Communities." *AEA Papers and Proceedings*, vol. 112, May 2022, https://www.aeaweb.org/articles?id=10.1257/pandp.20221028.

36. Lei Li and Philip E. Strahan, "Who Supplies PPP Loans (and Does It Matter)? Banks, Relationships and the COVID Crisis," *Social Science Research Network*, June 2021, https://ssrn.com/abstract=3710929; Gustavo Joaquim and Felipe Netto, "Bank Incentives and the Impact of the Paycheck Protection Program," *Social Science Research Network*, October 2021, https://ssrn.com/abstract=3704518; João Granja, Christos Makridis, Constantine Yannelis, and Eric Zwick, "Did the Paycheck Protection Program Hit the Target?" *Journal of Financial Economics 145*, no. 3 (September 2022), https://doi.org/10.1016/j.jfineco.2022.05.006; Ran Duchin, Xiumin Martin, Roni Michaely, and Hanmeng Wang, "Concierge treatment from banks: Evidence from the paycheck protection program," *Journal of Corporate Finance 71* (February 2022), https://www.sciencedirect.com/science/article/pii/S0929119921002467.

37. Sabrina T. Howell, Theresa Kuchler, David Snitkof, Johannes Stroebel and Jun Wong "Lender Automation and Racial Disparities in Credit Access," *The Journal of Finance*, 2023; Robert W. Fairlie and Frank M. Fossen, "The 2021 Paycheck Protection Program Reboot: Loan Disbursement to Employer and Nonemployer Businesses in Minority Communities," *AEA Papers and Proceedings*, vol. 112, May 2022, https://www.aeaweb.org/articles?id=10.1257/pandp.20221028; Kristopher Deming and Stephan Weiler, "Banking Deserts and the Paycheck Protection Program," *Economic Development Quarterly*, *37*, no. 3 (February 2023), https://doi.org/10.1177/08912424231152873; T. William Lester and Matthew D. Wilson, "The Racial and Spatial Impacts of the Paycheck Protection Program," *Economic Development Quarterly 37*, no. 3 (February 2023), https://doi.org/10.1177/08912424231157693.

38. David Glancy, "Bank Relationships and the Geography of PPP Lending," *Federal Reserve Finance and Economics Discussion Series*, February 2023, https://www.federalreserve.gov/econres/feds/bank-relationships-and-the-geography-of-ppp-lending.htm.

39. Sabrina T. Howell, Theresa Kuchler, David Snitkof, Johannes Stroebel and Jun Wong "Lender Automation and Racial Disparities in Credit Access," *The Journal of Finance*, 2023; Robert W. Fairlie and Frank M. Fossen, "The 2021 Paycheck Protection Program Reboot: Loan Disbursement to Employer and Nonemployer Businesses in Minority Communities," *AEA Papers and Proceedings*, vol. 112, May 2022, https://www.aeaweb.org/articles?id=10.1257/pandp.20221028; Isil Erel and Jack Liebersohn, "Does FinTech Substitute for Banks? Evidence from the Paycheck Protection Program," *NBER Working Paper*, no. 27659, December 2020, https://www.nber.org/papers/w27659.

40. Isil Erel and Jack Liebersohn, "Does FinTech Substitute for Banks? Evidence from the Paycheck Protection Program," *NBER Working Paper*, no. 27659, December 2020, https://www.nber.org/papers/w27659.

41. Author's analysis of data from "The PPP Experience for Small Business Owners at CDFIs," *60 Decibels*, 2022, https://60decibels.com/expertise/micro-and-small-businesses/.

42. Sabrina T. Howell, Theresa Kuchler, David Snitkof, Johannes Stroebel and Jun Wong "Lender Automation and Racial Disparities in Credit Access," *The Journal of Finance*, 2023.

43. Ibid.

44. Center for Disease Control and Prevention, accessed August 2023, https://www.cdc.gov/index.htm.

45. "Testimony of Patrick Kelley Associate Administrator Office of Capital Access U.S. Small Business Administration Before the Committee on Small Business and Entrepreneurship United States Senate," Small Business Administration, August 2, 2022, https://www.sbc.senate.gov/public/_cache/files/a/b/ab3b24c9-86dc-4a15-a0b8-46cc63fdef73/6DF327 25E45B76CDD56FE8EFD91A5414.kelley-testimony.pdf.

46. Jean Folger, "Federal Pandemic Unemployment Programs: How They Worked," *Investopedia*, January 3, 2023, https://www.investopedia.com/federal-pandemic-unemployment-programs-how-they-worked-480 1925.

47. Note: On June 5, 2020, the "Paycheck Protection Program Flexibility Act of 2020" was signed. This act led to changes in PPP forgiveness eligibility in which the payroll costs needed to make up 60% of the loan amount, down from 75%. Robert W. Fairlie and Frank M. Fossen, "The 2021 Paycheck Protection Program Reboot: Loan Disbursement to Employer and Nonemployer Businesses in Minority Communities," *AEA Papers and Proceedings*, vol. 112, May 2022, https://www.aeaweb.org/articles?id=10.1257/pandp.20221028.

48. "FAQ for PPP Borrowers and Lenders," *Small Business Administration*, accessed November 7, 2023, https://www.sba.gov/document/support-faq-ppp-borrowers-lenders.

49. "2022 Forgiveness Platform Lender Submission Metrics Report", *Small Business Administration Office of Capital Access*, October 24, 2022, https://www.sba.gov/document/report-2022-ppp-forgiveness-platform-lender-submission-metrics-reports.

50. "SBA's Response to the Deepwater Horizon Oil Spill", *Small Business Administration*, April 7, 2011, https://www.sba.gov/sites/sbagov/files/2019-07/Report-11-12-SBAs-Response-to-the-Deepwater-Horizon-Oil-Spill.pdf.

51. "Covid-19 Economic Injury Disaster Loan," *Small Business Administration Funding Programs*, accessed August 2023 https://www.sba.gov/funding-programs/loans/covid-19-relief-options/eidl.

52. Note: Businesses were allowed to receive both an EIDL loan and a PPP grant but had to use the funds for different costs.

53. "Four Million Hard-Hit Businesses Approved for Nearly $390 Billion in COVID Economic Injury Disaster Loans," *Small Business Administration Press Release*, June 13, 2022, https://www.sba.gov/article/2022/jun/13/four-million-hard-hit-businesses-approved-nearly-390-billion-covid-economic-injury-disaster-loans.

54. "Restaurant Revitalization Fund," *Small Business Administration Funding Programs*, accessed August 2023, https://www.sba.gov/funding-programs/loans/covid-19-relief-options/restaurant-revitalization-fund.

55. "SBA Administrator Announces Closure of Restaurant Revitalization Fund Program," *Small Business Administration Press Release*, July 2, 2021, https://www.sba.gov/article/2021/jul/02/sba-administrator-announces-closure-restaurant-revitalization-fund-program.

56. Note: The program was created as part of the Economic Aid to Hard-Hit Small Businesses, Nonprofits, and Venues Act, which was passed by Congress on December 27, 2020.

57. "Shuttered Venue Operators Grant," *Small Business Administration Funding Programs*, accessed August 2023, https://www.sba.gov/funding-programs/loans/covid-19-relief-options/shuttered-venue-operators-grant.

58. Jeff Drew, "Shuttered Venue Operator Grant Awards top $7.5 Billion, SBA Says," July 27, 2021, https://www.journalofaccountancy.com/news/2021/jul/sba-svog-shuttered-venue-operator-grant-awards.html.

59. Note: Estimate based on SBA program data: 8.9 million businesses received first draw PPP loans and 3.9 million received Covid EIDL loans, excluding the EIDL Supplements and EIDL Advances (https://www.sba.gov/funding-programs/loans/covid-19-relief-options/paycheck-protection-program/ppp-data#id-program-reports; https://www.sba.gov/funding-programs/loans/covid-19-relief-options/eidl/eidl-data).

Chapter 9

1. Michelle Toh, "Shake Shack Returns $10 Million Emergency Loan to the US Government," *CNN Business*, April 20, 2020, https://edition.cnn.com/2020/04/20/business/shake-shack-ppp-loan-sba/index.html.
2. Kevin Arnovitz, "Lakers Got Money from Loan Program, Returned It," *ESPN*, April 27 2020, https://www.espn.com/nba/story/_/id/29104444/lakers-got-money-loan-program-returned-it.
3. Bruce Brumberg, "88% of Public Companies That Got PPP Loans Kept the Funds," *Forbes*, September 15, 2020, https://www.forbes.com/sites/brucebrumberg/2020/09/15/88-of-public-companies-that-got-ppp-loans-kept-the-funds/.
4. "Protecting the Integrity of the Pandemic Relief Programs," *Small Business Administration Report*, June 27, 2023, https://www.sba.gov/document/report-protecting-integrity-pandemic-relief-programs.
5. "Small Business Administration loan program performance, Table 5 - Charge Off Amount by Program", Small Business Administration, accessed June 2024, https://www.sba.gov/document/report-small-business-administration-loan-program-performance. Note: The $52 billion charge-offs include defaults by small business who legitimately obtained a Covid EIDL loan but were unable to repay the obligation.
6. John M. Griffin, Samuel Kruger and Prateek Mahajan, "Did FinTech Lenders Facilitate PPP Fraud?" *Journal of Finance*, forthcoming, August 17, 2022, https://ssrn.com/abstract=3906395.
7. "How Fintechs Facilitated Fraud in the Paycheck Protection Program," *The House Select Subcommittee on the Coronavirus Crisis*, December 2022, https://coronavirus-democrats-oversight.house.gov/news/reports/new-select-subcommittee-report-reveals-how-fintech-companies-facilitated-fraud-paycheck.
8. "Protecting the Integrity of the Pandemic Relief Programs," *Small Business Administration Report*, June 27, 2023, https://www.sba.gov/document/report-protecting-integrity-pandemic-relief-programs.

9. "How Fintechs Facilitated Fraud in the Paycheck Protection Program," *The House Select Subcommittee on the Coronavirus Crisis*, December 2022, https://coronavirus-democrats-oversight.house.gov/news/reports/new-select-subcommittee-report-reveals-how-fintech-companies-facilitated-fraud-paycheck.

10. "Small Business Administration Paycheck Protection Program Phase III Fraud Controls," *Pandemic Response Accountability Committee*, January 21, 2022, https://www.oversight.gov/sites/default/files/oig-reports/PRAC/SBAFraudControlsFinal02Jan21.pdf.

11. "Protecting the Integrity of the Pandemic Relief Programs," *Small Business Administration Report*, June 27, 2023, https://www.sba.gov/document/report-protecting-integrity-pandemic-relief-programs.

12. "Technology Solutions for PPP and Beyond", *FinReg Lab Research Brief*, June 2020, https://finreglab.org/wp-content/uploads/2020/06/FinRegLab-Brief_Technology-Solutions-for-PPP-and-Beyond.pdf.

13. "Lessons Learned in Oversight of Pandemic Relief Funds," *Pandemic Response Accountability Committee*, June 8, 2022, https://www.pandemicoversight.gov/media/file/prac-lessons-learned-update-june-2022pdf.

14. Chuck Casto, "Special Report: Small Biz Labor Shortage Worsens, 65% Can't Find Workers, Up 5%," *Alignable Blog*, March 4, 2022, https://www.alignable.com/forum/small-biz-labor-shortage-worsens-65-cant-find-workers-up-5.

15. "Special Report on Inflation and Supply Chain Shocks on Small Business," *U.S. Chamber of Commerce*, March 3, 2022, https://www.uschamber.com/small-business/special-report-on-inflation-and-supply-chain-shocks-on-small-business.

16. David Autor, David Cho, Leland D. Crane, Mita Goldar, Byron Lutz, Joshua Montes, William B. Peterman, David Ratner, Daniel Villar, and Ahu Yildirmaz, "The $800 Billion Paycheck Protection Program: Where Did the Money Go and Why Did It Go There?" *Journal of Economic Perspectives 36* (Spring 2022), https://www.aeaweb.org/articles?id=10.1257/jep.36.2.55. Note: Measure of job saved in job-year, that is, one worker for one year.

17. Michael W Faulkender, Robert Jackman, and Stephen Mira, "The Job Preservation Effects of Paycheck Protection Program Loans" *Social Science Research Network Electronic Journal* (February 15, 2023), https://ssrn.com/abstract=3767509.

18. Ibid.

19. Robert P. Bartlett III, and Adair Morse, "Small Business Survival Capabilities and Policy Effectiveness: Evidence from Oakland," *NBER Working Papers*, no. 27629, July 2020, https://www.nber.org/papers/w27629.
20. Allison Cole, "The Impact of the Paycheck Protection Program on (Really) Small Businesses," *Social Science Research Network Electronic Journal*, May 13, 2022, https://ssrn.com/abstract=3730268.
21. Allison Cole, "The Impact of the Paycheck Protection Program on (Really) Small Businesses," *Social Science Research Network Electronic Journal*, May 13, 2022, https://ssrn.com/abstract=3730268; Gustavo Joaquim, and Christina J. Wang, "What Do 25 Million Records of Small Businesses Say About the Effects of the PPP?" *Federal Reserve Bank of Boston Research Department Working Papers*, No. 22-23, August 2022, https://doi.org/10.29412/res.wp.2022.23; Michael W. Faulkender, Robert Jackman, and Stephen Mira, "The Job Preservation Effects of Paycheck Protection Program Loans," *Social Science Research Network Electronic Journal*, February 15, 2023, https://ssrn.com/abstract=3767509; David Autor, David Cho, Leland D. Crane, Mita Goldar, Byron Lutz, Joshua Montes, William B. Peterman, David Ratner, Daniel Villar, and Ahu Yildirmaz, "The $800 Billion Paycheck Protection Program: Where Did the Money Go and Why Did It Go There?" *Journal of Economic Perspectives 36* (Spring 2022), https://www.aeaweb.org/articles?id=10.1257/jep.36.2.55.
22. Alexander Bartik, Marianne Bertrand, Zoe Cullen, Edward L. Glaeser, Michael Luca, and Christopher Stanton, "The Impact of COVID-19 on Small Business Outcomes and Expectations," *Proceedings of the National Academy of Sciences*, vol. 117, no. 30 (July 2020), https://doi.org/10.1073/pnas.2006991117.
23. Michael Dalton, "Putting the Paycheck Protection Program into Perspective: An Analysis Using Administrative and Survey Data," *BLS Working Paper*, November 2021, https://www.bls.gov/osmr/research-papers/2021/pdf/ec210080.pdf; Alexander W. Bartik, Zoe B. Cullen, Edward L. Glaeser, Michael Luca, Christopher T. Stanton, and Adi Sunderam, "When Should Public Programs Be Privately Administered? Theory and Evidence from the Paycheck Protection Program," *NBER Working Paper*, no. 27623, July 2023, https://www.nber.org/papers/w27623.
24. Note: For example, Dalton estimates that within the first month of PPP approval, an establishment is about 5.8% less likely to close relative to an establishment that did not receive approval for a PPP

loan. Michael Dalton, "Putting the Paycheck Protection Program into Perspective: An Analysis Using Administrative and Survey Data," *BLS Working Paper*, November 2021, https://www.bls.gov/osmr/research-pap ers/2021/pdf/ec210080.pdf; Alexander Bartik, Marianne Bertrand, Zoe Cullen, Edward L. Glaeser, Michael Luca, and Christopher Stanton, "The Impact of COVID-19 on Small Business Outcomes and Expectations," *Proceedings of the National Academy of Sciences*, vol. 117 no. 30, July 2020, https://doi.org/10.1073/pnas.2006991117; Robert P. Bartlett III, and Adair Morse, "Small Business Survival Capabilities and Policy Effectiveness: Evidence from Oakland," *NBER Working Papers*, no. 27629, July 2020, https://www.nber.org/papers/w27629.

25. "Business Entry and Exit in the COVID-19 Pandemic: A Preliminary Look at Official Data," *Federal Reserve FEDS Notes*, May 6, 2022, https://www.federalreserve.gov/econres/notes/feds-notes/business-entry-and-exit-in-the-covid-19-pandemic-a-preliminary-look-at-official-data-20220506.html.

26. Sabrina T. Howell, Theresa Kuchler, David Snitkof, Johannes Stroebel and Jun Wong, "Lender Automation and Racial Disparities in Credit Access," *The Journal of Finance*, 2023; Robert W. Fairlie and Frank M. Fossen, "The 2021 Paycheck Protection Program Reboot: Loan Disbursement to Employer and Nonemployer Businesses in Minority Communities." *AEA Papers and Proceedings*, vol. 112, May 2022, https://www.aeaweb.org/articles?id=10.1257/pandp.20221028; Isil Erel and Jack Liebersohn, "Does FinTech Substitute for Banks? Evidence from the Paycheck Protection Program," *NBER Working Paper*, no. 27659, December 2020, https://www.nber.org/papers/w27659; Gustavo Joaquim and Felipe Netto, "Bank Incentives and the Impact of the Paycheck Protection Program," *Social Science Research Network*, October 2021, https://ssrn.com/abstract=3704518.

27. David Autor, David Cho, Leland D. Crane, Mita Goldar, Byron Lutz, Joshua Montes, William B. Peterman, David Ratner, Daniel Villar, and Ahu Yildirmaz, "The $800 Billion Paycheck Protection Program: Where Did the Money Go and Why Did It Go There?" *Journal of Economic Perspectives 36* (Spring 2022), https://www.aeaweb.org/articles?id=10.1257/jep.36.2.55; Alexander W. Bartik, Zoe B. Cullen, Edward L. Glaeser, Michael Luca, Christopher T. Stanton, and Adi Sunderam, "When Should Public Programs be Privately Administered? Theory and Evidence from the Paycheck Protection Program," *NBER Working Paper*, no. 27623, July 2023, https://www.nber.org/papers/w27623.

Chapter 10

1. "Shopify Magic", *Shopify*, accessed November 5, 2023, https://www.sho pify.com/magic.
2. Rockwell Anyoha, "The History of Artificial Intelligence," *Harvard University Blog*, Special Edition on Artificial Intelligence, August 28, 2017, https://sitn.hms.harvard.edu/flash/2017/history-artificial-intellige nce/.
3. "The Use of Cash-Flow Data in Underwriting Credit", *FinReg Small Business Spotlight*, September 2019, https://finreglab.org/wp-content/upl oads/2019/09/FinRegLab-Small-Business-Spotlight-Report.pdf.
4. Mia Ellis, Cynthia Kinnan, Margaret S. McMillan and Sarah Shaukat, "What Predicts the Growth of Small Firms? Evidence from Tanzanian Commercial Loan Data," *NBER Working Paper*, no. 31620, August 2023, https://www.nber.org/papers/w31620.
5. "The Use of Cash-Flow Data in Underwriting Credit", *FinReg Small Business Spotlight*, September 2019, https://finreglab.org/wp-content/upl oads/2019/09/FinRegLab-Small-Business-Spotlight-Report.pdf.
6. "Enigma Raises Another $95M to Bridge the Gap Between Data and Business Decisions," *AlleyWatch*, September 2018, https://www.alleyw atch.com/2018/09/enigma-raises-another-95m-to-bridge-the-gap-bet ween-public-data-and-business-decisions/.
7. "Tala," *CNBC Disruptor 50*, May 15, 2023, https://www.cnbc.com/ 2023/05/09/tala-disruptor-50.html.
8. Victor Oluwole, "M-Pesa: Kenya's Mobile Money Success Story Celebrates 15 Years," *Business Insider Africa*, March 7, 2022, https://afr ica.businessinsider.com/local/markets/m-pesa-kenyas-mobile-money-suc cess-story-celebrates-15-years/srp9gne.
9. AJ Chen, Omri Even-Tov, Jung Koo Kang, and Regina Wittenberg Moerman, "Digital Lending and Financial Well-Being: Through the Lens of Mobile Phone Data," *Harvard Business School Research Paper Series Working Paper*, no. 23-076, July 2023.
10. Vindu Goel, "The New York Times, India's Top Court Limits Sweep of Biometric ID Program," *The New York Times*, September 2018, https:// www.nytimes.com/2018/09/26/technology/india-id-aadhaar-supreme-court.html.
11. Benjamin Parkin, John Reed and Jyotsna Singh, "The India Stack: Opening the Digital Marketplace to the Masses," *Financial Times*, April 20, 2023, https://www.ft.com/content/cf75a136-c6c7-49d0-8c1c-89e046b8a170?sharetype=blocked.

12. Karen G. Mills and Ahmed Dahawy, "Chari: Exploring Fintech in Morocco," *Harvard Business School Case*, no. N2-323-082, February 27, 2023.

13. Ibid.

14. Iain M. Cockburn, Rebecca Henderson, and Scott Stern, "The Impact of Artificial Intelligence on Innovation: An Exploratory Analysis," *University of Chicago Press*, Chapter 4 in the Economics of Artificial Intelligence: An Agenda, 2019.

15. Zvi Griliches, "Hybrid Corn: An Exploration in the Economics of Technological Change," *Econometrica 25*, no. 4 (1957): 501–522.

Chapter 11

1. "Small Businesses Are Hurting. Our Survey Shows How Banks Can Help." *PwC*, Pulse Small Business Survey, April 2020.

2. Joshua Franklin, "Goldman Sachs Pulls Back from Retail Banking in Latest Overhaul," *Financial Times*, October 18, 2022, https://www.ft.com/content/cac2059d-4ead-4415-a7ef-74cdfc3c13d2.

3. "Annual Report & Proxy," *J.P. Morgan Chase & Co*, accessed October 3, 2023, https://www.jpmorganchase.com/ir/annual-report; "7(a) & 504 Lender Report," *Small Business Administration*, accessed October 3, 2023, https://careports.sba.gov/views/7a504LenderReport/LenderRep ort?%3Aembed=yes&%3Atoolbar=no.

4. Sabrina T. Howell, Theresa Kuchler, David Snitkof, Johannes Stroebel and Jun Wong "Lender Automation and Racial Disparities in Credit Access," *The Journal of Finance*, 2023. Note: Researchers noted that J.P. Morgan and Wells Fargo served 70.2 and 73.7% of their own customers respectively (from NBER Working Paper 29364, version of October 2021, Table 1, Panel C).

5. Vishal Dalal, Ondrej Dusek, Anand Mohanrangan, "Core Systems Strategy for Banks," *McKinsey & Company*, May 4, 2020, https://www.mckinsey.com/industries/financial-services/our-insights/banking-mat ters/core-systems-strategy-for-banks; "Should US Banks Be Moving to Next-Generation Core Banking Platforms?" *McKinsey & Company*, June 26, 2022, https://www.mckinsey.com/industries/financial-services/our-insights/should-us-banks-be-moving-to-next-generation-core-banking-platforms.

6. "The Argument for an Open Approach to Banking Technology & Culture," *Jack Henry White Paper*, 2022, https://www.jackhenry.com/hubfs/resources/white-papers/jh-white-paper-digital-banking-the-argument-for-an-open-approach.pdf.

7. Interview with Gina Taylor, October 23, 2023.

8. "Business Blueprint," *American Express*, accessed October 5, 2023, https://www.americanexpress.com/en-us/business/blueprint/.

9. Sarah K. White, "Investing in IT Careers Pays Off at Capital One," *CIO*, April 5, 2022, https://www.cio.com/article/307683/investing-in-it-careers-pays-off-at-capital-one.html.

10. Miriam Cross, "Small-Bank Rarity: A Digital Launch That Happened on Time," *American Banker*, August 10, 2023, https://www.americanbanker.com/news/small-bank-rarity-a-digital-launch-that-happened-on-time.

11. "A Retail Incubator for the Shopkeeper Experience." *Citizens Bank RISE*, accessed October 30, 2023, https://mycitizens.bank/rise.

12. "The Big Tech in Fintech Report: How Meta, Apple, Google, & Amazon Are Battling for the Future of Financial Services", *CB Insights*, October 2022, https://www.cbinsights.com/research/report/big-tech-fintech/#:~:text=Apple%20and%20Google%20are%20now,competing%20for%20Amazon's%20market%20share.

13. Ibid.

14. "Annual Report 2022," *Amazon*, 2023, https://s2.q4cdn.com/299287126/files/doc_financials/2023/ar/Amazon-2022-Annual-Report.pdf.

15. "Amazon Business Prime American Express Card," *Amazon*, accessed November 2023, https://www.amazon.com/dp/B07984JN3L?plattr=30215.

16. "Pay By Invoice",*Amazon Business*, accessed August 2023, https://www.amazon.com/Amazon-Business-Pay-by-Invoice/dp/B07GZY6QJK.

17. "The Big Tech in Fintech Report: How Meta, Apple, Google, & Amazon Are Battling for the Future of Financial Services", *CB Insights*, October 2022, https://www.cbinsights.com/research/report/big-tech-fintech/#:~:text=Apple%20and%20Google%20are%20now,competing%20for%20Amazon's%20market%20share.

18. "Apple Working to Bring More Financial Services In-House," *Bloomberg*, March 30, 2022, https://www.bloomberg.com/news/articles/2022-03-30/apple-is-working-on-project-to-bring-financial-services-in-house.

19. "Apple Acquires Credit Kudos, UK Data Tool for Lenders," *PYMTS*, March 23, 2022, https://www.pymnts.com/news/digital-banking/2022/apple-acquires-credit-kudos-uk-data-tool-for-lenders/#:~:text=Apple%20has%20bought%20the%20U.K.,transaction%20and%20loan%20outcome%20data.

20. "Google Kills The Google Plex: It Could Have Been A Digital Checking Account Killer App," *Forbes*,October 2021, https://www.forbes.com/sites/ronshevlin/2021/10/01/google-kills-the-google-plex-it-could-have-been-a-digital-checking-account-killer-app/?sh=564631ed20d5.

21. "Big Tech in Fintech Report," *CB Insights*, October 2022, https://www.altfi.com/article/10594_neobanks-10-now-use-app-only-bank-as-main-account.

22. Oliver Smith, "Challenger Bank SME Lending Hit £35.5bn in 2022, Overtaking Incumbents," *Altfi*, March 1, 2023, https://www.altfi.com/article/10462_challenger-bank-sme-lending-hit-355bn-in-2022-overtaking-incumbents.

23. Daniel Lanyon, "Neobanks: 10% Now Use App-Only Bank as Main Account," *Altfi*, April 11, 2023, https://www.altfi.com/article/10594_neobanks-10-now-use-app-only-bank-as-main-account.

24. "The Road to Starling," *Starling Bank*, accessed November 5, 2023, https://www.starlingbank.com/about/road-to-starling/.

25. "Organise Your Finances with Saving Spaces," *Starling Bank*, accessed November 5, 2023, https://www.starlingbank.com/features/saving-spaces/.

26. "How Consumers Use Digital Banks," *PYMNTS & Treasury Prime*, September 2022, https://www.pymnts.com/news/digital-banking/2023/only-25-percent-consumers-have-used-neobank-digital-bank-fintech/.

27. Ibid.

28. "Only 25% of Consumers Have Ever Used a FinTech Bank," *PYMNTS*, May 25, 2023, https://www.pymnts.com/news/digital-banking/2023/only-25-percent-consumers-have-used-neobank-digital-bank-fintech/.

29. "7(a) & 504 Lender Report," *Small Business Administration*, accessed November 5, 2023, https://careports.sba.gov/views/7a504LenderReport/LenderReport?%3Aembed=yes&%3Atoolbar=no.

30. Vishal Dalal, Ondrej Dusek, Anand Mohanrangan, "Core Systems Strategy for Banks," *McKinsey & Company*, May 4, 2020, https://www.mckinsey.com/industries/financial-services/our-insights/banking-matters/core-systems-strategy-for-banks; "Should US Banks Be Moving to Next-Generation Core Banking Platforms?" *McKinsey & Company*, June 26, 2022, https://www.mckinsey.com/industries/financial-services/our-insights/should-us-banks-be-moving-to-next-generation-core-banking-platforms.

31. "Embedded Finance: What It Takes to Prosper in the New Value Chain," *Bain & Company and Bain Capital Report*, September 2022, https://www.bain.com/insights/embedded-finance/.

32. Jeffrey Bussgang, "Bussgang's Bullets Linkedin, Vertical SaaS: Flipping the Playbook," *Linkedin*, August 2023, https://www.linkedin.com/pulse/vertical-saas-flipping-playbook-jeffrey-bussgang/.

Chapter 12

1. Portions of this story are adapted from Karen Gordon Mills, Dennis Campbell, and Aaron Mukerjee, *Eastern Bank: Innovating Through Eastern Labs*, HBS No. 9-318-068 (Boston: Harvard Business School Publishing, 2017), https://www.hbs.edu/faculty/Pages/item.aspx?num=53399. Unless otherwise noted, all quotes come from this case. Note: The author is an investor in Numerated Growth Technologies.
2. "The Future of Banks: A $20 Trillion Breakup Opportunity", *McKinsey & Company*, December 20, 2022, https://www.mckinsey.com/industries/financial-services/our-insights/the-future-of-banks-a-20-trillion-dollar-breakup-opportunity#/; "Global Fintech 2023: Reimagining the Future of Finance," *BCG*, May 3, 2023, https://www.bcg.com/publications/2023/future-of-fintech-and-banking; "Embedded Finance: What It Takes to Prosper in the New Value Chain," *Bain & Company and Bain Capital Report*, September 2022, https://www.bain.com/insights/embedded-finance/.
3. "Comprehensive New Data Reassesses the MSME Finance Gap in Developing Countries," *International Finance Corporation*, November 3, 2017, https://pressroom.ifc.org/all/pages/PressDetail.aspx?ID=18268.
4. "How Community Banks Can Embrace the Small Business Market," *Amount and Cornestone Advisors*, November 2022, https://www.amount.com/small-business-big-ambitions-report.
5. Ibid.
6. Note: Total assets, which include reserves, loans and securities, were 0.017 trillion in 2008 versus 3.7 trillion in 2022. Author's analysis of "Annual Report 2008 of J.P. Morgan AG," *J.P. Morgan Chase & Co*, accessed October 3, 2023, https://www.jpmorgan.com/content/dam/jpm/global/disclosures/de/english-version-of-disclosures/2008-annual-report-english.pdf; "JPMorgan Chase Acquires Substantial Majority of Assets and Assumes Certain Liabilities of First Republic Bank", *J.P. Morgan Chase & Co Press Releases*, May 1, 2023, https://www.jpmorganchase.com/ir/news/2023/jpmc-acquires-substantial-majority-of-assets-and-assumes-certain-liabilities-of-first-republic-bank#:~:text=About%20JPMorgan%20Chase&text=(NYSE%3A%20JPM)%20is%20a,as%20of%20March%2031%2C%202023.

7. Note: Total assets, which include reserves, loans and securities, were 1.74 trillion in 2008 versus 3.05 trillion in 2022. Author's analysis of "Bank of America Earns $1.21 Billion, or $0.23 Per Share, in the First Quarter," *Bank of America Press Release*, April 21, 2008, https://investor.bankofamerica.com/regulatory-and-other-filings/all-sec-filings/content/0001193125-08-085232/dex991.htm#:~:text=Period%2Dend%20assets%20were%20%241.74,of%20preferred%20stock%20in%20January; "Annual Report 2022," *Bank of America*, 2023, https://d1io3yog0oux5.cloudfront.net/bankofamerica/files/pages/bankofamerica/db/809/content/BAC_AR22_final_030523_%281%29.pdf.

8. Ron Shevlin, "What's Going on in Banking 2023," *Cornerstone Advisors Report*, 2023, https://www.crnrstone.com/whats-going-on-in-banking-2023.

9. Ibid.

10. Juan Antonio Bahillo, Frank Gerhard, Abhimanyu Harlalka, András Havas, and Andreas Kremer, "How Banks Can Reimagine Lending to Small and Medium-Size Enterprises," *Mckinsey & Company*, May 24, 2022, https://www.mckinsey.com/capabilities/risk-and-resilience/our-insights/how-banks-can-reimagine-lending-to-small-and-medium-size-enterprises.

11. Michael T. Tushman, Wendy K. Smith, and Andy Binns, "The Ambidextrous CEO," *Harvard Business Review*, June 2011, https://hbr.org/2011/06/the-ambidextrous-ceo; Charles A. O'Reilly and Michael L. Tushman, "The Ambidextrous Organization," *Harvard Business Review*, April 2004, https://hbr.org/2004/04/the-ambidextrous-organization.

12. "The Opportunities of Banking as a Service", *MasterCard Data & Services*, October 2022, https://www.mastercardservices.com/en/reports-insights/opportunities-banking-service.

13. "Banking as a Service: Banks' $25 Billion Revenue Opportunity in FinTech Banking," *Synctera*, February 2022, https://www.synctera.com/post/banking-as-a-service-banks-25-billion-revenue-opportunity-in-fintech-banking.

Chapter 13

1. Sandra K. Hoffman and Tracy G. McGinley, *Identity Theft: A Reference Handbook* (ABC-CLIO, 2010), 11.

2. Sean Vanatta, "The Great Chicago Christmas Credit Card Fiasco of 1966: Echoes," *Bloomberg*, December 24, 2012, https://www.bloomberg.com/view/articles/2012-12-24/the-great-chicago-christmas-credit-card-fiasco-of-1966-echoes.

3. "Financial Regulation: Complex and Fragmented Structure Could Be Streamlined to Improve Effectiveness," *United States Government Accountability Office*, February 2016, http://www.gao.gov/assets/680/675400.pdf.

4. Elizabeth F. Brown, "Prior Proposals to Consolidate Federal Financial Regulators," *The Volcker Alliance*, February 14, 2016, https://www.volckeralliance.org/sites/default/files/attachments/Background%20Paper%201_Prior%20Proposals%20to%20Consolidate%20Federal%20Financial%20Regulators.pdf.

5. "About the Federal Reserve System," Board of Governors of the Federal Reserve System, last updated August 24, 2022, https://www.federalreserve.gov/aboutthefed/structure-federal-reserve-system.htm.

6. "What We Do," *Federal Deposit Insurance Corporation*, last updated May 15, 2020, https://www.fdic.gov/about/what-we-do/.

7. "About us," *Office of the Comptroller of the Currency*, accessed October 4, 2023, https://www.occ.gov/about/index-about.html.

8. "Fair Credit Reporting Act," *Federal Trade Commission*, accessed November 7, 2023, https://www.ftc.gov/legal-library/browse/statutes/fair-credit-reporting-act.

9. "The CFPB," *Consumer Financial Protection Bureau*, accessed January 2024, https://www.consumerfinance.gov/about-us/the-bureau/#:~:text=We%20protect%20consumers%20from%20unfair,to%20make%20smart%20financial%20decisions.

10. Kevin V. Tu, "Regulating the New Cashless World," *Alabama Law Review 65*, no. 1 (2013): 109, accessed March 27, 2018, https://www.law.ua.edu/pubs/lrarticles/Volume%2065/Issue%201/2%20Tu%2077-138.pdf.

11. "Vision 2020 for Fintech and Non-Bank Regulation," *Conference of State Bank Supervisors*, June 7, 2018, https://www.csbs.org/vision2020.

12. "SES Consumer Finance Standards Expand State Exam Uniformity", *CSBS*, April 3, 2023, https://www.csbs.org/ses-consumer-finance-standards-expand-state-exam-uniformity.

13. "OCC Begins Accepting National Bank Charter Applications From Financial Technology Companies," *Office of the Comptroller of The Currency*, July 31, 2018, https://www.occ.gov/news-issuances/news-releases/2018/nr-occ-2018-74.html.

14. "Interagency Guidance on Third-Party Relationships: Risk Management," *The Board of Governors of the Federal Reserve System (Board), the Federal Deposit Insurance Corporation (FDIC), and the Office of the Comptroller of the Currency (OCC), Treasury*, June 6, 2023, https://www.occ.gov/news-issuances/news-releases/2023/nr-ia-2023-53a.pdf.

15. "Guidance on Managing Outsourcing Risk," *Board of Governors of the Federal Reserve System*, June 7, 2023.

16. "Guidance for Managing Third-Party Risk", *FDIC*, June 6, 2008.

17. OCC Bulletin, "Third-Party Relationships: Risk Management Guidance," *OCC Bulletin*, 2013; "Third-Party Relationships: Frequently Asked Questions to Supplement OCC Bulletin 2013-29," *OCC Bulletin*, 2020.

18. "Guidance on Managing Outsourcing Risk," *Board of Governors of the Federal Reserve System*, December 5, 2013, updated February 26, 2021.

19. "Interagency Guidance on Third-Party Relationships: Risk Management," *The Board of Governors of the Federal Reserve System (Board), the Federal Deposit Insurance Corporation (FDIC), and the Office of the Comptroller of the Currency (OCC), Treasury*, June 6, 2023, https://www.occ.gov/news-issuances/news-releases/2023/nr-ia-2023-53a.pdf.

20. Barbara J. Lipman and Ann Marie Wiersch, "Alternative Lending Through the Eyes of 'Mom & Pop' Small-Business Owners: Findings from Online Focus Groups," *Federal Reserve Bank of Cleveland*, August 25, 2015, https://www.clevelandfed.org/newsroom-and-events/publications/spe-cial-reports/sr-20150825-alternative-lending-through-the-eyes-of-mom-and-pop-small-business-owners.aspx.

21. Barbara J. Lipman and Ann Marie Wiersch, "Browsing to Borrow: Mom & Pop Small Business Perspectives on Online Lenders," *Federal Reserve Board and Federal Reserve Bank of Cleveland*, June 2018, https://www.federalreserve.gov/publications/files/2018-small-business-lending.pdf.

22. "Unaffordable and Unsustainable: The New Business Lending on Main Street," *Opportunity Fund*, May 2016, https://aofund.org/app/uploads/2021/03/Unaffordable-and-Unsustainable-The-New-Business-Lending-on-Main-Street_Opportunity-Fund-Research-Report_May-2016.pdf.

23. Patrick Clark, "How Much Is Too Much to Pay for a Small Business Loan," *Bloomberg*, May 16, 2014, http://www.bloomberg.com/news/articles/2014-05-16/how-much-is-too-much-to-pay-for-a-small-busi-ness-loan.

24. Ben Wieder, "Even Finance Whizzes Say It's Impossible to Compare Online Small Business Loan Options," *McClatchy*, June 8, 2018, http://www.mcclatchydc.com/news/nation-world/national/article212491199.html.

25. Leonard J. Kennedy, "Memorandum to Chief Executive Officers of Financial Institutions Under Section 1071 of the Dodd-Frank Act," *Consumer Financial Protection Bureau*, April 11, 2011, http://files.consumerfinance.gov/f/2011/04/GC-letter-re-1071.pdf.

26. Consumer Financial Protection Bureau, "Request for Information Regarding the Small Business Lending Market," *Federal Register*, May 15, 2017, https://www.federalregister.gov/documents/2017/05/15/2017-09732/request-for-information-regarding-the-small-business-lending-market.

Chapter 14

1. "Small Business Borrowers' Bill of Rights," *The Aspen Institute*, accessed October 5, 2023, https://www.aspeninstitute.org/programs/business-ownership-initiative/small-business-borrowers-bill-rights/.

2. "The Small Business Borrowers' Bill of Rights," *Responsible Business Lending Coalition*, accessed September 22, 2018, http://www.borrowers-billofrights.org/.

3. Interview with George Osborne, September 2016.

4. "About the FCA," *Financial Conduct Authority*, accessed March 30, 2018, https://www.fca.org.uk/about/the-fca.

5. "Regulatory Sandbox," *Financial Conduct Authority*, November 2015, https://www.fca.org.uk/publication/research/regulatory-sandbox.pdf.

6. Note: These modifications would apply as long as the waiver or modification did not conflict with FCA objectives or violate U.K. or international law.

7. "Project Innovate and Innovation Hub," *Financial Conduct Authority*, accessed March 30, 2018, https://www.fca.org.uk/firms/fca-innovate.

8. "Regulatory Sandbox Lessons Learned Report," *Financial Conduct Authority*, October 2017, https://www.fca.org.uk/publication/research-and-data/regulatory-sandbox-lessons-learned-report.pdf.

9. "Regulatory Sandbox," *Financial Conduct Authority*, accessed August 2023, https://www.fca.org.uk/firms/innovation/regulatory-sandbox.

10. Rowland Manthorpe, "What Is Open Banking and PSD2? WIRED Explains," *WIRED*, April 17, 2018, https://www.wired.co.uk/article/open-banking-cma-psd2-explained.

11. "Open Banking," *Databricks*, accessed November 7, 2023, https://www.databricks.com/glossary/open-banking.

12. Authors' analysis based on: Moira O'Neill, "An Open Door for Open Banking," *Financial Times*, April 21, 2023, https://www.ft.com/content/2b227007-3468-4b15-8117-68a30e0023a0.

13. Martin Chorzempa, "P2P Series Part 1: Peering into China's Growing Peer-to-Peer Lending Market," *Peterson Institute for International Economics*, June 27, 2016, https://piie.com/blogs/china-economic-watch/p2p-series-part-1-peering-chinas-growing-peer-peer-lending-market.

14. Joseph Luc Ngai, John Qu, Nicole Zhou, Xiao Liu, Joshua Lan, Xiyuan Fang, Feng Han, and Vera Chen, "Disruption and Connection: Cracking the Myths of China Internet Finance Innovation," *McKinsey Greater China FIG Practice*, July 2016, https://www.mckinsey.com/~/media/mckinsey/industries/financial%20services/our%20insights/whats%20next%20for%20chinas%20booming%20fintech%20sector/disruption-and-connection-cracking-the-myths-of-china-internet-finance-innovation.ashx.

15. (Robin) Hui Huang, "Online P2P Lending and Regulatory Responses in China: Opportunities and Challenges," *Centre for Financial Regulation & Economic Development*, May 8, 2018, https://papers.ssrn.com/sol3/papers.cfm?abstract_id=2991993.

16. Sidney Leng, "One Third of China's 3,000 Peer-to-Peer Lending Platforms 'Problematic': New Report," *South China Morning Post*, September 24, 2016, http://www.scmp.com/news/hong-kong/economy/article/2022317/one-third-chinas-3000-peer-peer-lending-platforms-problematic.

17. Matthew Miller, "Leader of China's $9 Billion Ezubao Online Scam Gets Life; 26 Jailed," *Reuters*, September 12, 2017, https://www.reuters.com/article/us-china-fraud/leader-of-chinas-9-billion-ezubao-online-scam-gets-life-26-jailed-idUSKCN1BN0J6.

18. Neil Gough, "Online Lender Ezubao Took $7.6 Billion in Ponzi Scheme, China Says," *New York Times*, February 1, 2016, https://www.nytimes.com/2016/02/02/business/dealbook/ezubao-china-fraud.html.

19. (Robin) Hui Huang, "Online P2P Lending and Regulatory Responses in China: Opportunities and Challenges," *Centre for Financial Regulation & Economic Development*, May 8, 2018, https://papers.ssrn.com/sol3/papers.cfm?abstract_id=2991993.

20. Martin Chorzempa and Yiping Huang, "Chinese Fintech Innovation and Regulation," *Asian Economic Policy Review*, February 2022, https://onlinelibrary.wiley.com/doi/abs/10.1111/aepr.12384.

21. David Meyer, "Jack Ma's Chinese Fintech Firm Just Raised So Much Money It's Now Worth More Than Goldman Sachs," *Fortune*, June 8, 2018, http://fortune.com/2018/06/08/ant-financial-alipay-14-billion-funding/.

22. Martin Chorzempa and Yiping Huang, "Chinese Fintech Innovation and Regulation," *Asian Economic Policy Review*, February 2022, https://onlinelibrary.wiley.com/doi/abs/10.1111/aepr.12384.

23. Yingzhi Yang, Brenda Goh and Kane Wu, "Ant Group Founder Jack Ma to Give Up Control in Key Revamp," *Reuters Business*, January 7, 2023, https://www.reuters.com/business/ant-group-says-jack-ma-relinquishes-control-company-2023-01-07/.

24. Harald Hau, Yi Huang, Hongzhe Shan and Zixia Sheng, "FinTech Credit and Entrepreneurial Growth," *Swiss Finance Institute*, Research Paper No. 21-47, https://papers.ssrn.com/sol3/papers.cfm?abstract_id=3899863.

25. Martin Chorzempa, "The Cashless Revolution: China's Reinvention of Money and the End of America's Domination of Finance and Technology," 2022.

26. Giulio Cornelli, Jon Frost, Leonardo Gambacorta, Raghavendra Rau, Robert Wardrop and Tania Ziegle, "Fintech and Big Tech Credit: A New Database," *BIS Working Paper*, no. 887, September 2020. https://www.bis.org/publ/work887.htm.

27. Raghuram Rajan and Luigi Zingales, *Saving Capitalism from the Capitalists* (New York: Crown Business, 2003), 1.

28. "Sound Practices, Implications of Fintech Developments for Banks and Bank Supervisors," *Bank for International Settlements: Basel Committee on Banking Supervision*, October 5, 2023, https://www.bis.org/bcbs/publ/d431.pdf.

29. "The Kalifa Review of UK FinTech," February 26, 2021, https://assets.publishing.service.gov.uk/media/607979c7d3bf7f400f5b3c65/KalifaReviewofUKFintech01.pdf.

30. James M. Lacko and Janis K. Pappalardo, "Improving Consumer Mortgage Disclosures: An Empirical Assessment of Current and Prototype Disclosure Forms: A Bureau of Economics Staff Report," *Federal Trade Commission*, June 2007, https://www.ftc.gov/reports/improving-con sumer-mortgage-disclosures-empirical-assessment-current-prototype-dis closure.

31. Note: Industry players have made recommendations on what these regulations might look like through the Small Business Lending Subgroup of the CSBS Fintech Industry Advisory Panel, https://www.csbs.org/csbs-fintech-industry-advisory-panel.

32. Note: The 1968 Truth in Lending Act (TILA) provides strong protections for consumer borrowers by requiring lenders to disclose terms and costs. TILA applies to banks and fintech lenders that make consumer loans, but does not apply to small business borrowers. There are other laws, such as the Equal Credit Opportunity Act (ECOA), which guarantees non-discrimination and applies to any borrower whether they are interacting with a bank or non-bank lender. The operating principle of TILA should be expanded to follow that of ECOA, providing equal protections to both small businesses and consumers when they borrow, regardless of the source of their loans.

33. Claire Williams, "Biden's Order Marks the Beginning of AI Regulation for Banks," *American Banker*, October 30, 2023, https://www.americ anbanker.com/news/bidens-order-marks-the-beginning-of-ai-regulation-for-banks.

34. "Blueprint for an AI Bill of Rights," *The White House*, accessed October 10, 2023, https://www.whitehouse.gov/ostp/ai-bill-of-rights/.

35. Ibid.

36. Interview with Jo Ann Barefoot, November 4, 2023.

37. "Dodd-Frank's Missed Opportunity: A Road Map for a More Effective Regulatory Architecture," *Economic Policy Program Financial Regulatory Reform Initiative*, April 2014, https://bipartisanpolicy.org/download/? file=/wp-content/uploads/2019/03/BPC-Dodd-Frank-Missed-Opport unity.pdf.

38. "Assessing Impacts of New Entrant Non-bank Firms on Competition in Consumer Finance Markets," *U.S. Department of the Treasury Report to the White House Competition Council*, November 2022, https://home.treasury.gov/system/files/136/Assessing-the-Impact-of-New-Entrant-Nonbank-Firms.pdf.

39. Ibid.

40. Small Business Borrowers' Bill of Rights, http://www.borrowersbillofrig
    hts.org/

Chapter 15

1. William Goetzmann, *Money Changes Everything: How Finance Made
   Civilization Possible* (Princeton, NJ: Princeton University Press, 2016), 50.
2. "Chart 3. Survival Rates of Establishments, by Year Started and Number
   of Years Since Starting, 1994–2015, in Percent," *Business Labor of
   Statistics*, Business Employment Dynamics, accessed November 2, 2023,
   https://www.bls.gov/bdm/entrepreneurship/bdm_chart3.htm.
3. "Availability of Credit to Small Businesses," *Federal Reserve Banks Publications*, October 2022. https://www.federalreserve.gov/publications/2022-
   october-availability-of-credit-to-small-businesses.htm.
4. Note: All estimates are merely guesswork, but if 34% of small businesses
   are seeking capital (Chapter 5), a 5% improvement in the number of businesses funded would mean 561,000 additional creditworthy businesses
   served by the market. The 5% estimate is based on the level of the Small
   Business Administration (SBA) loan portfolio which runs between 5 and
   10% of the total market. The calculation assumes that the SBA is a proxy
   for the market gap as it only guarantees loans that banks would not make
   under market conditions. Since the SBA loss rate is less than 4%, 96% of
   the borrowers it serves are creditworthy businesses that the current lending
   marketplace is not serving.
5. Frank Rotman, "The Copernican Revolution in Banking," *QED Investors*,
   April 8, 2018.
6. Note: The mortgage lending environment leading up to the financial
   crisis is an example of where lenders' incentives were not aligned with
   full disclosure of terms or the best interests of their borrowers.
7. Ross Levine, "Financial Development and Economic Growth: Views and
   Agenda," Journal of Economic Literature 35, no. 2 (June 1997): 688–726,
   https://www.jstor.org/stable/2729790.
8. "About Us," When Pigs Fly Bakery, accessed October 10, 2023, https://
   sendbread.com/about-us/.

Index

Printed by Wilco bv, the Netherlands